106/6/8 √2

Kir Darroch

S

July 1959

THE
LAMBETH CONFERENCE
1958

THE
LAMBETH
CONFERENCE
1958

*The Encyclical Letter
from the Bishops
together with the
Resolutions and Reports*

S · P · C · K

AND

SEABURY PRESS

1958

First published in 1958
by S.P.C.K.
Holy Trinity Church, Marylebone Road, London, N.W.1
and The Seabury Press
Havemeyer Place, Greenwich, Connecticut
Made and printed in Great Britain by
William Clowes and Sons, Limited, London and Beccles

NOTE

The Biblical quotations in this volume are taken generally from *The Revised Standard Version of the Bible*, copyrighted in 1946 and 1952 and used here by permission of The Division of Christian Education of The National Council of Churches, New York, and Thomas Nelson and Sons, Ltd, Edinburgh.

Contents

Part 1

Part 2

Contents

PART 1

List of Bishops attending the Lambeth Conference of 1958

G. F. FISHER	Primate of All England and Archbishop of Canterbury
H. C. MONTGOMERY CAMPBELL	Bishop of London
A. T. P. WILLIAMS	Bishop of Winchester
P. M. HERBERT	Bishop of Norwich
A. E. J. RAWLINSON	Bishop of Derby
C. M. CHAVASSE	Bishop of Rochester
N. B. HUDSON	Bishop of Ely
W. L. ANDERSON	Bishop of Salisbury
B. F. SIMPSON	Bishop of Southwark
W. M. ASKWITH	Bishop of Gloucester
H. W. BRADFIELD	Bishop of Bath and Wells
F. A. COCKIN	Bishop of Bristol
R. P. WILSON	Bishop of Chichester
R. C. MORTIMER	Bishop of Exeter
T. LONGWORTH	Bishop of Hereford
W. L. S. FLEMING	Bishop of Portsmouth
E. M. GRESFORD JONES	Bishop of St Albans
S. F. ALLISON	Bishop of Chelmsford
E. R. MORGAN	Bishop of Truro
J. L. WILSON	Bishop of Birmingham
A. S. REEVE	Bishop of Lichfield
R. R. WILLIAMS	Bishop of Leicester
A. H. MORRIS	Bishop of St Edmundsbury and Ipswich
H. J. CARPENTER	Bishop of Oxford
L. M. CHARLES-EDWARDS	Bishop of Worcester
C. K. N. BARDSLEY	Bishop of Coventry
I. S. WATKINS	Bishop of Guildford

A*

R. W. Stopford	Bishop of Peterborough
K. Riches	Bishop of Lincoln
G. K. A. Bell	Formerly Bishop of Chichester
C. E. Stuart	Formerly Bishop of Uganda
D. C. Dunlop	Assistant Bishop of Lincoln
G. F. Allen	Assistant Bishop of Oxford
G. Sinker	Assistant Bishop of Derby
R. N. Coote	Bishop Suffragan of Fulham

Province of York

A. M. Ramsey	Primate of England and Archbishop of York
M. H. Harland	Bishop of Durham
L. S. Hunter	Bishop of Sheffield
F. R. Barry	Bishop of Southwell
C. A. Martin	Bishop of Liverpool
T. Bloomer	Bishop of Carlisle
G. A. Chase	Bishop of Ripon
W. D. L. Greer	Bishop of Manchester
W. H. Baddeley	Bishop of Blackburn
B. Pollard	Bishop of Sodor and Man
G. A. Ellison	Bishop of Chester
F. D. Coggan	Bishop of Bradford
H. E. Ashdown	Bishop of Newcastle
J. A. Ramsbotham	Bishop of Wakefield
C. R. Claxton	Bishop Suffragan of Warrington

Wales

A. E. Morris	Archbishop of Wales and Bishop of Monmouth
D. D. Bartlett	Bishop of St Asaph
W. G. H. Simon	Bishop of Llandaff
J. R. Richards	Bishop of St David's
G. O. Williams	Bishop of Bangor
J. J. A. Thomas	Bishop of Swansea and Brecon

Ireland

J. A. F. GREGG	Primate of All Ireland and Archbishop of Armagh
G. O. SIMMS	Primate of Ireland and Archbishop of Dublin
J. McCANN	Bishop of Meath
E. C. HODGES	Bishop of Limerick, Ardfert, and Aghadoe
F. J. MITCHELL	Bishop of Down and Dromore
R. G. PERDUE	Bishop of Cork, Cloyne, and Ross
C. J. TYNDALL	Bishop of Kilmore and Elphin and Ardagh
R. C. H. G. ELLIOTT	Bishop of Connor
H. A. STANISTREET	Bishop of Killaloe, Kilfenora, Clonfert, and Kilmacduagh
A. H. BUTLER	Bishop of Tuam, Killala, and Achonry

Scotland

T. HANNAY	Primus of the Scottish Episcopal Church and Bishop of Argyll and The Isles
E. GRAHAM	Bishop of Brechin
K. C. H. WARNER	Bishop of Edinburgh
F. H. MONCREIFF	Bishop of Glasgow and Galloway
D. MacINNES	Bishop of Moray, Ross, and Caithness
J. W. A. HOWE	Bishop of St Andrews, Dunkeld, and Dunblane
E. F. EASSON	Bishop of Aberdeen and Orkney

United States of America

H. K. SHERRILL	Presiding Bishop of the Protestant Episcopal Church in the United States of America
H. W. HOBSON	Bishop of Southern Ohio
F. D. GOODWIN	Bishop of Virginia
C. C. J. CARPENTER	Bishop of Alabama
M. E. PEABODY	Bishop of Central New York
A. H. BLANKINGSHIP	Bishop of Cuba
W. H. GRAY	Bishop of Connecticut
O. L. LORING	Bishop of Maine

N. C. POWELL	Bishop of Maryland
J. P. DEWOLFE	Bishop of Long Island
W. F. LEWIS	Bishop of Nevada
O. J. HART	Bishop of Pennsylvania
J. T. HEISTAND	Bishop of Harrisburg
E. H. JONES	Bishop of West Texas
C. A. VOEGELI	Bishop of Haiti
S. F. D. WALTERS	Bishop of San Joaquin
H. S. KENNEDY	Bishop of Honolulu
A. PARDUE	Bishop of Pittsburgh
A. DUN	Bishop of Washington
T. N. CARRUTHERS	Bishop of South Carolina
W. W. HORSTICK	Bishop of Eau Claire
R. MALLETT	Bishop of Northern Indiana
B. W. HARRIS	Bishop of Liberia
R. H. GOODEN	Bishop of Panama Canal Zone
H. I. LOUTTIT	Bishop of South Florida
A. B. KINSOLVING	Bishop of Arizona
F. L. BARRY	Bishop of Albany
C. A. MASON	Bishop of Dallas
T. H. WRIGHT	Bishop of East Carolina
J. E. HINES	Bishop of Texas
W. R. MOODY	Bishop of Lexington
R. S. EMRICH	Bishop of Michigan
L. W. BARTON	Bishop of Eastern Oregon
S. F. BAYNE	Bishop of Olympia
H. W. B. DONEGAN	Bishop of New York
G. P. GUNN	Bishop of Southern Virginia
C. F. HALL	Bishop of New Hampshire
J. W. HUNTER	Bishop of Wyoming
F. E. BLOY	Bishop of Los Angeles
L. L. SCAIFE	Bishop of Western New York
W. J. GORDON	Bishop of Alaska
R. S. HUBBARD	Bishop of Spokane
T. N. BARTH	Bishop of Tennessee
M. G. HENRY	Bishop of Western North Carolina
E. H. WEST	Bishop of Florida
G. M. JONES	Bishop of Louisiana

R. R. CLAIBORNE	Bishop of Atlanta
A. J. MILLER	Bishop of Easton
N. M. BURROUGHS	Bishop of Ohio
E. M. KRISCHKE	Bishop of Southern Brazil
D. S. STARK	Bishop of Rochester
E. R. WELLES	Bishop of West Missouri
G. V. SMITH	Bishop of Iowa
W. C. CAMPBELL	Bishop of West Virginia
G. F. BURRILL	Bishop of Chicago
A. C. LICHTENBERGER	Bishop of Missouri
R. M. HATCH	Bishop of Western Massachusetts
R. S. WATSON	Bishop of Utah
A. E. SWIFT	Bishop of Puerto Rico
W. R. C. POWELL	Bishop of Oklahoma
D. H. V. HALLOCK	Bishop of Milwaukee
H. H. KELLOGG	Bishop of Minnesota
W. CRITTENDEN	Bishop of Erie
J. S. HIGGINS	Bishop of Rhode Island
F. J. WARNECKE	Bishop of Bethlehem
W. H. BRADY	Bishop of Fond Du Lac
D. B. MCNEIL	Bishop of Western Michigan
C. A. COLE	Bishop of Upper South Carolina
J. B. MOSLEY	Bishop of Delaware
C. G. MARMION	Bishop of Kentucky
W. H. MARMION	Bishop of South-Western Virginia
J. S. MINNIS	Bishop of Colorado
A. R. STUART	Bishop of Georgia
A. P. STOKES	Bishop of Massachusetts
R. R. BROWN	Bishop of Arkansas
A. M. LEWIS	Bishop of Salina
P. L. SIMOES	Bishop of South-Western Brazil
C. R. HADEN	Bishop of Sacramento
J. G. SAUCEDO	Bishop of Mexico
J. B. BENTLEY	Director, Overseas Department of the National Council of P.E.C.U.S.A.
N. B. NASH	Bishop-in-Charge, Convocation of American Churches in Europe
R. F. GIBSON	Bishop Coadjutor of Virginia

R. H. BAKER	Bishop Coadjutor of North Carolina
L. W. F. STARK	Bishop Coadjutor of Newark
H. L. DOLL	Bishop Coadjutor of Maryland
J. W. F. CARMAN	Bishop Coadjutor of Oregon
E. C. TURNER	Bishop Coadjutor of Kansas
J. P. CRAINE	Bishop Coadjutor of Indianapolis
J. A. PIKE	Bishop Coadjutor of California

Canada

W. F. BARFOOT	Primate of All Canada, Archbishop and Metropolitan of Rupert's Land
H. E. SEXTON	Archbishop and Metropolitan of British Columbia
P. CARRINGTON	Archbishop of Quebec and Metropolitan of the Province of Canada
W. L. WRIGHT	Archbishop of Algoma and Metropolitan of Ontario
H. D. MARTIN	Bishop of Saskatchewan
J. DIXON	Bishop of Montreal
R. H. WATERMAN	Bishop of Nova Scotia
G. N. LUXTON	Bishop of Huron
W. E. BAGNALL	Bishop of Niagara
I. A. NORRIS	Bishop of Brandon
D. B. MARSH	Bishop of The Arctic
S. C. STEER	Bishop of Saskatoon
M. E. COLEMAN	Bishop of Qu'Appelle
R. J. PIERCE	Bishop of Athabasca
G. P. GOWER	Bishop of New Westminster
G. R. CALVERT	Bishop of Calgary
T. GREENWOOD	Bishop of Yukon
K. C. EVANS	Bishop of Ontario
F. H. WILKINSON	Bishop of Toronto
H. G. WATTS	Bishop of Caledonia
H. E. HIVES	Bishop of Keewatin
H. H. CLARK	Bishop of Edmonton
E. S. REED	Bishop of Ottawa
C. C. ROBINSON	Bishop of Moosonee

P. R. BEATTIE   Bishop of Kootenay
R. S. DEAN   Bishop of Cariboo
A. H. O'NEIL   Bishop of Fredericton
N. R. CLARKE   Bishop Suffragan of James Bay
W. A. TOWNSHEND   Bishop Suffragan of Huron
G. B. SNELL   Bishop Suffragan of Toronto

India, Pakistan, Burma, and Ceylon

A. N. MUKERJEE   Metropolitan of India, Pakistan, Burma
                           and Ceylon and Bishop of Calcutta
H. L. J. DE MEL   Bishop of Kurunagala
W. Q. LASH   Bishop of Bombay
C. J. G. ROBINSON   Bishop of Lucknow
A. R. GRAHAM-   Bishop of Colombo
  CAMPBELL
J. AMRITANAND   Bishop of Assam
L. H. WOOLMER   Bishop of Lahore
F. R. WILLIS   Bishop of Delhi
R. W. BRYAN   Bishop of Barrackpore
J. D. BLAIR   Bishop of East Bengal
P. PARMAR   Bishop of Bhagalpur
V. G. SHEARBURN   Bishop of Rangoon
A. W. LUTHER   Bishop of Nasik
J. W. SADIQ   Bishop of Nagpur
S. A. B. DILBAR HANS   Bishop of Chota Nagpur
J. AUNG HLA   Assistant Bishop of Rangoon
W. A. PARTRIDGE   Assistant Bishop of Calcutta
CHANDU RAY   Assistant Bishop of Lahore

Australia

R. C. HALSE   Archbishop of Brisbane and Metropolitan
                           of Queensland
R. W. H. MOLINE   Archbishop of Perth and Metropolitan of
                           West Australia
F. WOODS   Archbishop of Melbourne and Metropolitan
                           of Victoria

J. Frewer	Bishop of North-West Australia
J. S. Moyes	Bishop of Armidale
E. H. Burgmann	Bishop of Canberra and Goulburn
P. N. W. Strong	Bishop of New Guinea
W. H. Johnson	Bishop of Ballarat
T. M. Armour	Bishop of Wangaratta
G. F. Cranswick	Bishop of Tasmania
J. A. G. Housden	Bishop of Rockhampton
K. J. Clements	Bishop of Grafton
W. J. Hudson	Bishop of Carpentaria
C. E. B. Muschamp	Bishop of Kalgoorlie
A. E. Winter	Bishop of St Arnaud
I. W. A. Shevill	Bishop of North Queensland
R. E. Richards	Bishop of Bendigo
T. T. Reed	Bishop of Adelaide
M. L. Loane	Bishop Coadjutor of Sydney

New Zealand

R. H. Owen	Primate and Archbishop of New Zealand and Bishop of Wellington
L. S. Kempthorne	Bishop in Polynesia
W. J. Simkin	Bishop of Auckland
J. T. Holland	Bishop of Waikato
A. K. Warren	Bishop of Christchurch
A. H. Johnston	Bishop of Dunedin
W. N. Panapa	Bishop Suffragan of Aotearoa

South Africa

J. de Blank	Metropolitan of South Africa and Archbishop of Cape Town
A. H. Cullen	Bishop of Grahamstown
G. P. L. Turner	Bishop of St Helena
R. S. Taylor	Bishop of Pretoria
J. Hunter	Bishop of George
J. Boys	Bishop of Kimberley and Kuruman
R. A. Reeves	Bishop of Johannesburg

J. A. A. MAUND	Bishop of Basutoland
T. G. V. INMAN	Bishop of Natal
J. D. VINCENT	Bishop of Damaraland
J. L. SCHUSTER	Bishop of St John's, Kaffiaria
B. B. BURNETT	Bishop of Bloemfontein
T. J. SAVAGE	Bishop of Zululand

West Indies

A. J. KNIGHT	Archbishop of the West Indies and Bishop of Guiana
S. BURTON	Bishop of Nassau and the Bahamas
P. W. GIBSON	Bishop of Jamaica
G. H. BROOKS	Bishop of British Honduras
G. L. G. MANDEVILLE	Bishop of Barbados
D. R. KNOWLES	Bishop of Antigua
F. N. CHAMBERLAIN	Bishop of Trinidad and Tobago

Japan

M. H. YASHIRO	Presiding Bishop of the Nippon Sei Ko Ka and Bishop of Kobe
P. K. UEDA	Bishop of Hokkaido
I. H. NOSSÉ	Bishop of South Tokyo
P. Y. KUROSE	Bishop of Mid-Japan

China

R. O. HALL	Bishop of Hong Kong

West Africa

J. L. C. HORSTEAD	Archbishop of West Africa and Bishop of Sierra Leone
C. J. PATTERSON	Bishop on the Niger
E. T. DIMIEARI	Bishop of the Niger Delta
S. O. ODUTOLA	Bishop of Ondo-Benin
J. E. L. MORT	Bishop of Northern Nigeria

A. W. Howells	Bishop of Lagos
D. R. Oyebode	Bishop of Ibadan
R. R. Roseveare	Bishop of Accra
St John S. Pike	Bishop of Gambia and the Rio Pongas
P. J. Jones	Assistant Bishop of Sierra Leone
E. D. Martinson	Assistant Bishop of Accra
S. M. Nkemena	Assistant Bishop on the Niger
D. O. Awosika	Assistant Bishop of Ondo-Benin
H. A. I. Afonya	Assistant Bishop of the Niger Delta

Central Africa

W. J. Hughes	Archbishop of Central Africa and Bishop of Matabeleland
F. O. Thorne	Bishop of Nyasaland
C .W. Alderson	Bishop of Mashonaland
F. O. Green-Wilkinson	Bishop of Northern Rhodesia

Overseas Bishops of the Canterbury Jurisdiction

A. C. MacInnes	Archbishop in Jerusalem
W. J. Thompson	Bishop in Iran
F. F. Johnston	Bishop in Egypt and Libya
O. C. Allison	Bishop in the Sudan
D. Deng Atong	Assistant Bishop in the Sudan
N. A. Cuba'in	Bishop in Jordan, Lebanon, and Syria
F. W. T. Craske	Bishop of Gibraltar
L. C. Usher-Wilson	Bishop on the Upper Nile
S. Tomusange	Assistant Bishop on the Upper Nile
L. W. Brown	Bishop of Uganda
P. J. Brazier	Assistant Bishop of Uganda
F. Lutaya	Assistant Bishop of Uganda
K. Shalita	Assistant Bishop of Uganda
W. S. Baker	Bishop of Zanzibar
L. E. Stradling	Bishop of South-West Tanganyika
W. L. M. Way	Bishop of Masasi
A. Stanway	Bishop of Central Tanganyika

Y. M. OMARI	Assistant Bishop of Central Tanganyika
L. J. BEECHER	Bishop of Mombasa
F. H. OLANG'	Assistant Bishop of Mombasa
H. OTTER-BARRY	Bishop of Mauritius
T. R. PARFITT	Bishop in Madagascar
G. MILES	Assistant Bishop in Madagascar
J. MARCEL	Assistant Bishop in Madagascar
H. W. BAINES	Bishop of Singapore
R. P.-C. KOH	Assistant Bishop of Singapore
J. C. S. DALY	Bishop in Korea
A. E. CHADWELL	Assistant Bishop in Korea
N. E. CORNWALL	Bishop of Borneo
D. I. EVANS	Bishop of Argentina and Eastern South America with the Falkland Islands
A. L. E. WILLIAMS	Bishop of Bermuda

ENCYCLICAL LETTER

Encyclical Letter
to the Faithful in Jesus Christ

We, Archbishops and Bishops of the Holy Catholic and Apostolic Church in communion with the See of Canterbury, three hundred and ten in number, assembled from forty-six countries, under the Presidency of Geoffrey, Archbishop of Canterbury, in the year of our Lord one thousand nine hundred and fifty-eight, send you greeting in the name of our Lord and Saviour Jesus Christ.

In his Name we desire to set before you the outcome of the deliberations to which, with earnest prayer and Eucharist, we have for five weeks devoted ourselves day by day. We thank all those who, in so many parts of the world, have supported us with their prayers. We hope that the results of our work may bring help and encouragement to them in their labours for the extension of the Kingdom of our Lord.

From the opening service of our Conference in Canterbury Cathedral we have been conscious of a fellowship with each other in the faith of Christ which has given to our discussions a unity of purpose which has inspired us all. We have been granted a deeper understanding of the meaning of the Anglican Communion and of the tasks to which God is calling his Church in the years that lie ahead.

In this letter we survey the main results of our deliberations, which are set out in detail in the Resolutions adopted by the Conference. These Resolutions themselves are based on the Reports of the five Committees, which we commend to the careful study of our people. To the letter we attach a brief message which, if desired, a bishop may direct to be read in the churches of his diocese during the month of October 1958, as a simple word of encouragement from the Conference to all the members of our Communion. We hope that, wherever suitable, the Encyclical Letter itself will be read and expounded from the pulpit, or otherwise, as an introduction to the study of the Reports themselves.

We set ourselves to consider not only domestic problems concerning the Anglican Communion and Christendom, but also some of the fundamental issues which confront the whole of mankind. There are no simple answers to many of these baffling questions, and we believe that we should have misled ourselves and others if we had sought to find such answers. What we have tried to do, is to think out again the principles, as we find them in God's Word and revelation, by which we believe nations, Churches, and individual men and women will be judged, and on which their conduct and policies should be based.

At the heart of the Christian gospel is that thought of reconciliation which has been the keynote of our Conference. At the heart of the world's confusion is the failure of men to understand and accept the way God offers by which they may be reconciled to him. In such a situation it is the urgent duty of the Church to be the channel of Christ's reconciling power. We have tried to see all problems as problems of reconciliation, for the solution of which the spirit of renunciation and self-sacrifice is an essential condition. Tensions and differences there must be: they become creative when they are brought under the power and influence of God. When men, or groups, or nations find themselves in conflict because their opinions or their interests clash, though the flesh is weak the way is open for advance into a new and richer partnership. "When any man is in Christ, there is a new creation."

THE WORD OF RECONCILIATION

We begin, as the faith of the Church must always begin, with the Bible, through which God has spoken his word of reconciliation.

One of the distinguishing marks of our Anglican Communion is the supreme importance which is attached to the authority of the Bible in the formulation of doctrine. We give great prominence to the reading of the Bible in the services of the Church. But questions have arisen in recent years about the nature of the authority of the Scriptures and the relevance of their message, which seem to many to have seriously weakened the position of esteem in which our forefathers held the Bible.

Those who have been brought up in a scientific world may be mystified by the language of the Bible which is, broadly, prescientific. On the other hand, some who love the Bible deeply may lack a clear grasp of the relationship between its different parts, and may fail to see the connection between the content of the Bible and the faith of the Church. All too often there is a lack of personal familiarity with the Bible and sometimes a regrettable indifference when it is read and preached.

In this situation many Christians do not gain from the Bible the understanding of God's will that the world should be reconciled to him, nor of Christ's reconciling power which should be the inspiration of their witness in the world.

This present age urgently needs the Divine Message of the Bible if its predicament is to be met. Our Lord Jesus Christ is God's ultimate Word to man. In his light all Scripture is to be interpreted, the Old Testament in terms of Promise, the New in terms of Fulfilment. Though our understanding of the Bible has been greatly assisted by those scholars who have taught us to see more clearly the varied ways in which the human factor has contributed to the books we call the Bible, and to the history which they record, the great realities—life and death, sin and righteousness, war and peace, famine and plenty, good and evil—remain always the same, and the Bible speaks to these situations as it did when its various books were written.

Developments in the life of the Church hold out promise that there may lie before us a new experience of the living power of the Bible in the worship of the Church and in the hearts of Christian people. We are coming to see once more that the Bible has a deep underlying unity, in spite of its many different facets. We are seeing in a new way the unity of the Word and the Sacraments. The Christ who feeds us with himself in the Eucharist speaks to us through his own Word in the Gospel. In the Epistle we hear those Apostles whom he sent to guide and teach us. The pulpit is being seen not as a rival to the altar, but as its necessary counterpart. Group study of the Bible is being vigorously revived. New translations in many languages, both for those who have had the Bible for centuries and for those who have not, are now appearing, and are opening up the Scriptures to new generations.

In all this there is hope. But there is much yet to be done. Church people everywhere—clergy and laity alike—must join in this great rediscovery of the Bible as a means of grace to the individual and as the inspiration of corporate worship and witness. It is the duty of the clergy to exert their imaginative efforts so that the Bible may "come alive" for their hearers. It is the duty of the laity to bring to the hearing of the Bible an expectant heart, and to learn again the art of private Bible study and meditation. We all need to discover that the language of poetry and drama retains its deep truths even in a scientific age.

So we invite the Churches of the Anglican Communion to make a new effort to extend the scope and deepen the quality of both the personal and the corporate study of the Bible. If we thus prepare

the way, we believe that God will speak to our day and generation
his quickening word.

RECONCILIATION IN SOCIETY

The conflicts and tensions of our day in part arise from man's
basic needs, as nations grow up and long to be free, or feel the
pressure of material wants; in part they spring from man's sin—
from selfish fears, greed, false ambitions. Though the scientific
and technological achievements of our age have encouraged a spirit
of self-confidence which feels no need for God, yet underneath there
is a spiritual emptiness, which only a faith in the reconciling love
of God can satisfy.

Christians, therefore, called to share in the ministry of reconciliation, must first seek to create centres of reconciliation in their own
parishes and congregations, by faith and intercession, by fellowship
rooted in mutual forgiveness, by love which reflects the love of
Christ: Anglicans will also remember that, as members of their own
world-wide Communion, they are linked in worship with peoples
of many races, and given opportunities of friendship and mutual
service. "In one Spirit were we all baptized into one body, whether
Jew or Greek, whether bond or free."

In the Church they share a heavenly citizenship. But they have
also an earthly citizenship, with its own proper duties. In the conflicts which threaten the security of nations, Christians must recognize their share of responsibility for the policies of their own
countries. The Church cannot be identified with any particular
political or social system; its members cannot support policies proceeding from a selfish nationalism or lust for power, wherever they
are found, nor uphold the claims of a State to an absolute authority
which denies the purpose of God for men. They are called to work
positively for peace, to promote confidence by respecting the peoples
of other nations in their rights to freedom, and to encourage
generosity and compassion by pressing for a greater sharing of the
world's resources with countries in need and for the relief of the
countless millions of refugees.

The urgency of this is apparent to-day. The evil of war has become
more vile through the hideous weapons of destruction which man's
ingenuity has placed in his hands. Successive Lambeth Conferences
have asserted their belief that war as a method of settling international disputes is incompatible with the teaching and example of
our Lord Jesus Christ, and we are united both in hating war and
in pressing for its abolition.

The use of nuclear weapons is repugnant to the Christian conscience. Some of us would go further and regard such use in any circumstances as morally indefensible, while others of us, with equal conviction, would hold that so long as such weapons exist there are circumstances in which to use them might be preferable to political enslavement. We believe that the abolition of nuclear weapons of indiscriminate effect and destructive power by international agreement is an essential step towards the abolition of war itself. So we appeal to all Christians to press through their governments for the banning of such weapons, accepting such limitation of their own sovereignty as may be required to ensure inspection and control, so that no government may make them. We urge governments to devote their utmost efforts towards comprehensive international disarmament. We appeal for more enlightened support for the United Nations, so that it may become a more effective instrument of world peace and of that free co-operation between nations which is the condition of that world order for which we must pray.

Within nations as well as between them, conflicts mar that partnership in society through which men should express their membership one of another. Our report draws attention to the unsettlement which rapid industrialization has caused, and to some of those areas in the world where racial tension threatens the stability of whole communities and is a challenge to the Christian conscience. In many countries the Church is bearing courageous witness to the principle that every man, of whatever colour or race, possesses a natural dignity and value as created in the image of God, and should be given the right to exercise responsible freedom in all aspects of our human life. To that principle all Christians are committed, and for its recognition they are called to work, by supporting their brothers in prayer, by sharing in the task of reconciling those involved in conflict, and by patient understanding. Conflict, indeed, there will be, but it may be turned to creative purpose. The Christian must live his life amid tension, yet ever supported by the faith that by humble obedience to Christ he may share in his reconciling work. For Christ is our peace; and through him comes hope and inspiration to all who work for peace throughout the world.

But it is not only where there are conflicts between nations and within them that the world needs the reconciling work of Christ and of his Church. The family, which is the basic unit of human society, is to-day subjected to pressures from without and from within. We believe that the Christian faith has something unique which must be said both on the idea of the human family as rooted in the God-head and on its creative possibilities under God.

It has long been held that a primary obligation of Christian marriage is that children may be born within the supporting framework of parental love and family concern, with a right to an opportunity for a full and spiritually wholesome life. Yet we believe that the procreation of children is not the sole purpose of Christian marriage. Implicit within the bond between husband and wife is the relationship of love with its sacramental expression in physical union. Because these two great purposes of Christian marriage illumine each other and form the focal points of constructive home life, we believe that family planning, in such ways as are mutually acceptable to husband and wife in Christian conscience, and secure from the corruptions of sensuality and selfishness, is a right and important factor in Christian family life.

Realizing that no family can achieve true depth except through the firm assurance of a steadfast faithfulness, we reaffirm the permanence of the marriage bond. There is an obligation for Christian parents to work together with their children to form home life in which the lessons of human individuality and dignity, of discipline and responsible freedom, of forgiveness and redemptive love, are learned as prerequisites for the adequate discharge of the wider family obligations to which they are called.

We are agreed that one of the most valuable contributions the Church can make towards the stability of marriage and home life is to help young people to marry in the right way. The clergy should provide pre-marital instruction based on Christian principles, so that young couples can marry with a clear understanding of their imperative duties and high responsibilities. A home based on family prayers and worship, wherein mutual self-sacrifice is practised, gives its young people their sure foundations. And, as a family matures, the Church can help further by defining Christian service, not merely as work done within the Church and parish, but work in the wider community where social and industrial life require the participation of men and women informed by the Christian faith.

Family life suffers from the movement and resettlement which an increasingly industrialized society demands. Such movement makes parents and children lose their sense of security. This involves a new sense of responsibility for each other on the part both of parents and of children. We believe also that it is the moral obligation of those people who frame and finance policies in industry to be sensitive to the damage done to the family by demands which separate parents from children or make inordinate claims upon a family's stability. We urge that the organization of industry should be so modified that a worker is not prevented from enjoying the wholeness of life and from fulfilling his duties, both as a man in a family and as a citizen.

There are many lands to-day where population is increasing so fast that the survival of young and old is threatened. We believe that it is the duty of the better developed countries to help such countries to become self-supporting in food supplies and health measures through technical and other aids. In such countries population control has become a necessity. Abortion and infanticide are to be condemned, but methods of control, medically endorsed and morally acceptable, may help the people of these lands so to plan family life that children may be born without a likelihood of starvation. As the expectation of life in many parts of the world increases, the need to care for the aged therefore becomes more insistent.

To strengthen family life and to restore its unity where it is broken are essential parts of the ministry of reconciliation. To-day we can begin to see them not as problems of our own society alone, but as concerns of the whole human family: if one member suffers all must suffer, whether the one be a peasant in dire poverty through famine or a victim of too rapid industrialization. All are children of our Father: all are made in his image. The work of reconciliation must go forward.

RECONCILIATION IN THE CHURCH OF GOD

The Church can be effective as an agent of Christ's reconciling power only in proportion as it is itself reconciled to God and is seeking reconciliation between its members. Every Lambeth Conference since 1878 has recognized this by its concern for the unity of the Body of Christ. We believe that the Anglican Communion has a special opportunity and a corresponding responsibility to help in the healing of the divisions which hinder the Church's ministry of reconciliation. We rejoice in the many signs of closer Christian fellowship, and we thank God for the warmth of friendship between the Churches shown in the World Council of Churches and in other relations between our own and other Communions, of which the greetings conveyed to us by their delegations in our Opening Sessions were outstanding evidence. We thank God for all these signs of our fellowship in the faith, and we thank God that we have been able to share a little in the difficulties and trials of so many of our Christian brethren. Our Lord forewarned his Church that it must expect to be persecuted and despised; he taught us to rejoice and be glad when men despitefully use us. We praise God for the triumphant witness of the Church in persecution. We ask all our people to hold continually in their prayers our brethren in Christ who suffer for his Name.

The world is often critical because we seem to move so slowly towards the goal of the visible unity of the whole Church of God. Yet we can thank God that the last ten years have shown so much progress, and we rejoice in the many signs of the strengthening of the fellowship of our Communion with Churches of other and different traditions. In our last Conference we could not make one unanimous recommendation with regard to the relations between our Churches and Provinces and the newly-united Church of South India. In the ten years that have passed, visits by delegations and individuals have dispelled misunderstandings, and we record with thankfulness that many of our Provinces have been able to establish a limited inter-communion with that Church on which the grace of God has been so abundantly and manifestly bestowed.

The Church of India, Pakistan, Burma, and Ceylon asked that the Lambeth Conference should give advice upon three further schemes for united Churches in Ceylon, North India, and Pakistan. We examined these schemes with the greatest care, and we would express our gratitude to God for the clear evidence of the guidance of his Holy Spirit in the negotiations, which have led to schemes of union which we believe to mark a great and significant step towards the recovery of the visible unity of the Church Universal. We believe that it will be possible for the Church of Lanka to be from the outset in full communion with Churches and Provinces of the Anglican Communion. With some modification, the Churches of North India and Pakistan could have the same expectation. It is the earnest hope and prayer of all our members that these unions may go forward.

In West Africa and in the Jerusalem Archbishopric plans for reunion are under discussion. In Britain and America conversations are taking place between Churches of our Communion and Churches of the Presbyterian and Methodist traditions. We thank God for drawing us towards a wider and richer Christian unity. Because of our urgent desire to further negotiations and conversations with other Churches we have put forth in penitence and hope a fresh statement of our convictions, believing that we are called to a fresh effort in the cause of the unity of the one Church of God in the love of Christ, in faith and in order, and in fullness of sacramental communion.

As we set ourselves afresh to work and pray for such unity, we realize anew that we must seek also so to strengthen the life of our Communion that it may bring the full riches of our traditions and our heritage into the Church that is to be.

The Anglican Communion is faced in this mid-twentieth century with problems of great complexity, both in its witness to the world and in the strengthening of its inner life. The very recognition of these problems might cause despair, save for our faith that in the worship of Almighty God the Church can learn the will of God and receive power to do it. In worship we become aware that just as surely as God *calls* and *sends*, so also God *reigns*. He sends forth his Church to proclaim his reign to the end of the earth, to all nations, and to the end of time. In this total mission, every baptized member has his particular vocation and ministry. The seriousness of our problems and the urgency of our task alike demand that each of us shall ask anew, "Lord, what wilt thou have me do?"

Because worship is the well-spring of all our activity, it is essential that we grow in our understanding and practice of personal prayer and corporate devotion. A cherished part of our heritage in the Anglican Communion is the Book of Common Prayer, which is a bond of unity between us and which provides the forms whereby we live the life of the Catholic Church. We are in the midst of a time when these forms are being revised in various branches of our Communion. We value the enrichment that comes from a variety of usage and the constant effort to keep worship close to life, though we are concerned that no liturgical innovation should make difficult that unity in worship and in faith which we now enjoy. Through our growing knowledge of biblical teaching and of primitive Christian norms of worship, there is a movement towards greater understanding in doctrinal matters between churchmen of differing traditions, and we have tried to suggest principles which may guide gradual and careful revision of our Prayer Books towards a fuller unity in worship within our Communion.

Our Lord called his first disciples that they might be with him and that he might send them forth to preach. This is always the proper sequence in Christian life. We are called that we may be sent; we receive in order that we may give. The world-wide task of evangelism is not an "optional extra"; it is the high calling of every disciple. Our responsibility becomes all the greater as we look upon a world filled with confusion, fear, frustration, and prejudice; men need a power beyond their own to live victoriously in such a world. The power comes to mankind only through Christ and his Church.

If our missionary obligation is to be fulfilled effectively, we need wise planning and maximum co-ordination of effort. We need a wider and more imaginative use of all the modern media of communication, including television, radio, films, religious drama, and the secular and religious press. We need to use our joint resources of manpower and money to the best possible advantage. To this end we have strengthened the Advisory Council on Missionary Strategy, with wider responsibilities, world-wide representation, and a full-time Secretary. Moreover, the Central College of the Anglican Communion established at St Augustine's College, Canterbury, after the Lambeth Conference of 1948, has become a striking symbol of the fellowship which binds all together.

There can be no forward steps without a full acceptance of Christian stewardship. By stewardship we mean the regarding of ourselves—our time, our talents, and our money—as a trust from God to be utilized in his service. This teaching is an urgent need in every congregation; a parish without a sense of stewardship has within it the seeds of decay.

There is a growing recognition to-day that too sharp a distinction has been made between clergy and laity. All baptized persons have the priestly vocation of offering life as a living sacrifice, acceptable to God through Jesus Christ. There is a ministry for every member of Christ; every man and woman who is confirmed is commissioned to this ministry in the Church, the home, the community, the world of business, and social life.

The clergy throughout the world fulfil their ministry with devotion and zeal. Many of them are in lonely situations, many of them face daily difficulties and frequent discouragement with unflinching courage. We thank God for their loyalty and their devotion to his people. But we must face the fact that they are inadequate in numbers, though not in faith, to the ever growing opportunities for carrying on our Lord's reconciling work. Our Communion has far too few of the men required for the special tasks of the ordained ministry, and the shortage cripples our existing work and prevents the seizing of new opportunities. One reason for this situation is the lack of a sense of vocation on the part of all Christian people—the lack of realization that every man is called by God to make some special contribution to the life of the world. Another reason is that financial resources for maintaining the ministry at a reasonable standard of subsistence are not always available. There is need for the whole Church to be concerned in a new way with regard to the finding, the training, and the support of ordained ministers.

What of the future? We have had encouraging reports of the growth of the Anglican Communion in spiritual power and numerical strength. We have been humbled by a fresh realization of the responsibility which our Communion carries in so many parts of the world. Yet we believe that the spiritual gifts which our Lord has given to our part of his Church are ours in trust for the whole Body of Christ. We know that we must pray and work with a new sense of urgency for unity with the non-episcopal Churches, for harmony of spirit and agreement in doctrine with the Eastern Orthodox Church and other ancient Churches, and for the healing of the breach between ourselves and the Church of Rome. There has come before us a vision of a wider fellowship of episcopal Churches finding, if God wills, a focus of unity in the Anglican Communion. So we have recommended that there may be conferences of representative bishops from each Province of our Communion and from each Church possessing the historic episcopate with which we are in full communion or in a relation of intercommunion.

In 1948 the Lambeth Conference recorded that four dioceses of the Church of India, Burma, and Ceylon had left the fellowship of our Communion to enter into the new united Church of South India. In the near future it may be expected that fifteen dioceses of that Province will take their place in the new Churches of Lanka, North India, and Pakistan, though remaining in full communion with the Anglican Communion. The Lambeth Conference of 1948 set before our people a vision of what, if God wills, might come to pass: "There would be, in every country where there now exists the Anglican Church and others separated from it, a united Church, Catholic and Evangelical, but no longer in the limiting sense of the word, Anglican."

That vision is still in the distant future, and until the time comes when God brings us all together in that unity we believe that the Anglican Communion has its own life which it must sustain and its own distinctive witness which it must give. Over the years the fellowship of the Lambeth Conferences has helped to make the Anglican Communion a more worthy instrument of God's purpose. Until the unity of the whole Church of Christ is realized, we believe that they will still have their essential part to play. Our Communion, strengthened in fellowship by these Conferences, and by the Anglican Congress, which we hope will meet again in 1963, enriched by the ever growing interchange of visits between one Province and another, must ever dedicate itself anew to the task of making God's message of reconciliation known throughout the world.

Signed on behalf of the Conference,

GEOFFREY CANTUAR: *President*

ROBERT PETRIBURG: *Episcopal Secretary*

ERIC JAY, *Assistant Secretary*

8 August 1958

A Message

Before our Conference ends, we would seek to share with all our people in the Church throughout the world something of the experience which has come to us, in a fresh and wonderful way, by the power of God's Spirit among us.

From the first, and throughout our work, we have been conscious of two clear facts.

First, that we ourselves have been knit together by the Holy Spirit in mutual understanding and trust.

Second, that, because we ourselves have been thus drawn together, God has given us a message of reconciliation for the Church and for the world. It is of that message of reconciliation that we would speak to you.

A divided Church cannot heal the wounds of a divided world. Therefore our most urgent concern has been with our own divisions. We thank God for the unmistakable evidence which has come before us that in Asia and Africa as well as in Britain and America, Christian Churches are actively moving towards a greater measure of unity.

But the message of reconciliation is needed equally to meet the strife, suspicion, and fear which set races, nations, and classes at variance with one another. As we have studied these situations, which many of you know at first-hand in your own countries, we have been led to see the clear call to the Church to act as a channel of God's reconciling power. And this means that each one of you as a member of the Church must think out what you in your own neighbourhood can do to further trust, forgiveness, charity among those who are at present divided by misunderstanding or hate.

This is the heart of the missionary task which confronts the Church everywhere. The task is one and the same in Europe or America, in Asia or Africa or the Southern Seas. The Church exists to bring home to men the meaning and the power of the truth that "God was in Christ reconciling the world to himself".

No one can bring home this truth to others unless he has experienced it in his own life. And the natural place for this to start is within the home. We have tried to understand some of the dangers which threaten family life in a world in which so many of the established standards and habits are disappearing under the influence of immensely rapid change. Do everything in your power to make your own home a witness to Christian faith, practice, and character, and help others to do the same.

None of us can do these things in our own strength: we can only do them in the power which God gives to those who will trust him and seek to do his will.

That power is given to us through private prayer and joining in corporate worship and sacrament. It is given to us through regular and instructed reading of the Bible. That is why the Bible is given the first place among the Reports of this Conference. In the Bible God speaks to us all, making known his nature and will, bringing home to us our need of his forgiving grace, assuring us that in spite of our sin and blindness his eternal purpose stands secure.

But our religion must be expressed not only at home and in Church but in our working life in the world. This working life is just as truly God's concern. Therefore we call upon you all to seek to understand God's purpose amid the perplexities of the social, industrial, and political life of your country and to offer yourselves as instruments of this purpose in these spheres.

In our Lord's prayer we are bidden to ask that God's Kingdom may come, and his will be done, on earth as in heaven. We cannot rightly pray this prayer unless at the same time we are working, each according to his ability, for the advancement of this Kingdom on earth. But we are not working alone. "It is God who is at work within you, giving you the will and the power to achieve his purpose".

Signed on behalf of the Conference,

GEOFFREY CANTUAR: *President*

ROBERT PETRIBURG: *Episcopal Secretary*

ERIC JAY, *Assistant Secretary*

8 August 1958

THE RESOLUTIONS

formally adopted by

THE LAMBETH CONFERENCE

1958

The Resolutions

1. THE BIBLE

1. The Conference affirms its belief that the Bible discloses the truths about the relation of God and Man which are the key to the world's predicament and is therefore deeply relevant to the modern world.

2. The Conference affirms that our Lord Jesus Christ is God's final Word to man, and that in his light all Holy Scripture must be seen and interpreted, the Old Testament in terms of Promise and the New Testament in terms of Fulfilment.

3. The Conference affirms that Jesus Christ lives in his Church through the Holy Spirit according to his promise, and that the Church is therefore both guardian and interpreter of Holy Scripture; nevertheless the Church may teach nothing as "necessary for eternal salvation but what may be concluded and proved by the Scripture".

4. The Conference gratefully acknowledges our debt to the host of devoted scholars who, worshipping the God of Truth, have enriched and deepened our understanding of the Bible, not least by facing with intellectual integrity the questions raised by modern knowledge and modern criticism. It also acknowledges the Church's debt to the men and women in our universities, colleges, and schools who by their teaching and example inspire new generations to love the Scriptures.

5. The Conference welcomes every sign of the revival of Bible Study within the common life of the Church. It calls on all Church people to re-establish the habit of Bible-reading at home, and commends the growing practice of group Bible study.

6. The Conference recognizes with gratitude the dominant place which the Anglican Communion has always given to the Holy Scriptures in all its public worship. It welcomes in the contemporary Liturgical Revival the growing realization of the close relation of Word and Sacrament.

7. The Conference affirms the importance of preaching, both evangelistic and expository, ministered as a means of grace, by men who have experienced the power of the Gospel in their own lives.

8. The Conference acknowledges gratefully the work of scientists in increasing man's knowledge of the universe, wherein is seen the majesty of God in his creative activity. It therefore calls upon Christian people both to learn reverently from every new disclosure of truth, and at the same time to bear witness to the Biblical message of a God and Saviour apart from whom no gift can be rightly used.

9. In view of the lack of understanding which can develop in consequence of the different thought and language of the Bible and the modern world, the Conference urges Christian scholars and leaders to co-operate with men of science and other kinds of modern learning in the study of their respective modes of thought and speech.

10. The Conference believes that the presentation of the message of the Bible to the world requires great sensitiveness to the outlook of the people of to-day, and urges that imaginative use be made of all the resources of literature, art, music, and drama, and of new techniques appealing to eye as well as to ear.

11. The Conference welcomes the new translations of the Scriptures in many languages, and would encourage our people to give all possible support to those societies whose concern is the distribution of the Scriptures to all lands. Much still remains to be done in this field and the need is urgent.

12. In the light of the previous eleven resolutions the Conference invites the Churches of the Anglican Communion to engage in a special effort during the next ten years to extend the scope and deepen the quality of personal and corporate study of the Bible.

2. CHURCH UNITY AND THE CHURCH UNIVERSAL

Christian Unity

13. The Conference welcomes and endorses the Statement on Christian Unity contained in the Report of the Committee on *Church Unity and the Church Universal*.

Full Communion and Intercommunion

14. The Conference endorses the paragraph in the Report of the Committee on Church Unity and the Church Universal which refers to the use of the terms "full communion" and "intercom-

munion", and recommends accordingly that where between two Churches not of the same denominational or confessional family, there is unrestricted *communio in sacris*, including mutual recognition and acceptance of ministries, the appropriate term to use is "full communion", and that where varying degrees of relation other than "full communion" are established by agreement between two such Churches the appropriate term is "intercommunion".

15. The Conference therefore requests the Archbishop of Canterbury to communicate this resolution to the Faith and Order Commission of the World Council of Churches for its information.

Wider Episcopal Fellowship

16. The Conference re-affirms Resolution 74, passed by the Lambeth Conference 1948, regarding "A Larger Episcopal Unity", and strongly recommends that within the next five years the Archbishop of Canterbury should invite to a conference representative bishops from each Province of the Anglican Communion, together with representative bishops from each Church possessing the historic episcopate with which Churches and Provinces of the Anglican Communion are in full communion or in a relation of intercommunion.

17. The Conference notes the recommendation of the Committee on Church Unity and the Church Universal concerning future Lambeth Conferences, and commends it to the attention of the President and the Consultative Body for consideration before the next Lambeth Conference.

The Church of South India

18. The Conference welcomes and endorses the Report of the Committee on Church Unity and the Church Universal concerning the Church of South India.

Nandyal

19. The Conference is agreed that, notwithstanding the recommendations of the Lambeth Conferences of 1930 and 1948 that no Province of the Anglican Communion should set up dioceses or congregations in the area of the Church of South India, the Church of India, Pakistan, Burma, and Ceylon should be left free to make the arrangements which seem best to that Church for the spiritual oversight of Christians in the Nandyal area, after consulting the

Church of South India and with the good will of that Church, bearing in mind that the union of Christians in that area is the ultimate aim.

The Scheme of Church Union in Ceylon and
The Plan of Church Union in North India and Pakistan

20. The Conference endorses generally the paragraphs of the Committee on Church Unity and the Church Universal which refer to the Scheme of Church Union in Ceylon and the Plan of Church Union in North India and Pakistan, and gives thanks to God for manifest signs of the work of the Holy Spirit in the negotiations which have brought the Scheme and Plan to this stage.

21. The Conference advises that when Churches have united in such a way that the whole ministry of the United Church has been episcopally united, permission to visiting ministers, not episcopally ordained, of Churches in communion with the United Churches at the time of the union, to celebrate the Holy Communion occasionally when visiting a United Church, be not regarded as a bar to relations of full communion between the United Church and the Churches and Provinces of the Anglican Communion; provided that due constitutional provisions are made to safeguard the conscience of worshippers.

Ceylon

22. The Conference calls attention to the recommendation of the Committee on Church Unity and the Church Universal concerning the Unification of the Ministry in the Scheme of Church Union in Ceylon, and advises the Church of India, Pakistan, Burma, and Ceylon to recommend to the Negotiating Committee the suggested amendments to the Scheme.

23. The Conference advises the Churches and Provinces of the Anglican Communion that they should be willing to enter into full communion with the resulting Church of Lanka on its inauguration.

The Church of North India and the Church of Pakistan

24. (*a*) The Conference wholeheartedly desires that the Plan for reunion in North India and Pakistan may go forward, and that the intention of the Plan may be secured, that the ministry of the United Church shall be "fully accredited in the eyes of all its members, and so far as may be of the Church throughout the world".

(*b*) The Conference wholly shares the desire of the Church of India, Pakistan, Burma, and Ceylon that the Anglican Communion should be able to enter into full communion with the United Church; it believes that the Churches and Provinces of the Anglican Communion could enter into full communion if the recommendations concerning the service for the unification of the ministry could be accepted.

(*c*) Should further explanation and discussion concerning the recommendations be desired, the Conference requests the President to appoint a small commission of bishops to be immediately available for consultation with the Church of India, Pakistan, Burma, and Ceylon.

Relations between Anglican and Presbyterian Churches

25. The Conference welcomes the taking up in a new spirit of the problem of the relations between the Episcopalian and Presbyterian systems of Church Order of which the Report on *Relations between Anglican and Presbyterian Churches* (published in 1957) is a signal illustration.

26. The Conference, having noted the careful study which has been given to this Report by the Inter-Church Relations Committee of the Church of Scotland and the six questions addressed to Anglicans by that Committee, commends for further discussion the comments made on these questions by the Committee on Church Unity and the Church Universal.

27. The Conference commends this Report for wider study by clergy and laity throughout the Anglican Churches, especially in those parts of the world in which Churches of the Anglican and Presbyterian traditions are in contact with one another.

28. The Conference notes with satisfaction and thankfulness the remarkable measure of constructive theological agreement which the theologians on both sides were able to reach and record, and expresses the hope that serious consideration may be given to the possibility of drawing the Anglican and Presbyterian traditions more closely together by a process of mutual assimilation of their respective Church Orders such as is suggested in the Report.

The Methodist Church

29. The Conference has heard with interest and sympathy of the conversations now proceeding between representatives of the Church of England and representatives of the Methodist Church

in England, and between representatives of the Protestant Episcopal Church, and representatives of the Methodist Church in the U.S.A.

30. The Conference calls attention to the Report of the Committee on Unity; and encourages continuance of the conversations with a view to the making of concrete proposals, as offering a possible first step on the way to reunion in the particular historic situations in which the Churches concerned are placed; but on the understanding that organic union is definitely accepted as the final goal, and that any plans for the interim stage of intercommunion are definitely linked with provisions for the steady growing together of the Churches concerned.

West Africa

31. The Conference expresses its sincere thankfulness at the growing interest within the Province of West Africa in conversations on reunion, having had before it the proposed Scheme of Union for Nigeria and the Cameroons which is at present receiving the prayerful consideration of the dioceses of the Province of West Africa and of the Methodist and Presbyterian Churches in Nigeria and the Cameroons.

32. The Conference, while recognizing the weight to be attached to arguments in favour of retaining the model of the Church of South India and the policy of gradualness therein expressed, but aware also of the desire within the Province that from the outset full communion should be maintained between Churches of the Anglican Communion and any united Church which might be formed, strongly recommends to the Province of West Africa further consideration of the Ceylon Scheme as a model, since only so does it seem likely that the desired result will be achieved.

33. The Conference recommends that in any Reunion Scheme the Ceylon or North India/Pakistan statement as to the Faith of the Church should be followed.

34. The Conference further recommends that should any far-reaching decision be reached by the Dioceses of the Province, the advice of the Lambeth Consultative Body should be sought.

The Jerusalem Archbishopric

35. The Conference welcomes such action toward Church unity as has been taken by the bishoprics in the Middle East and recog-

nizes the peculiar importance there of our relationship with the Orthodox and other Eastern Churches.

36. The Conference commends to the bishoprics concerned the Ceylon scheme for Church union as a model for any further discussions which it is hoped will take place.

37. The Conference urges that at every stage reference be made to the Lambeth Consultative Body.

The Roman Catholic Church

38. The Conference welcomes the permission given by Roman Catholic authority for contacts, discussions, and co-operation between Roman Catholics and other Christians, as contained in the document, *Instruction to Local Ordinaries on the Oecumenical Movement*, issued by the Supreme Sacred Congregation of the Holy Office in December 1949; and expresses the hope, first, that these permissions may be more widely and generously used, secondly, that they may be further extended in the interests of Christian understanding and fellowship, and thirdly, that Anglicans will make full use of these and all other available opportunities for promoting charitable understanding.

The Eastern Orthodox Church

39. The Conference deeply appreciates the presence of a distinguished group of Eastern Orthodox leaders at the opening of its proceedings, and is grateful for the opportunity thus given of having informal talks with them. It sincerely hopes that the relations between Orthodox and Anglicans may grow ever closer, and that advantages will be taken of every opportunity to further that aim, both in the interests of Christian Unity and as an important contribution to understanding and confidence between peoples.

40. The Conference has learned with satisfaction of the correspondence between the Archbishop of Canterbury and the Oecumenical Patriarch, and warmly endorses the desire of the Patriarch for a continuation of joint Anglican-Orthodox doctrinal discussion on the pattern of the Joint Doctrinal Commission of 1931.

41. The Conference has heard with keen interest and approval of the conversations between representatives of the Russian Orthodox Church and those of the Church of England held in Moscow in 1956, and draws attention to the Report of the proceedings since published.

Other Eastern Churches

42. The Conference welcomes the prospect of discussion with representatives of the Armenian Church with the object of promoting closer fellowship between the Anglican and the Armenian Churches. It views with sorrow the present internal difficulties experienced by the members of this ancient Church, and prays that they may soon be overcome. The Conference asks the Archbishop of Canterbury to take steps to arrange discussions with representatives of the Armenian Church when the time seems to him to be propitious.

43. The Conference encourages the Metropolitan of the Church of India, Pakistan, Burma, and Ceylon, to continue the plan to have further discussions with the Malankara Jacobite Syrian Church. It recommends that as the next step, other Churches, Provinces, and Dioceses of the Anglican Communion which have a direct interest in these questions should be consulted, and that they should be represented in any further discussions with the Syrian Orthodox Church.

44. The Conference notes with interest the discussions now in progress between the Church of India, Pakistan, Burma, and Ceylon and the Mar Thoma Church. It recommends that before these discussions are brought to a conclusion, other Churches, Provinces, and Dioceses of the Anglican Communion which are concerned with relations with Mar Thoma Christians should be taken into consultation so that if possible a common agreement may be reached by all the authorities concerned.

45. The Conference hopes that in all such negotiations any steps taken should be such as to encourage the recovery of unity among Syrian Christians.

Old Catholic Churches

46. The Conference notes with satisfaction that the Bonn Agreement has now been adopted by nearly all the Provinces of the Anglican Communion.

47. The Conference welcomes the suggestions made by a meeting between some Anglicans and Old Catholics in Holland, that the two Churches should co-operate in practical action to meet the spiritual needs of Dutch-speaking Christians who wish to resort to Anglican Churches in that country. It is of the opinion that such practical action would not only be a valuable demonstration of

the inter-communion which exists between the Anglican and Old Catholic Churches, but also a means of deepening the fellowship that exists between the members of those Churches.

Scandinavian Churches

48. The Conference welcomes the action taken by several Churches and Provinces in accordance with Resolutions 69, 70, and 71 of the Lambeth Conference of 1948.

49. The Conference welcomes the report of the discussions with the Churches of Norway, Denmark, and Iceland in accordance with Resolution 72 of the Lambeth Conference of 1948, and encourages their continuance.

Netherlands Reformed Church

50. The Conference, having heard with interest of discussions held between Anglican and Dutch theologians at the official request of the Netherlands Reformed Church—the first official discussion of the kind held with a Reformed Church on the Continent of Europe in recent years—requests the Archbishop of Canterbury to encourage the continuation of such discussions when opportunity offers.

Spanish Reformed Episcopal Church and Lusitanian Church

51. The Conference, being entirely satisfied with Reports received on the present doctrine and discipline of the Spanish Reformed Episcopal Church and the Lusitanian Church, welcomes the news of the consecration of Bishop Molina in Spain and of Bishop Fiandor in Portugal by bishops of the Episcopal Church of the United States and of the Church of Ireland, and prays that these Churches may be blessed by God in the service of his Kingdom. The Conference hopes that the desire of these Churches for the same relationship with Churches of the Anglican Communion as have the Old Catholic Churches will soon be fulfilled.

52. The Conference suggests that the bishops of these two Churches be invited to any conference arranged in accordance with the recommendation of Resolution 74—"A Larger Episcopal Unity"—of the Lambeth Conference of 1948.

Philippine Independent Church (Aglipayan)

53. The Conference records its pleasure at the vigorous growth of the Philippine Independent Church and welcomes the progress

being made in the relations between this Church and the Protestant Episcopal Church in the United States of America since the consecration of three bishops of the Philippine Independent Church by bishops of the Protestant Episcopal Church in the United States of America in 1948. The Conference is gratified to learn that priests of the Philippine Independent Church are receiving their theological training at St Andrew's Theological Seminary in Manila.

Episcopi Vagantes

54. The Conference draws attention to the fact that there are Episcopi Vagantes who call themselves either "Old Catholic" or "Orthodox", in combination with other names. It warns its members of the danger of accepting such persons at their own valuation without making further enquiries. The Conference reiterates the principle contained in Resolution 27 of the 1920 Lambeth Conference, that it cannot recognize the Churches of such *episcopi vagantes* as properly constituted Churches, or recognize the orders of their ministers, and recommends that any such ministers desiring to join an Anglican Church, who are in other respects duly qualified, should be ordained *sub conditione* in accordance with the provisions suggested in the Report of the relevant Committee of the 1920 Lambeth Conference.

The World Council of Churches

55. The Conference records its thankfulness to Almighty God for the formation, growth, and achievements of the World Council of Churches, and urges all the Churches and Provinces of the Anglican Communion to ensure that they are adequately represented in its counsels, take a full share in its work, and assume a just part of its financial responsibility.

Inter-Church Aid

56. The Conference commends to all members of the Anglican Communion the outstanding work of relief and reconciliation carried out by the World Council of Churches Department of Inter-Church Aid and Service to Refugees, in which they have gladly participated. It urges them to support it wholeheartedly and, when possible, themselves to offer sanctuary and the deepest charity to those who, for whatever cause, have lost their home and citizenship.

Prayer for Christian Unity

57. The Conference wishes to emphasize the importance of widespread prayer for the unity of all Christian people, and commends to all Anglicans the observance of the Week of Prayer for Christian Unity in the spirit of the late Abbé Paul Couturier, who taught many to pray for the unity of Christ's people in the way he wills and by the means he chooses. It welcomes the remarkable growth of such prayer and commends the formation of local groups of Christians of different traditions for the purpose of promoting prayer for Christian unity.

3. PROGRESS IN THE ANGLICAN COMMUNION

MISSIONARY APPEAL AND STRATEGY

The Mission of the Church

58. The Conference calls on every Church member, clergy and laity alike, to take an active part in the Mission of the Church. It is a Mission to the whole world, not only in area but in all the concerns of mankind. It has no frontiers between "Home" and "Foreign" but is concerned to present Christ to people everywhere.

Each generation needs to be evangelized and to this all-important task we summon the people of God in every land.

59. The Conference affirms that while the Church of Jesus Christ transcends all national or racial limitations, every Church should endeavour to share fully in the life of the people in the country in which it exists. The Conference rejoices that, in all parts of the world, a strong ministry is growing up from among the people. It notes with satisfaction that, under the guidance of the Holy Spirit, and in accordance with Catholic practice, bishops are being appointed and elected without reference to race or nationality.

Advisory Council on Missionary Strategy

60. The Conference accepts the recommendations of the Committee on Progress in the Anglican Communion concerning the Advisory Council on Missionary Strategy, and respectfully requests that action be taken by His Grace the President as soon as possible.

The Consultative Body

61. The Conference, while reaffirming the opinion expressed in Resolution 44 of the Lambeth Conference of 1920 that the

Consultative Body is of the nature of a Continuation Committee of the Lambeth Conference, recommends that its duties and composition should be redefined as follows:

(*a*) The duties of the Consultative Body shall be:

(i) to carry on work left to it by the preceding Conference;

(ii) to assist the Archbishop of Canterbury in the preparation of business of the ensuing Conference;

(iii) to consider matters referred to the Archbishop of Canterbury on which he requests its aid and to advise him;

(iv) to advise on questions of faith, order, policy, or administration referred to it by any Bishop or group of Bishops, calling in expert advisers at its discretion, and reserving the right to decline to entertain any particular question;

(v) to deal with matters referred to it by the Archbishop of Canterbury or by any Bishop or group of Bishops, subject to any limitations upon such references which may be imposed by the regulations of local and regional Churches;

(vi) to take such action in the discharge of the above duties as may be appropriate, subject to the condition that with regard to churches, provinces, and dioceses of the Anglican Communion its functions are advisory only and without executive or administrative power.

(*b*) The Consultative Body shall consist of:

(i) The Archbishop of Canterbury as ex officio Chairman and the Archbishop of York;

(ii) The Primates or Presiding Bishops of National or Provincial Churches in the following countries or areas:
Wales: Ireland: Scotland: U.S.A.: Canada: India, Pakistan, Burma, and Ceylon: Australia: New Zealand: South Africa: West Indies: Japan: China: West Africa: Central Africa: Middle East.

(iii) Such Members to represent other dioceses under the jurisdiction of the Archbishop of Canterbury as he may appoint.

Each member shall have the right to nominate a bishop to take his place at any meeting which he is unable to attend.

(*c*) The Archbishop of Canterbury with the approval of the Consultative Body shall appoint a secretary to serve under the directions of the Archbishop, who may, if the Advisory Council so agrees, be also the Secretary of that Council.

(*d*) The Consultative Body shall meet when summoned by the Archbishop of Canterbury or on his behalf; and in between meetings may conduct business by correspondence. All minutes and papers shall be sent to every member and if so desired to alternates also.

(*e*) Expenses incurred on behalf of the Consultative Body shall be borne by the fund provided for the Advisory Council on Missionary Strategy, if that Council so agrees.

Communication

62. The Conference urges that every opportunity be taken, at the local and provincial level, to make effective use of such channels of communication as television, radio, films, religious drama, and the secular and religious press.

63. The Conference suggests that through the Advisory Council on Missionary Strategy there could be an exchange of material, talent, skill, and technical knowledge between regional Churches of the Anglican Communion.

Christian Stewardship

64. The Conference recalls Church people to the duty and privilege of stewardship, of which sacrificial, planned, and systematic giving is a part, to the end that the souls of the people may be enriched, and the needs of the Church met, including the adequate support of its ministry and provision for the extension of its work. The Conference urges that the Church in every field be encouraged to become self-supporting.

Movement of Peoples

65. The Conference emphasizes the importance of the witness for Christ which can be borne when Christians go from one country to another, especially to countries where Christians are a small minority, and urges that ways and means be developed to assist both clergy and members of the laity to do so effectively. It also urges that every effort be made, especially on the parochial level, to practise Christian fellowship with people of other nations and races who come to live permanently in a new land.

Regional Councils

66. The Conference welcomes the fact that regional councils have been formed in the South-East Pacific and the South-West Pacific to assist common counsel and co-operation.

Religious Freedom

67. The Conference is deeply concerned by restrictions upon religious freedom in many areas, imposed in some cases by the State alone and in others by the State influenced by a dominant religious group. To those who suffer under these conditions the Conference extends the assurance of its sympathy and support. It affirms its conviction that freedom of religion includes not only freedom to worship but also freedom to propagate and to teach, as essential parts of the Christian faith.

Anglican Congress

68. The Conference, holding the Anglican Congress to be of great value to the life of the Anglican Communion,

    (a) re-affirms the desire expressed at the Anglican Congress of 1954 that another such Congress be held;

    (b) respectfully requests the Archbishop of Canterbury and the Presiding Bishop of the Protestant Episcopal Church in the United States of America to appoint a committee of bishops, priests, and lay persons to make arrangements, in accordance with the resolution of the Anglican Congress 1954;

    (c) asks that special consideration be given by this committee to the question of holding this Congress outside the English speaking countries;

    (d) suggests that the date of the Congress be 1963; and

    (e) recommends that the major topic should be "The World-wide Mission of the Church".

The Anglican Cycle of Prayer

69. The Conference calls attention to the Anglican Communion Cycle of Prayer prepared by the Overseas Council of the National Assembly of the Church of England, issued in response to the request of the Lambeth Conference, 1948, and commends it for the widest possible use in all our Churches by circulation in the Dioceses.

The Pan-Anglican Review

70. The Conference appreciates the value of the *Pan-Anglican* review, and commends it to the attention of the Churches and Provinces of the Anglican Communion, as a means of disseminating information about the Anglican Communion.

Christian Literature

71. The Conference recommends that literature should be recognized as an important instrument of the Church in fulfilling its mission; and that steps should be taken to secure that in every language area suitable literature is made available for the training of ordinands, the use of the clergy, the instruction and equipment of the laity, and not least for the commending of Christianity to those outside the Church.

72. The Conference urges that men and women ready to devote themselves to Christian literary work, including journalism, should be enlisted and trained to regard such work as a true vocation in the service of the Church.

THE BOOK OF COMMON PRAYER

Prayer Book Revision

73. The Conference welcomes the contemporary movement towards unanimity in doctrinal and liturgical matters by those of differing traditions in the Anglican Communion as a result of new knowledge gained from Biblical and liturgical studies, and is happy to know of parallel progress in this sphere by some Roman Catholic and Reformed theologians. It commends the Report of the sub-committee on the Book of Common Prayer on this subject to the careful study of all sections of the Anglican Communion.

74. The Conference, recognizing the work of Prayer Book Revision being done in different parts of the Anglican Communion,

(a) calls attention to those features in the Books of Common Prayer which are essential to the safeguarding of our unity: i.e. the use of the Canonical Scriptures and the Creeds, Holy Baptism, Confirmation, Holy Communion, and the Ordinal;

(b) notes that there are other features in these books which are effective in maintaining the traditional doctrinal emphasis and ecclesiastical culture of Anglicanism and therefore should be preserved;

(c) and urges that a chief aim of Prayer Book Revision should be to further that recovery of the worship of the Primitive Church which was the aim of the compilers of the first Prayer Books of the Church of England.

75. The Conference commends to the study of the whole Anglican Communion the counsel on Prayer Book Revision given in the Report of the sub-committee on the Book of Common Prayer.

The Holy Communion Service

76. The Conference requests the Archbishop of Canterbury, in co-operation with the Consultative Body, to appoint an Advisory Committee to prepare recommendations for the structure of the Holy Communion service which could be taken into consideration by any Church or Province revising its Eucharistic rite, and which would both conserve the doctrinal balance of the Anglican tradition and take account of present liturgical knowledge.

The Commemoration of Saints and Heroes of the Christian Church in the Anglican Communion

77. The Conference holds that the purpose of a Kalendar is to increase our thankfulness to God and to strengthen our faith by recalling regularly the great truths of the Gospel, the principal events in the life of our Lord, and the lives and examples of men and women who have borne pre-eminent witness to the power of the Holy Spirit, and are with us in the communion of saints.

78. The Conference considers that the power to revise or amend Kalendars should be exercised by the same authority as is required for the revision of the Book of Common Prayer within each several Church or Province, which authority may allow supplementary commemorations for local use in addition to the Kalendar at the request of a diocese.

79. The Conference is of opinion that the following principles should guide the selection of saints and heroes for commemoration:

(*a*) In the case of scriptural saints, care should be taken to commemorate men or women in terms which are in strict accord with the facts made known in Holy Scripture.

(*b*) In the case of other names, the Kalendar should be limited to those whose historical character and devotion are beyond doubt.

(*c*) In the choice of new names economy should be observed and controversial names should not be inserted until they can be seen in the perspective of history.

(*d*) The addition of a new name should normally result from a widespread desire expressed in the region concerned over a reasonable period of time.

80. The Conference recommends that the Church should continue to commemorate the saints in three ways: by Red Letter days, Black Letter days, or a memorial collect alone.

MINISTRIES AND MANPOWER

The Needs of the Ministry

81. The Conference, while feeling deep concern about the numerical inadequacy of the ministry available to consolidate the Church's present work, and to serve its expanding mission, nevertheless recognizes that there is no short cut to the solution of problems of manpower, and that nothing less than a wide response in terms of vocational dedication to the ministry will meet present needs and provide for expansion.

It therefore urges upon every diocese and upon every priest the need for presenting the vocation to the ministry in terms which will challenge the laymen of the Church to consider a call to this life of sacrifice and devotion.

Areas of Special Need

82. The Conference desires to emphasize that there is a continuing need in "missionary" provinces and dioceses for a supply of men for the ordinary ministerial needs of the Church from outside their own area.

It recognizes that from time to time there is need also for men of mature experience, sound learning, and pastoral gifts, to undertake work of special responsibility. It therefore recommends that the missionary agencies of the Church throughout the Anglican Communion should keep this in mind, and seek to have available priests and lay workers for this purpose.

The Staffing of Theological Colleges

83. The Conference desires to emphasize the need for first-class theological teachers for colleges in the developing areas of the Church, and calls upon the missionary agencies of the Anglican Communion to take such steps as are practicable to meet this pressing need. Financial aid is also needed for the improvement of buildings and for the provision of adequate library facilities.

United Colleges

84. The Conference, recognizing that there is much common ground in theological training which can be covered in united

colleges, and that such colleges can exert a considerable influence in creating better understanding between the several Churches which they serve and in fostering the growth towards greater unity, welcomes the development of united colleges. Nevertheless it considers it essential to secure for Anglican students adequate arrangements for the worship and discipline customary in the Church and to ensure that the Anglican theological contribution is fully and worthily made in the united college.

Theological Faculties or Departments

85. The Conference urges that every endeavour should be made to provide resources whereby theological faculties or departments may be established and supported at the newer universities which are coming into being throughout the area covered by the Anglican Communion. The Conference welcomes the progress which has already been made towards this end, and urges the Church to make the fullest use of these faculties when they are created, both as training centres for the ministry, and as providing opportunities for a real integration of Christian faith and scholarship with the intellectual life of other academic disciplines.

Standards of Training

86. The Conference urges each Province of the Anglican Communion to keep under continuous review its standards for training for ordination, both with regard to the period required and the content of the course, having regard to the demands made upon the clergy in modern conditions.

Post-Ordination Training

87. The Conference draws attention to the importance of post-ordination training, and recommends that adequate opportunity and financial provision may be available for such training.

The Office of Deacon

88. The Conference recommends that each province of the Anglican Communion shall consider whether the office of Deacon shall be restored to its primitive place as a distinctive order in the Church, instead of being regarded as a probationary period for the priesthood.

The Supplementary Ministry

89. The Conference considers that, while the fully-trained and full-time priesthood is essential to the continuing life of the Church, there is no theological principle which forbids a suitable man from being ordained priest while continuing in his lay occupation. While calling attention to Resolution 65 of the Lambeth Conference of 1930, the Conference now wishes to go further and to encourage provinces to make provision on these lines in cases where conditions make it desirable. Such provision is not to be regarded as a substitute for the full-time ministry of the Church, but as an addition to it.

The Office of Reader

90. The Conference, gratefully recognizing the value of the Lay Ministry (i.e. Sub-Deacon, Reader, and Catechist), whether stipendiary or voluntary, is of opinion that it should be controlled and directed (a) by admission to office by the Bishop or his deputy, and (b) by the Bishop's formal licence. The Conference is of opinion that the work of these ministries should be described as an office, not an order, nor should the office be deemed to possess the character of indelibility. The Conference urges the importance of adequate training and examination before admission to office.

91. The Conference emphasizes the necessity for due care in the exercise of the facility recommended in the latter part of Resolution 65 of the Lambeth Conference of 1930, for the authorizing by a Bishop of certain Readers to assist in the Administration of the Holy Communion. It recommends that this should be done only to meet pressing need, and that this authority should be given explicitly in writing from time to time.

Religious Orders and Communities

92. The Conference, greatly valuing the special form of vocation evident in Religious Orders and Communities, hopes that this form of vocation may find its expression in a wide range of ecclesiastical tradition within the Anglican Communion.

The Contribution of Women

93. The Conference thankfully recognizes the particular contribution of women to the mission of the Church: and urges that fuller use should be made of trained and qualified women, and that

spheres of progressive responsibility and greater security in service should be planned for them.

The Task of the Laity

94. The Conference, believing that the laity, as baptized members of the Body of Christ, share in the priestly ministry of the Church and in responsibility for its work, calls upon Anglican men and women throughout the world to realize their Christian vocation both by taking their full part in the Church's life and by Christian witness and dedication in seeking to serve God's purpose in the world.

St Augustine's College, Canterbury

95. The Conference expresses its satisfaction at the establishment and progress of St Augustine's College, Canterbury, as a Central College for the Anglican Communion. It approves of the way in which its work is developing and would encourage its continuance on the present lines.

96. The Conference requests the College Consultative Council to continue its work as a necessary link between the College and the Anglican Communion as a whole.

97. The Conference recommends that, in view of the financial needs of the College, the Provinces of the Anglican Communion should be asked to increase their contributions for the upkeep of the College from £11,000 to £14,000 *per annum.*

98. The Conference endorses the policy whereby St Augustine's College awards a Diploma to students who have satisfactorily completed a prescribed course.

99. The Conference requests Provinces of the Anglican Communion to seek to ensure that suitable men are set free for a course of study at St Augustine's.

4. THE RECONCILING OF CONFLICTS BETWEEN AND WITHIN NATIONS

The Church's Work of Reconciliation

100. The Conference is convinced that the Church's work of reconciliation must be powerfully expressed within the parish or local congregation. Consequently here it would lay emphasis upon the following points:

(a) There is a need for Christians to understand more deeply the meaning of God's providence in history and the ground of Christian hope, as distinct from a belief in automatic social progress. This needs to be emphasized in preaching and teaching.

(b) There is need for persistent intercessory prayer, not only in general terms but specifically and by name for those in positions of great responsibility. Such prayers should be offered for those in nations which oppose us as well as those friendly to us.

(c) There is need to emphasize the disastrous effect on the common life of those who come to the Lord's Table unreconciled to their neighbours and with bitterness towards them in their hearts. We would recall that the Invitation to the Holy Communion is addressed to those who are "in love and charity with their neighbours".

(d) Where there are divisions in the local community, the Christian congregation in that place should face them fearlessly and, by the action of its members, should serve as an agent of reconciliation.

(e) While there are many elements in the reconciling of conflicts, none are more important than the character and conduct of individual people. Success or failure in any particular instance may in the end depend on the individual: not only on his knowledge, his judgement, and his zeal, but also on the spirit of Christ mirrored in a life which bears the marks of the Cross and the fruits of the Spirit.

101. The Conference urges all members of the Anglican Communion to further the ministry of reconciliation by

(a) developing deeper understanding and fellowship with churchmen of every land;

(b) extending the use of clergy and lay workers in lands other than their own, the exchange of teachers and seminarians, and the participation by lay visitors in the Church life of the countries they visit;

(c) the general use of the Anglican Cycle of Prayer to under-gird this wider sense of community;

(d) participation everywhere in the wider community of all Christian people in the ecumenical opportunities open to them.

Christian Citizenship

102. The Conference calls upon all Christian people to recognize their duty of exercising to the full their responsibility as citizens in the national and international policies of their governments.

103. The Conference calls upon all Christian people to strive by the exercise of mutual understanding, calm reason, and constant prayer, to reconcile all those who are involved in racial, political, economic, or other conflicts.

The Rights of Men and Nations

104. The Conference declares that the Church is not to be identified with any particular political or social system, and calls upon all Christians to encourage their governments to respect the dignity and freedom of people within their own nations and the right of people of other nations to govern themselves.

Sharing Material Resources

105. The Conference draws attention to the widespread poverty in many parts of the world; it notes with thankfulness the measures taken to help under-developed countries to become self-supporting, and calls upon Christians in more favoured lands to use their influence to encourage their governments in the task of relieving poverty by a generous sharing of their material and technical resources with those in need.

Modern Warfare and Christian Responsibility

106. The Conference reaffirms that war as a method of settling international disputes is incompatible with the teaching and example of our Lord Jesus Christ, and declares that nothing less than the abolition of war itself should be the goal of the nations, their leaders, and all citizens. As an essential step towards achieving this goal the Conference calls upon Christians to press through their governments, as a matter of the utmost urgency, for the abolition by international agreement of nuclear bombs and other weapons of similar indiscriminate destructive power, the use of which is repugnant to the Christian conscience. To this end governments should accept such limitations of their own sovereignty as effective control demands.

The Conference further urges the governments of the leading

nations of the world to devote their utmost efforts at once to framing a comprehensive international disarmament treaty, which shall also provide for the progressive reduction of armed forces and conventional armaments to the minimum necessary for the maintenance of internal security and the fulfilment of the obligations of States to maintain peace and security in accordance with the United Nations Charter.

107. The Conference calls Christians to subject to intense prayer and study their attitudes to the issues involved in modern warfare, and urges the Church to continue to consult regularly with scientists and political leaders about the many problems of ethics and conscience which arise from advances in nuclear research.

The United Nations

108. The Conference affirms the need for strengthening the United Nations and to this end:

(a) urges that serious consideration be given to the revision of its Charter, the more effective use of, and respect for, the existing processes of international justice, and to the creation of adequate means for enforcing its decisions;

(b) commends wholeheartedly the work done under the aegis of the United Nations, whereby the skills and resources of member nations are made available for the benefit of the whole of humanity;

(c) recommends that all Church people be asked to pray for God's blessing upon the officers and declared purposes of the United Nations;

(d) urges that all Church people be asked to encourage community study regarding the constitution, the plans, and the needs of the United Nations.

109. The Conference draws attention to the work of the Committee of the Churches on International Affairs (within the World Council of Churches) and urges Anglicans to support its efforts to bring an informed Christian opinion to bear on international issues.

Condemnation of Racial Discrimination

110. The Conference affirms its belief in the natural dignity and value of every man, of whatever colour or race, as created in the

image of God. In the light of this belief the Conference affirms that neither race nor colour is in itself a barrier to any aspect of that life in family and community for which God created all men. It therefore condemns discrimination of any kind on the grounds of race or colour alone.

The Conference would urge that in multi-racial societies members of all races shall be allowed:

(a) a fair and just share in the government of their country;

(b) a fair and just share in the control, development, and rewards of the natural resources of their country, including advancement to the highest level of attainment;

(c) the right to associate freely in worship, in education, in industry, in recreation, and in all other departments of the common life.

The Church in an Industrial Age

111. The Conference urges the Provinces of the Anglican Communion to give special study to the task, strategy, and ministry of the Church within industrial society, and by the use of bold and imaginative experiments to strengthen the impact of the Christian Faith upon the whole life and pattern of industry.

5. THE FAMILY IN CONTEMPORARY SOCIETY

Marriage

112. The Conference records its profound conviction that the idea of the human family is rooted in the Godhead and that consequently all problems of sex relations, the procreation of children, and the organization of family life must be related, consciously and directly, to the creative, redemptive, and sanctifying power of God.

113. The Conference affirms that marriage is a vocation to holiness, through which men and women may share in the love and creative purpose of God. The sins of self-indulgence and sensuality, born of selfishness and a refusal to accept marriage as a divine vocation, destroy its true nature and depth, and the right fullness and balance of the relationship between men and women. Christians need always to remember that sexual love is not an end in itself nor

a means to self-gratification, and that self-discipline and restraint are essential conditions of the responsible freedom of marriage and family planning.

114. The Conference welcomes, with thankfulness, the increasing care given by the clergy to preparation for marriage both in instructing youth, through confirmation classes and other means, and also immediately before marriage. It urges that the importance of this ministry should continue to be emphasized and that special attention should be given to our Lord's principle of life-long union as the basis of all true marriage.

115. The Conference believes that the responsibility for deciding upon the number and frequency of children has been laid by God upon the consciences of parents everywhere: that this planning, in such ways as are mutually acceptable to husband and wife in Christian conscience, is a right and important factor in Christian family life and should be the result of positive choice before God. Such responsible parenthood, built on obedience to all the duties of marriage, requires a wise stewardship of the resources and abilities of the family as well as a thoughtful consideration of the varying population needs and problems of society and the claims of future generations.

116. The Conference calls upon all Church people to have in mind that, since our Lord's ministry gave a new depth and significance to forgiveness, his Church and the families within it must be a forgiving society, and that there are no wrongs done by its members, one to another, that are unforgivable, or in which a costly forgiveness may not lead to repentance and, through repentance, to reconciliation and a new beginning in living together.

The Conference believes that many tensions in marriage and family life are allowed to reach a breaking point because self-righteousness or a sense of injury takes priority of forgiveness, and that marital relations also break down because those involved do not in time take counsel with a wise advisor. It affirms that no husband or wife has the right to contemplate even legal separation until every opportunity of reconciliation and forgiveness has been exhausted.

117. The Conference welcomes the growth of Marriage Guidance Councils, which prepare people for marriage and assist in maintaining stable married life. It recommends that the clergy and Church

people of mature faith and with the right qualifications should be encouraged to offer themselves for training as counsellors. It believes that such counsel, given as a Christian vocation by well-trained Christian husbands and wives, is a volunteer service of great value, makes an important contribution to the community, and deserves government support.

118. The Conference recognizes that divorce is granted by the secular authority in many lands on grounds which the Church cannot acknowledge, and recognizes also that in certain cases, where a decree of divorce has been sought and may even have been granted, there may in fact have been no marital bond in the eyes of the Church. It therefore commends for further consideration by the Churches and Provinces of the Anglican Communion a procedure for defining marital status, such as already exists in some of its Provinces.

119. The Conference believes that the Resolutions of the 1948 Lambeth Conference concerning marriage discipline have been of great value as witnessing to Christ's teaching about the life-long nature of marriage, and urges that these Resolutions, and their implications, should continue to be studied in every Province.

Polygamy

120. (*a*) The Conference bears witness to the truth that monogamy is the Divine will, testified by the teaching of Christ himself, and therefore true for every race of men.

(*b*) It acknowledges that the introduction of monogamy into societies that practise polygamy involves a social and economic revolution and raises problems which the Christian Church has as yet not solved.

(*c*) The Conference urges upon Church members the continuance of thorough study and earnest prayer that God may lead his Church to know the manner of its witness and discipline in this issue.

(*d*) The Conference, recognizing that the problem of polygamy is bound up with the limitation of opportunities for women in society, urges that the Church should make every effort to advance the status of women in every possible way, especially in the sphere of education.

(*e*) The Conference further requests his Grace the President to refer this problem to the Advisory Council on Missionary Strategy.

The Christian Family

121. The Conference commends, as an aid to better teaching about marriage and home life, the following summary of the marks of a Christian family. Such a family—

(*a*) Seeks to live by the teaching and example of Jesus Christ;

(*b*) Joins in the worship of Almighty God on Sundays in church;

(*c*) Joins in common prayer and Bible reading, and grace at meals;

(*d*) Is forgiving one to another, and accepts responsibility for one another;

(*e*) Shares together in common tasks and recreation;

(*f*) Uses abilities, time, and possessions responsibly in society;

(*g*) Is a good neighbour, hospitable to friend and stranger.

122. The Conference believes that a most important answer to the crushing impact of secularism on family life lies in a return to the discipline of family prayer and in a faithful common Christian life in the household. It urges that the clergy work towards this end by teaching both the privilege and the means of such worship, and of Bible reading, in which fathers should take their due place with mothers and children as members and ministers of a worshipping community.

123. The Conference, recognizing that there is a world-wide need for decent and suitable housing, records its belief that every married couple should have adequate privacy and shelter, for the better bringing up of the family as well as for the benefit of its own married life; and that national and local government share fully with private enterprise the community's obligation to meet this need.

124. The Conference, noting the increasing proportion of older people in many parts of the world, calls attention to the fact that, although some are entirely dependent upon the care of others, many of them, by reason of experience or special skills, still have much to give. It expresses its warm appreciation of the studies and projects, bearing on this problem, which have already been made, and records its belief that the Church, in all its Provinces, should initiate and assist such studies, and should also seek practical means of meeting the needs they reveal. It further emphasizes the responsibility of sons and daughters for the needs of elderly parents and, where possible, for making such provision as will keep them closely within the life and activity of their family circle.

The Duties of the Laity

125. The Conference rejoices that, more and more, lay men and women are finding their true Christian ministry in their daily work in the world, as well as in the organized life of the Church. All of us need to remember that the field of Christian service for the laity lies mainly in the secular sphere, where their integrity and competence can best serve the needs of the world and the glory of God. The clergy need to understand this, and to help, by their teaching and by sharing in the thoughts and problems of the laity in their daily work, to deepen this ministry. The laity need equally to understand it, to help one another by Christian discussion and loyal comradeship to bear a better witness, and to offer in their work both their responsible, skilled gifts, and a deeper understanding of the Christian faith about God and man.

Gambling, Drunkenness, and the Use of Drugs

126. The Conference draws attention to the widespread and growing reliance on undesirable and artificial means of responding to the restlessness of our present age, and to the resulting weakening of family life. It utters a warning against the dangers implicit in gambling, drunkenness, and the use of drugs, and calls for renewed teaching of responsible and disciplined standards of behaviour.

Migratory Labour

127. The Conference, recognizing the family as the God-given unit of human life and society, condemns those systems of migratory labour that break up family life by enforcing the unjustified residential separation of man and wife, or of parents and children.

Refugees and Stateless Persons

128. The Conference calls the attention of churchmen to the tragic plight of refugees and stateless persons, as a continuing feature of the world to-day. It believes their plight is a cause both of intense personal suffering and of political unrest; and that neither this, nor the size of the problem, is sufficiently appreciated. It therefore calls:

(a) for continuing support, in the form of both gifts and personal service, for the Inter-Church Aid and Refugee Service Department of the World Council of Churches, so that such people may be assisted;

(*b*) for more sustained action through the United Nations and through the governments concerned, to finance migrants and place them in new countries; and

(*c*) for special care in keeping together the members of families in such distress.

The Religious Duties of Churchmen

129. The Conference urges that the sections of the Report on the Family in Contemporary Society dealing with industrial pressures on the family, and, by implication, upon the religious duties of churchmen, should be carefully studied by Christians in industry and should be made a basis for discussions between representatives of the Churches and industrial managers and trade unionists.

Co-operation with Secular Agencies

130. The Conference believes it to be most desirable that the clergy and Church workers should take every opportunity of meeting health and social workers, as well as teachers, in a locality, and discussing with them the welfare of the community and its family life.

The Mutual Exchange of Information

131. The Conference, believing that a need exists within the Anglican Communion for a far greater sharing of study, and that, especially in areas where research is advancing rapidly, and where social and political changes are pressing, the usefulness of the Anglican Communion, under God, depends upon the maintenance of the closest possible relations between the Provinces and their various activities of exploration and investigation, recommends that his Grace the President and the Consultative Body consider and adopt appropriate means of establishing and maintaining such common conversations and mutual exchange.

A Statement on Peace

We all know that in the hearts of the vast majority of men and women of all races there is a haunting fear of war and a deep desire for peace. In our experience of Christ, we who represent many countries and peoples have found a unity which helps us to transcend our differences: and because we believe that God is the Father of all men we speak not only to our fellow Christians but to all who will listen to us.

Unless war and its causes can be banished, nuclear weapons threaten the annihilation of whole peoples, the destruction of our material civilization, and the corruption of mankind. But merely to banish war is not to achieve true peace. True peace means an order in which men are free to live under justice and according to righteousness; in which the resources of the world are developed and distributed for the benefit of all; in which the only war is against poverty, ignorance, disease, and oppression; in which the results of man's knowledge and discovery are used not for destruction but for enlightenment and health.

To create such an order will demand sacrifices from all. Nations have their own legitimate interests which it is their duty to preserve but, too often, they exaggerate their own claims and ignore those of others. That leads inevitably to jealousy and strife, with all the risks of bloodshed and open war.

We call, then, upon the nations to forgo those policies of self-interest which deny the interests of others. We call on people of all faiths, and those who lead them, to work and pray persistently for the development of a community of peoples wherein, with whatever limitations of national sovereignty may be necessary, all shall live under the rule of law. Only in such a community can the present unequal division of resources be remedied and assistance brought to nations which are struggling with dire poverty and distress.

Not in a day can trust replace mistrust, partnership replace selfishness. Disagreements and rivalries will long remain between nations and individuals, and for these every nation bears, and will continue to bear, a share of the guilt. But even so, in this human situation, men must practise patience, humility, generosity, and sacrifice. They must make the strenuous effort of mind and will required to understand and overcome, with a new urgency, the practical problems which divide the human family. They must pray for that peace which, because it is the will of God, is the one hope of mankind.

The Services and Meetings of the Conference

Thursday, 3 July

3.0 p.m.   Canterbury Cathedral: Service for the Reception of Archbishops and Bishops attending the Lambeth Conference.

Friday, 4 July

10.0 a.m.– Lambeth Parish Church: Mattins, Litany, and
12.30 p.m. Holy Communion.

2.30 p.m.   Lambeth Palace—Full Session.
Reception of Delegates:

Scandinavian Churches
The Right Rev. Dr Gösta Lundström, Bishop of Strängnäs
The Right Rev. Dr E. G. Gulin, Bishop of Tampere
The Right Rev. Dr Skat Hoffmeyer, Bishop of Aarhus

German Evangelical Church
The Right Rev. Dr Otto Dibelius, Bishop of Berlin and Brandenburg

Church of Scotland
The Right Rev. Dr John A. Fraser, Moderator of the General Assembly

The Free Church Federal Council of England
The Rev. Dr Ernest A. Payne, Moderator of the Free Church Federal Council
The Rev. Dr Harold Roberts, President of the Methodist Conference
The Rev. Dr T. G. Dunning, President of the Baptist Union
The Rev. John Huxtable, representative of the Congregational Union of England and Wales
The Right Rev. G. T. Bellhouse, Moderator of the General Assembly of the Presbyterian Church of England

Saturday, 5 July

10.30 a.m. Lambeth Palace and Church House: meetings of Committees.

2.15 p.m.   Lambeth Palace: Full Session.
Reception of the Mayor and Mayoress of Lambeth.
Reception of Delegates:

Old Catholics

The Most Rev. Dr Andreas Rinkel, Archbishop of Utrecht

The Orthodox Church

Archbishop Athenagoras of Thyateira

The Metropolitan James of Melita

Bishop Meletios of Reggio

of the Oecumenical Patriarchate of Constantinople.

The Metropolitan Pitirim of Minsk

Bishop Michael of Smolensk

Archpriest K. I. Ruzitsky

Professor N. D. Uspensky

Mr V. S. Alekseev

of the Church of Russia.

The Metropolitan Justin of Moldavia

The Rev. Alexander Jonescu

of the Church of Rumania.

The Metropolitan of Varna and Preslav

of the Church of Bulgaria.

Bishop Anthony of Sergievo

of the Russian Orthodox Church in London.

The Armenian Church

The Right Rev. Bessak Toumayan

special representative in England of the Armenian Supreme Catholicos.

(The Delegates also attended the services at Canterbury Cathedral and St Paul's Cathedral, but were not present at any other meetings of the Conference.)

Sunday, 6 July

    10.30 a.m.   St Paul's Cathedral: Sung Eucharist preceded by the Litany in procession.

Monday, 7 July–Friday, 11 July

    Lambeth Palace: Full Sessions.

Monday, 14 July–Friday, 25 July

    Lambeth Palace and Church House: meetings of Committees.

Monday, 28 July–Friday, 8 August

    Lambeth Palace: Full Sessions.

Sunday, 10 August

    10.30 a.m.   Westminster Abbey: closing service of the Lambeth Conference.

PART 2

THE REPORTS
OF THE COMMITTEES

NOTE

The following Reports must be taken as having the authority only of the Committees by which they were respectively prepared and presented.

The Conference as a whole is responsible only for the formal Resolutions agreed to after discussion and printed in Part 1 of this volume.

Contents of Part 2

1. The Holy Bible:
Its Authority and Message

MEMBERS OF THE COMMITTEE

ENGLAND

A. M. Ramsey, D.D. [York]
    (Chairman)
A. T. P. Williams, D.D. [Winchester]
M. H. Harland, D.D. [Durham]
G. A. Chase, M.C., D.D. [Ripon]
R. R. Williams, D.D. [Leicester]
B. Pollard, T.D., M.SC., D.D. [Sodor and Man]
H. E. Ashdown, D.D. [Newcastle]

WALES

W. G. H. Simon, D.D. [Llandaff]
    (Joint Secretary)
J. R. Richards, D.D. [St David's]
G. O. Williams, D.D. [Bangor]

IRELAND

R. G. Perdue, D.D. [Cork, Cloyne, and Ross]

SCOTLAND

J. W. A. Howe, M.A., B.D. [St Andrews, Dunkeld, and Dunblane]

UNITED STATES

A. B. Kinsolving, D.D. [Arizona]
W. R. Moody, D.D. [Lexington]
R. S. Emrich, PH.D. [Michigan]
    (Joint Secretary)
R. S. Hubbard, D.D. [Spokane]
E. H. West, D.D. [Florida]
A. J. Miller, PH.D. [Easton]
C. R. Haden, D.D. [Sacramento]
J. P. Craine, D.D. [Indianapolis (Coadj.)]

CANADA

P. Carrington, D.D., LITT.D. [Quebec]
    (Vice-Chairman)
H. D. Martin, D.D. [Saskatchewan]

M. E. Coleman, D.D. [Qu'Appelle]
R. J. Pierce, D.D. [Athabasca]
H. E. Hives, D.D. [Keewatin]
R. S. Dean, D.D. [Cariboo]
A. H. O'Neil, D.D. [Fredericton]

INDIA, PAKISTAN, BURMA, AND CEYLON

S. A. B. Dilbar Hans, B.A. [Chota Nagpur]
Chandu Ray [Lahore (Asst.)]

AUSTRALIA

E. H. Burgmann, M.A., TH.D. [Canberra and Goulburn]
W. H. Johnson, B.A., TH.D. [Ballarat]
A. E. Winter, M.A., TH.D. [St Arnaud]

NEW ZEALAND

A. H. Johnston, L.TH. [Dunedin]

SOUTH AFRICA

A. H. Cullen, D.D., B.SC. [Grahamstown]

WEST INDIES

P. W. Gibson, B.A., D.D. [Jamaica]

JAPAN

P. Y. Kurose [Mid-Japan]

WEST AFRICA

J. L. C. Horstead, D.D. [Sierra Leone]
E. T. Dimieari, C.B.E. [Niger Delta]
H. A. I. Afonya [Niger Delta (Asst.)]

EXTRA-PROVINCIAL

S. Tomusange [Upper Nile (Asst.)]
K. Shalita [Uganda (Asst.)]
L. E. Stradling, M.A. [South-West Tanganyika]
H. Otter-Barry, C.B.E., M.A. [Mauritius]

A+

The Bible and the modern world seem at first sight to be very far apart, and even among those who wish to see the bearing of the one upon the other there are many who are perplexed as to how to do so. This report is written in sensitiveness to this perplexity, but in the conviction that it is through the Bible that the modern world can come to understand itself.

The contrast is indeed great between the modes of thought of the Bible and of the modern world. The Bible contains the story of an ancient people, with a primitive culture, a pre-democratic polity, and a pre-scientific view of the universe. The modern world is conscious of the discoveries of science about the place of the world in the universe, and while a sense of poetry may help to find the Bible intelligible it is sometimes hard for those whose mental training has been scientific or technological to understand the Biblical language. It is not only that those whose moral outlook is conditioned by popular influences of an unethical kind find the moral emphasis of the Bible far removed from them; it is also that those who are deeply concerned about moral issues may find the God-centred morality of the Bible hard to understand.

On the other hand there is a difficulty of a totally different kind to which sensitiveness is also due. At a time when religious men and women are hungry for authority, many in different parts of the world have been turning to the Bible to find authority within it, but have often interpreted it in ways which lead to extravagance or sectarianism. This may result from reading it with too narrow a belief in the Holy Spirit, which does not take into account either scientific methods of study or the accumulated experience of the Church in the understanding of the Bible. Here also is a need to be met.

This Report is written in the belief that within the contemporary Church, and not least within the Anglican Communion, there is the power to present the Bible as possessing an urgent message to the modern world, probing deeply to the roots of its distress and bringing God's own remedy to it. The times seem in many ways to be propitious for this. There has been a revival of the use and study of the Bible in every part of Christendom. There has been amongst Biblical scholars a renewed emphasis not only upon the important work of literary and historical study, but upon the exposition of the great themes about God and Man which the Bible contains. There has been, in various liturgical movements, a recovery of the close relation between the Bible and the eucharistic worship of the Church; and there has been no less a recovery of the place of the Bible in the life of prayer and in the training of souls. Besides all this, there has been, especially in very recent years, a concern about the problems of language and thought-forms which are implicit in the presentation of the Biblical message to people of different cultures.

To pass from the modern world to the Bible and back again is in one sense to make a long journey. To the scholar it means the study of an ancient literature in its own ancient setting and the attempt to bring its message from its original setting into our own. But, if there is faith and imagination, the Bible and the modern world are not so far apart—for the modern world is restless, torn by calamity, and seemingly near to catastrophe. It was in such an environment that the Bible was first written, and to such an environment it has the power to speak yet again.

THE BIBLE AND THE CHURCH

It is right first that we should reaffirm the relation of the Bible and the Church, which Anglican teaching has always emphasized and the modern study of Christian origins has made more clear. Neither Bible nor Church is understood apart from the other.

At the time of the life of our Lord the Church of God already existed, for the nation of Israel was the Church: a people which God had called to a particular relation to himself as the messenger of his self-revelation to mankind. It was to this nation-Church, "the people of the old covenant", with the Old Testament scriptures as its Bible, that our Lord addressed his message; and when that national rejection of him which led to his death had begun, he had already gathered around him a remnant to be the nucleus of his new Church which was to embrace people of every nation. After the ascension we see this new Church in existence, continuous with the old through the person of our Lord himself, but now possessing the new covenant given on the night before the crucifixion and the Holy Spirit bestowed on the day of Pentecost.

As yet no New Testament had been written, and the Old Testament Scriptures remained as the only Bible of the Christians. But the Church possessed, as gifts consequent upon the coming of Christ, the sacraments of Baptism and the Holy Communion, an oral tradition of teaching, and an apostolic ministry. By all these its life was sustained, its service of the Gospel was set forward, and its fidelity to that Gospel was conserved.

1. Baptism was the way of admission of converts to the Church as the Body of Christ, and to union with Christ crucified and risen. The Eucharist united the members of the Church to one another in the partaking of the body of Christ and the blood of Christ, and showed forth his death till he come.

2. Preaching and teaching conveyed both to potential converts and to the members of the Church the knowledge of the Christian faith. From the earliest days there was the Gospel preached by the Apostles, with the Lord's death and resurrection as its central core. There was also oral teaching about the things which the Lord did and taught in his life on earth. We learn from the prologue of St Luke's Gospel that,

before even the writing of that book had been planned, much instruction about the story of Jesus had been given. There is, however,
evidence for the early use of brief written catechetical forms and
credal summaries such as would assist the process of oral teaching.

3. There were also men commissioned by Christ with authority to
teach and to rule in the Church: the Apostles. By exercising their
authority, which they were charged to do with personal humility and
self-effacement, they secured the unity of the Church and its fidelity
to the original Gospel.

As the Church advanced into the second and third generations after
the life and death of Jesus, developments took place in the means
whereby its fidelity to the Gospel was maintained. Eye-witnesses of
the original events existed no longer, and the original Apostles were
dead. While there was the need to present the Christian faith to
people of different kinds of culture and to interpret its meaning in
the light of the Church's experience under the guidance of the Holy
Spirit, the Spirit who should guide the Church into all truth, there
was the need no less to ensure that the essence of that faith was
preserved amid tendencies to false innovation and to syncretism with
other religious cults.

The new developments were these:

1. There were Baptismal Creeds, of which the one known as the
   Apostles' Creed was an example, which set before converts a
   summary of the Christian faith as the Apostles had taught it.
2. A process was begun whereby certain books held to possess
   authority were formed into the Canon of the New Testament, so
   as to constitute, together with the books of the Old Testament,
   the Bible of the Christian Church.
3. There was the office of bishop, now distinct from the office of
   presbyter, and exercising certain functions which the Apostles
   had exercised in relation to the unity and continuity of the Church.
   In particular, the succession of bishop to bishop in his see secured
   continuity of the true teaching in contrast to what was spurious.
   Each of these developments served the Church's apostolic character as its mission passed beyond the historical memories of the
   first days.

It is our belief that these developments were not fortuitous, but
were expressions of the rule of the Holy Spirit in the Church, and
were divinely given gifts to it. Accordingly, the Anglican Communion
appeals to the whole of that primitive tradition of which the Sacraments, the Creeds, the Canon of the Bible, and the historic episcopate
are all parts. The New Testament is thus not to be seen in isolation:
the Church preceded it in time, and it was within the Church, with
its Sacraments, Creeds, and Apostolic Ministry, that the New Testament was canonized. The Church is the witness and keeper of Holy

Writ, charged to interpret it and expound it by the aid of the Spirit of truth which is in the Church. But on the other hand the Church is not "over" the Holy Scriptures, but "under" them, in the sense that the process of canonization was not one whereby the Church conferred authority on the books but one whereby the Church acknowledged them to possess authority. And why? The books were recognized as giving the witness of the Apostles to the life, teaching, death, and resurrection of the Lord and the interpretation by the Apostles of these events. To that apostolic authority the Church must ever bow.

In the formation of the Canon of the New Testament, the books which composed it were added to the Canon of the Old Testament, as it came to be accepted as authoritative in the Church. A number of books familiar in the Synagogue and the Church were excluded from the Old Testament, but continued to be read in Church in connection with the complete Canon. These books are known as the Apocrypha. The Old Testament was not left behind. Rather was it now seen, not as a complete revelation in itself but as the first stage in a revelation of which the New Testament was the fulfilment. The conjunction of the Old Testament and the New was seen to be important both for the Christian belief in God and for the Christian belief in the Church. The God who revealed himself in Jesus, and through him overcame sin and death, was the self-same God who had created the world and ruled it by his providential government. That God the creator and God the redeemer are one is signally borne out by the unity of the two testaments. Similarly there is a continuity between the Church of God in the Old Testament and the New. Israel was the Church or "people of God", set free by the Exodus from Egypt to fulfil a divine mission for the sake of the human race. The Christian Church is the new Israel or "people of God" set free by Christ's death and resurrection to fulfil a divine mission unlimited in place or time.

CRITICISM AND AUTHORITY

It has always been the belief of the Christian Church that the Holy Scriptures are inspired, and not seldom they have been described as the Word of God. It is concerning the nature of their inspiration and their status as the Word of God that many difficulties have arisen in modern times; and these difficulties have had a considerable bearing upon the use of the Bible by Christian people and the authority of its message for the modern world.

It was in the nineteenth century that the clash between the belief in the Bible as the inspired word of God and modern critical and historical studies became acute. While at various stages in the history of the Church there had been room for the understanding of the Bible as allegory or as parable as well as in its literal meaning, it had been common for Christians to take as literal history the narrative portions of the Old Testament as of the New, and to regard this literal acceptance as part of a true belief in the Bible as the divine Word. It was thus a severe shock when geology challenged the account of the creation of the world in the book of Genesis, or when biological science challenged the belief that the human race originated in the special creation of two first human beings, Adam and Eve, or when the critical study of historical documents questioned the unity and the historicity of the books ascribed to Moses, or when historians drew attention to discrepancies in the narratives in the four Gospels such as raised a query as to the equal historical value of every detail which the Gospels contain. It is not too much to say that this clash between faith and criticism effected a revolution in the study of the Bible and caused great travail in its use amongst Christian people. It is, however, our conviction that the Bible has come through this travail with its authority not damaged but enhanced.

The work of criticism has been an inevitable consequence of the claim of the Christian Church to appeal to history. If we believe that God revealed himself through the history of Israel and especially through the events connected with Jesus, that history must bear the scrutiny of scientific study. Biblical criticism has brought about a number of widely accepted results: that certain narratives which had been taken to be literal history cannot be so taken; that certain books were not written by the writers traditionally ascribed to them; that some of the books were written in several stages at different periods; that some of the features of religion described in the Bible were less unique than had been supposed and were more interwoven with the religion and culture of other peoples. But these results are not only negative: they enable us to read the Bible less as a uniform oracle than as a library of books of many kinds—history, drama, poetry, law, proverbial wisdom, prophecy—reflecting in divers ways the story of a nation unique in the claims to be made for itself and for its literature, with Jesus Christ as the climax. Plainly the work of criticism has enlarged our understanding of the Bible in its human elements. We have to ask: How has it affected our attitude to the Bible as the revealed Word of God?

There was a phase in the work of Biblical criticism when it was often dominated by the presuppositions of what may be called evolutionary liberalism. This was the notion that man steadily progresses in morals and religion as well as in everything else; that nature is uniform, with no room for particular divine interventions; and that the Kingdom of God is to be equated with the progress of mankind to the fulfilment of God's will. With these presuppositions, students of the Bible tended to discard from it the elements which involved the supernatural action of the living God, and to present its message as a movement of moral and religious progress. But more recently amongst Biblical scholars in every part of the world there has been a strong reaction from this outlook. Scholars, thorough and rigorous in criticism and historical method, have studied the Bible without prejudice against belief in the living God who is active in history, and have shown how the very varied library of books in the Bible has its origin in the unique action of God in Israel and in Jesus Christ. This point of view, powerfully represented at the present day, is often called by the name of "Biblical theology". While subjecting the records about Jesus Christ, no less than those of the Old Testament, to a criticism which does not accept every detail of the narratives as historical, "Biblical theology" is able none the less to affirm that Jesus Christ is the divine Son of God whose life and death and resurrection are not understood apart from the Apostles' own interpretation of them as a Gospel of divine salvation.

Such is the background to the consideration to-day of the authority of the Bible. It is possible both to acknowledge the great debt which is owed to the work of critical scholarship and to affirm that divine authority is to be seen within the Bible. What is not easy is to define precisely the synthesis of authority and criticism. But we believe that the suggestions which follow will be of service.

1. Throughout the Bible there are many references to "the Word" or "the Word of the Lord", or to God as speaking. These phrases tell of a significant element in the conception of God within the Bible. God is a God who "speaks". This means both that God's declared purpose finds its expression in his actions in the world, and that his actions in the world are intended to have an impact upon the minds and consciences of men: revealing or commanding or judging or challenging. By God's Word the world was created, the world is sustained, the events of history are ruled, Israel was delivered. By God's Word law and prophecy came to Israel to reveal God to her, God's judgements fell upon her, and God's consolations restored her. In all these God's Word was disclosed. But finally in Jesus "the Word became flesh and dwelt among us". Here is the full and final disclosure. Jesus is himself the Word of God, final both in revelation and in redemptive act. And while, after the coming of Jesus, the term "Word" is used of his own teaching and of the Gospel concerning him which the Apostles preached, it is clear that he is himself the heart and centre of that Gospel. Since Jesus is the Word, he is the key to our understanding of the Word in the Old Testament which preceded his incarnation and of the Word in the New Testament writings which now show him forth.

It is clear that if we are to understand the way in which the Bible is the Word of God we need to take as our central thought the fact that Jesus Christ is the Word of God. With this to guide us we can read the Old Testament as God's Word of Promise and the New

Testament as God's Word of Fulfilment. It is because of their connection with Jesus Christ that the books have authority.

In the light of the relation of the Bible to Jesus Christ we can affirm that the Bible possesses the authority of God's truth and is the work of God's inspiration, without ascribing inerrancy to every statement which the Bible contains.

2. The *truth of God* in the Bible is conveyed in more ways than one. It is conveyed through significant actions of God in history, and through inspired interpretation of those events: thus the Exodus from Egypt is interpreted as disclosing God's providential care for the nation whom he had called to be his people with a mission in the world. It is conveyed sometimes through propositional statements— and the very limitations of language, even when it is inspired by God, are such that the truth of God transcends the propositions which convey it. It is conveyed sometimes through imagery, parable, and analogy. It is conveyed sometimes through moral commands. All these ways of conveying the truth of God appear in the books of the Old Testament, and they do not necessarily involve inerrancy of factual statement. Rather does the absence of inerrancy enable us to avoid the mistake of ascribing finality to stages of revelation which are incomplete, and remind us to use the Old Testament as God's Word of Promise of which Jesus Christ alone is the complete Fulfilment.

3. As to *inspiration,* it seems that perplexities may be greatly lessened by the line of thought which we have been following. There are obviously degrees within the Bible: degrees of significance as between books or portions of books, and degrees of religious and moral approximation to the full revelation of Jesus Christ. But it is doubtful whether we can rightly speak of "degrees of inspiration"; and those who have done so have sometimes thought of inspiration in terms of what we find inspiring to ourselves or of genius in religion or language. But inspiration means that the Spirit of God has been at work in a writer; and just as the Bible as a whole is the record of God's revelation of himself in Israel and in Jesus, so we believe that as a whole it is inspired by God. It is the whole of the Biblical drama and the whole of the Biblical literature which bears witness to God's revelation of himself in the story of Israel, with the shadows as well as the lights and the ups and downs of failure and recovery. Correlative with the divine revelation in the whole, is the belief that his Spirit was at work in all the books which serve that revelation.

It must not be forgotten that God has disclosed himself in many ways within the created world, in nature which reflects him and in man who is in his own image. Nor must it be forgotten that the Spirit of God has inspired men in every nation far beyond the covenants of the Bible. But the Christian truth is bound up with the belief that in Jesus Christ there has been a unique revelation and a unique redemptive act, prepared for by a unique action of the living God in Israel and interpreted by a unique action of his Spirit in the Apostolic Church. Therein lies the importance of the Bible for all time.

In the light of all these considerations it is possible, for all the variety of the contents of the Bible, to see its unity as a drama disclosing the truth about God and man. Here is the drama in its outline.

THE DRAMA OF THE BIBLE

The Hebrew mind sees the story of the world and of mankind as a drama, in which the author and chief actor is God. It visualizes the creation of the universe in a sequence of six scenes which it calls "days". The sixth picture is flashed upon the screen; it is the appearance of Man upon this planet—Adam, to use the Hebrew name. It is the epoch of Man, the "Day" in which we are still living.

Man is a fallen creature. He has transgressed the law of good and evil which is written in his heart; he is subject to sin and death. And so indeed he appears in history. There is a fatal element of evil even in his greatest achievements. He never enters with any security into his allotted kingdom of the earth. He dies, and they bury him.

Other stories in the book of Genesis illustrate his history. They are framed from ancient tales and poems; but in these Hebrew pictures God Almighty is the chief actor, or has the last word. The flood of evil overwhelms mankind; the tower of his civilization breaks in confusion; but a small remnant, a "righteous seed" is preserved and endures in every generation.

The story of the Hebrew people now begins. We are given the family portraits: Abraham and Isaac and Jacob—not perfect men, of course, or fully understanding the purposes of God, but leaving everything to follow the call which they receive. In them and in their seed all the nations of the world will be blessed.

The idea of Israel as a chosen nation does not exclude the idea that other nations, Egypt, Assyria, Babylon, Persia, Greece, or Rome, were also chosen for a purpose, which they fulfilled in their time. It runs through the Hebrew literature that God has a purpose and a destiny for every nation and every man, and that man can only realize himself fully when he becomes conscious of it and fulfils it.

The Bible follows the fortune of the descendants of Jacob, who was given the name of Israel.

The book of Exodus begins the epic of the formation of the chosen people. The descendants of Israel are slaves in the land of Egypt, and God brings them out into liberty, using that great leader of men, Moses, for his purpose; for God always works through flesh and blood in this divine story.

It is the passover night. He redeems them; he liberates them; they pass through the Red Sea; at the foot of Mount Sinai they are made

A*

his own people in a "covenant" or compact which was looked upon as a mystical marriage: "I will make my abode among you . . . and I will walk among you, and will be your God, and you shall be my people."

The power and glory and righteousness of God are thus revealed and embodied in a chosen people. The world receives through them the Ten Commandments which are the laws of life for nations and for men.

The reader of the books of Joshua and Judges will find much evidence that the Israelites were as yet a group of uncivilized or savage tribes, though they possessed the revelation of God. They took possession of the "promised land" by sword and fire: they slaughtered their enemies. This tradition of aggressive warfare was believed by them to be in accordance with the will of God. They had much to learn about the ways of God; and they took long to learn it.

The Books of Samuel and Kings tell the tale of the institution of the monarchy. In the character of David the paradoxes of this phase of the story meet. David is in part a savage, in part a civilized man, and also a man "after God's own heart". He has charm and chivalry in his character. In his person the twelve tribes do for a short time realize their unity. God continues to work through consecrated personality.

As a further centre of unity, David projected the building of a temple in the city of Jerusalem, to take the place of the old "tabernacle" of Moses; a work which was carried out by his son Solomon. The "ark of the covenant" was installed here; and it was believed that the glory of the Lord filled the temple. It was here that Isaiah saw his vision of the Lord seated upon his throne, and heard the angelic chorus: "Holy, holy, holy is the Lord of hosts; the whole earth is full of his glory."

The rest of the Books of the Kings is a tale of division and dissension, deterioration and reform. The kings, the priests, and the prophets play a great part in this exciting story which establishes all the main elements in the revelation of God through Israel; the monarchy and the temple as the centre of unity, the priesthood as the ministry of teaching and worship, and the prophets as the inspired messengers of repentance and reform. Many of the prophets left behind them written transcripts of their words, among them Isaiah and Jeremiah. They proclaim the righteousness and mercy of the God of Israel, and call upon the nation to repent and to trust in him; but they begin to see that the nation as a whole is far from the righteousness of God, and its unfaithfulness can only end in judgement and catastrophe. The climax of this phase of prophetic witness was the tragic period when God delivered his people into the hand of their enemies, the Assyrian and the Babylonian; the temple was burned, the city laid waste, and great numbers of the leading citizens, with their king, carried away as captives to Babylon.

In all human probability this would have been the end of the little backward nation which had dared to believe that it was the people of God Almighty; but the impossible happened; it emerged from this catastrophe or judgement with a purer faith and devotion. The prophet Ezekiel arose among the exiles in Babylon. Isaiah and Jeremiah had said that God would restore his people under a monarch descended from David. Jeremiah and Ezekiel spoke of a "new covenant" according to the spirit, which would be written in the heart.

The restoration actually began seventy years later under the patronage of the Persian monarch. Haggai and Zechariah uttered their prophecies at this time; Nehemiah and Ezra record some of its phases. It was slow, painstaking, and laborious; and it called for great faith and courage. The books of the law and the prophets and the psalms were preserved and studied and edited in their present form.

A strange development can be traced in the minds of the greater prophets. It was felt that the religion of Israel, even in the written law, was not yet a perfect expression of the mind of God for his people: Israel too had not responded as it should; there was need of a change of heart, a new covenant, a more spiritual law. "The days would come" when God would send them a saviour or deliverer, often pictured as coming from David's royal line; and in his days there would be universal peace, and the whole world would put *their* trust in him.

Another picture is given in the latter part of Isaiah; there is a servant of the Lord, who is a man of sorrows and acquainted with grief; it is through his sufferings and death that he will bear his witness, and yet he will be exalted and lifted up, after offering his life to God. He will bear the sins of his people.

The history of Jerusalem after the restoration is obscure and inglorious; but there were always those who held the faith. The oppression and persecutions in the Greek period were the occasion of successful military resistance and of heroic martyrdoms, the greatest spiritual monument of which was the Book of Daniel. Israel maintained its faith in God, and God preserved his people through their darkest hours: but they were subjected to the Roman rule and administered by Herodian kings and a Sadducee priesthood. Apocalyptic writers kept alive fantastic dreams of a glorious future. Simple people kept alive a genuine faith in God Almighty and his love for his people.

Then comes John the Baptist, heralding the coming of Jesus Christ the Son of God, to inherit the promises made to Abraham, and to fulfil the hopes and aspirations of the prophets. Christ takes it all up into himself; he is king, priest, and prophet; he perfects and transforms the whole content of the old Israel; he preaches the gospel in Galilee; he forms the apostolate; it is the passover season; he makes the "new covenant" with them in his flesh and blood. He offers his life for theirs, and goes to his death.

He was crucified. He was buried. But the sepulchre in the rock could not hold him down. He rose again. In spite of all the fires of modern criticism and scepticism, it remains a fact of history, the most important fact of history, that those who knew him best declared that they had seen him risen from the dead; they took this gospel round the world; they died for it.

What did this gospel mean to those who proclaimed it with his mandate and mission, and in the power of the Holy Spirit? It meant Jesus himself as the revelation of God, ascended into heaven, seated at God's right hand, and coming in power and glory. What did it mean to those who accepted it in simple faith, and were baptized in his Name, and incorporated into the apostolic fellowship? Words were not enough. It was righteousness, forgiveness, resurrection from the dead, hope, life, glory.

Two things happen. The old Jerusalem, with its temple and priesthood and sacrifice, was destroyed, and vanishes from history. It had fulfilled its purpose.

A new people was created, a new Israel continuous with the old, but gathered into the risen and victorious Christ, a Church for all nations filled with the power of the Holy Spirit. In this Church the literature of the New Testament (or "new covenant") came into existence. This Church maintained the tradition of great Apostles such as Peter and Paul and John, whose memory it revered as martyrs and witnesses. It believed itself to be the new Israel or new Jerusalem foretold by the prophets, and founded upon the Apostles, Jesus Christ himself being the chief corner-stone. They saw it expanding to the ends of the earth; but it was also one with the company of saints in heaven, from which they looked for the coming of the Lord in power and glory.

Even so, come, Lord Jesus.

THE BIBLE AND THE CHRISTIAN FAITH

Such is the drama of the Bible. While it sometimes speaks of the relation of God and Man in ways which belong more to poetry than to history, it rests upon a firm ground of history, inasmuch as the deliverance and mission of Israel were facts, and it is no less fact that Jesus lived, died, and rose again. Faith affirms that through these facts God has spoken to men. It affirms yet more that the Divine Son came and entered completely into the experience of human life in order to draw the human race into fellowship with himself.

The great Christian doctrines are no more and no less than interpretations of the Biblical drama which the Church made under the guidance of the Holy Spirit. God the righteous and omnipotent creator; the utter dependence of all created existence upon him; the human race as possessing the divine likeness and yet torn from the divine fellowship by sinfulness; the impotence of the human race to fulfil itself without the divine rescue brought by Jesus Christ; the act of rescue in Christ's life, death, and resurrection; his revelation of the

Triune God, Father, Son, and Holy Spirit; the Church as the community wherein by the indwelling of the Holy Spirit fellowship with God is found; the possession here and now of eternal life by those who are united to Christ in anticipation of life with him in the world to come: the presence already of the reign of God within history and its final vindication yet to come. Such is the pattern of Christian belief. The Creeds summarize it. The Church expounds it in systematic form. But it is from the Bible that every right exposition of it derives.

There have from time to time been attempts at radical reinterpretations of the Biblical message which try to discard the elements belonging to primitive culture and to retain an essential core relevant to the modern world. These attempts often involve a sceptical attitude towards the historical worth of much that is in the gospels, and an earnest desire to make the New Testament gospel the vehicle of a contemporary message of God to man in his modern predicament. Anglicans should not desire the free inquiries of scholarship to be restricted on dogmatic grounds; and they should be ready to learn from every effort to interpret the gospel to each successive age. But there is need to beware of re-interpretations which merely pick from the Biblical message the elements which happen to be congenial to a particular generation.

THE CHURCH LIVING BY THE BIBLE

The Church must live by the Bible. More than that, it must know itself as the Church of the Bible, the people of God.

It is right for the Church still to see itself as the people of God, even as the Old Testament describes it. It owes its existence to God's loving kindness in redemption. Its privileges are bound up with its obligation to obedience. Its obedience is to a mission for the sake of the whole human race, and if it becomes wrapped up in itself, God will judge and punish it: when he does so he will restore a remnant faithful to himself. It is by God's faithfulness alone that the Church endures to fulfil his purpose. Still to-day the Church reads the Old Testament, and recites the Psalms—to find in them these undying truths about itself and its mission.

But the Church is now under the new covenant, and it is Christ's Body, and Bride, and Temple. Christ lives in it, through the indwelling of the Holy Spirit. For all the sinfulness of the Church's members the divine life is there; and within the Church men and women already have union with God himself through the Word and the Sacraments. It is a fellowship including those who have departed this life in the faith of Christ no less than those now living in this world; it may truly be said to span this world and the world-to-come. It is called to reflect in the fellowship of its members their fellowship with Christ. Its mission towards the world is the overflowing of that divine love by which it is constituted.

It is for the Church therefore to be the Church *truly*, and so to bring home the meaning of the Bible wherein its own meaning is learned. The realization of this gives vitality to the Church's own use of the Bible.

In the public worship of the Church the Bible has always had a conspicuous place; and, thanks to the Book of Common Prayer and the liturgies derived from it, the Anglican Communion has given the ordered use of the Bible a dominant position in its worship. The full effect of this, however, rests upon constant teaching about it. Everything possible should be done to help worshippers discover that, in the services of the Church, the Bible is alive; so that they may consciously take part in the process through which the Holy Spirit is seeking to bring its message home to their minds and consciences. The reading of the Scriptures in the Church services needs the utmost care in order that it may be as worthy and helpful as can be; and no part of the work of the preacher matters more than the exposition of the Scriptures which are read in the services of the Church. The preacher will often find great value in modern translations.

The unity of the Bible and liturgy has been given a fresh emphasis in recent times, as a result of what is broadly called the "Liturgical Movement" in many parts of the Christian Church. In the Holy Communion, Epistle and Gospel and sermon proclaim the Word of Christ to the people, just before Christ—living and contemporary—feeds them with his Body and his Blood. Thus the Word in the Scriptures is the more vivid on account of the nearness of Jesus who is the Word in the sacramental presence and gift. So the Eucharist is illuminated by the Scriptures; and the power of the Scriptures is enhanced by their use within the Eucharist. In this way the Church may increasingly realize itself as the community which lives by the Bible no less than by the Sacraments which unite its members to their Lord. In the services of Morning and Evening Prayer also, the drama of the Church as the people of God is set forth in psalms, lessons, and canticles.

The preaching of the Word is far more than teaching about the Gospel. It is a means whereby Jesus, who is the Word, becomes vivid to the hearers in his presence, his gift, and his demand.

The reading of the Bible is a means of grace for Christians, and it is their duty to avail themselves of it according to their capacity. But much help is needed to enable them to do this. All should read the Bible as nourishment for the soul, with prayer that the Holy Spirit may stir mind and heart and will in response to it. Those who are capable of it should be given the opportunity of grasping its history, and of appreciating the help which critical study brings. There is need to call specially for the reading of the Bible by the members of a family or household together. In many parts of the Church there are groups who read the Bible together, sharing together their knowledge and understanding of its message.

The Church is called to confront the world with the righteousness of God, and to this end looks constantly to the moral teaching of the Bible. It is, however, never easy, and sometimes agonizingly difficult, to use this moral teaching in the right way.

There is first the moral law of God propounded in the Old Testament and summarized in the Ten Commandments. These commandments are not made obsolete by the new covenant; they declare the rudiments of moral obligation towards God which civilized men even now have failed to learn. But the Law, which had been given to lead men to Jesus Christ, was reinterpreted by him. He taught a more radical obedience, involving not only actions but the motives and inclinations of the heart, and he summarized the Law in the twofold commandment of love to God and love to one's neighbour. This twofold commandment finds illustration in all that Christ taught about purity of heart, forgiveness, and the abolition of any limits as to those who must be loved.

It is, however, impossible to draw upon the moral teaching of Christ as a code of rules or a set of definitions. Some of his teaching sets out the utter renunciation of self to which his disciples are called; and Christians, pledged as they always are to this, have to apply it in many changing conditions of society under the guidance of the Holy Spirit. Some of his teaching, as in the Beatitudes in the Sermon on the Mount, illustrates the character of those who belong to the Kingdom of God, and it is a character embodied perfectly in Christ himself. It is from Christ as example that this character is learned; and it is from Christ, through the Holy Spirit, that there comes the grace to practise it.

The morality drawn from the Bible involves therefore both constant reference to the person and teaching of Christ and belief that the conscience which takes Christ as its guide will be given new insight by the Holy Spirit. From time to time the Church itself uses its power of "binding and loosing" in the making of decisions about the duty of its members, and where it does so its members ought loyally to respect its authority. But both law and precept should always serve the purpose of God, revealed in the Bible, to deliver men through the obedience of faith into the liberty of sonship.

It is not only the individual but the community which Christ came to redeem. When a man responds to the converting power of Christ, he brings with him the whole sum of his personal relations and activities, so that all these may be brought beneath Christ's law of love. The Church therefore cannot bring men the Gospel in its fulness without trying always to learn and to teach the pattern of common life which discipleship demands in each particular human situation.

THE CHURCH PRESENTING THE BIBLICAL MESSAGE TO-DAY

The Gospel is the power of God unto salvation to them that believe, and its essence is ever the same. Its centre is the Cross of Christ, whereby God leads men to see themselves as sinners under the divine judgement and as recipients of the divine forgiveness when they repent and believe. It is a Gospel calling for decision, for when the mind and conscience have been truly confronted with it, the issue lies between fellowship with God, which is salvation, and the loss of it, which is a state of peril. The Church is charged until the end of time to preach the Gospel with the Cross as its centre and with the incisiveness of life and death.

The Gospel is "according to the scriptures", and the preaching of it includes the use of every aspect of the Bible. It is necessary to bring home the truth that God is creator and that men are made in his image, and so the foundation of the theology of the Bible is still part of the Church's proclamation. It is necessary for men to-day, as it was for those to whom the Gospel was first preached, to learn of the imperative character of God's moral law as the preparation for the Gospel and to hear the righteousness of God, as the prophets taught it, affirmed yet again. Furthermore, the Cross cannot be isolated from the Resurrection which made it effectual in redeeming power, or from the Holy Spirit and the Sacraments as a part of God's saving work. Nor must the emphasis upon Calvary and Easter cause any neglect of the life and teaching of Jesus, since these show us the perfect humanity which Christians are called to imitate and the moral demands made of those who live according to God's Kingdom. In all these ways the Bible serves the preaching of the Christian faith.

How then may it be shown that the message of the Bible, concerned as it is with past events, is not about the past alone but about the present also? How may it be grasped in its contemporary significance?

1. First, the message of the Bible becomes contemporary whenever the members of the Church witness truly to their fellowship with the present, living Christ. It is the rôle of the Word and the Sacraments to be the means of Christ's presence within the Christian community, and when its members respond in surrender to him and reflect him in their lives, the Bible can come alive to their contemporaries.

2. The message may no less be made contemporary by the faithful preaching of the Cross, so that here and now men see the judgement upon themselves, upon the Church, and upon the civilization of the day. In this way the Cross has timeless significance, as the Holy Spirit brings to men's consciences the conviction of the truth. Consequently, the love of God in the Cross is realized with new vividness.

3. The message of the Bible is about the Kingdom or sovereignty of God—present already and one day to be vindicated. But how is the

sovereignty of God to be believed amid the stresses of the present time? The Bible helps us to find the answer. It does so by its record of men who were faithful amid calamities, by its revelation of the sovereignty of God as omnipotent love working through the Cross, and by its message that the Creator has come to take upon him the pains and frustrations of his creatures and that the world is in his hands.

4. Above all, the Biblical message is seen to be contemporary whenever human lives are changed by the grace of God, with the surrender of heart and mind and will to him. Here are seen the authentic signs of the new creation which is still the proof of the Gospel.

In all these ways the Church can show how the message of the Bible bears upon to-day—and to-morrow—as well as yesterday. Indeed the Christian Year, which is observed from Advent to Whitsunday, can be felt by the members of the Church as a drama in which they themselves are sharing even now. But in presenting the message to those who are outside the Christian tradition, the Church has to face the needs and difficulties which are sometimes discussed under the word "communication". The message has to be given with awareness of the setting of the lives of those who hear it, and of the ways in which their mental outlook is formed.

1. The contrast is great between the traditional language of the Christian faith and the modes of thought of a scientific culture. This question needs much study within the Church, and it has no easy solution. While there is theological language which calls for constant paraphrase into contemporary idioms, there is also theological language which is difficult for many, not because it is old, but because it is poetical, and awareness of this can assist the work of Christian teaching. So can the use of good modern translations of the Bible. There is a special need of exponents of the Christian faith who have a knowledge of the scientific disciplines in which so many contemporary minds are trained. There is great need for personal co-operation between those who are working in the two fields. This would help to overcome the difficulties caused by the existence of different modes of thought.

2. It is not by speaking and hearing alone that the message of the Bible is conveyed. It is addressed to the eye and the imagination. Art and drama, no less than music and poetry, can be powerful means of serving the truth; and so can the techniques of television and radio. In the field of education much depends not only upon the teaching of religion in itself but upon the character of education as a whole with the awakening of minds to the many ways in which truth may be approached.

3. If the conflict which once existed between religion and science, through the misuse on both sides of their respective rôles, has largely changed its ground, it would be disastrous for us to lapse into a

neutrality in which each ignored the other. It is the conviction of Christian faith that all knowledge comes from God and is to be reverenced as his gift; and that in all the discoveries of the sciences God has a purpose that they may be used to reflect his glory in the world. The Christian Church is therefore called both to learn from all new disclosures of truth, and to proclaim constantly the Biblical message of the righteous God by whom and for whom all things were made.

It is, however, not only with the world of scientific culture that the need for "communication" exists. There are the many parts of the world where other faiths are dominant, and here too there is need for sympathetic understanding and knowledge in the approach which the evangelist makes. It is only thus that the Church can effectively witness to the uniqueness of the Gospel and the satisfaction by Christ of all man's hunger and search for God.

All these needs are urgent for the presentation of the message of the Bible to this generation, and many of them call for the service of scholars and thinkers and for the planning of new techniques. But amid all these needs none is greater than that the message should be brought by Christians with a burning love for God and for their fellows and with the experience of the power of Christ in their lives. Thus the Church may prepare the way, in prayer and expectation. But it is God who speaks; who knows what he may accomplish by his Word?

MICHAEL EBOR:
Chairman

2. Church Unity and the Church Universal

INDIA, PAKISTAN, BURMA, AND CEYLON

W. Q. Lash, M.A. [Bombay]
     (Joint Vice-Ch.)
A. R. Graham-Campbell, M.A. [Colombo]
L. H. Woolmer, M.A. [Lahore]
J. D. Blair, M.A. [East Bengal]
A. W. Luther, M.A., B.T., S.T.B. [Nasik]
W. A. Partridge, B.A. [Calcutta (Asst.)]

AUSTRALIA

R. C. Halse, D.D. [Brisbane]
F. Woods, D.D. [Melbourne] (B)
C. E. B. Muschamp, M.A., TH.L. [Kalgoorlie] (B)

NEW ZEALAND

A. K. Warren, M.A. [Christchurch]
     (Secretary B)

SOUTH AFRICA

B. B. Burnett, M.A., L.TH. [Bloemfontein]

WEST INDIES

S. Burton, S.S.J.E., D.D. [Nassau and the Bahamas]

JAPAN

M. H. Yashiro, D.D. [Kobe]
     (Joint Vice-Ch. B)

WEST AFRICA

C. J. Patterson, C.M.G., C.B.E., M.A. [Niger]
S. O. Odutola, M.A. [Ondo-Benin]
S. M. Nkemena [Niger (Asst.)]
D. O. Awosika, M.A. [Ondo-Benin (Asst.)]

CENTRAL AFRICA

C. W. Alderson, M.A., A.TH. [Mashonaland]

EXTRA-PROVINCIAL

A. C. MacInnes, D.D. [Jerusalem] (C)
F. F. Johnston, C.B.E., M.A. [Egypt and Libya] (B)
O. C. Allison, M.A. [Sudan]
N. A. Cuba'in [Jordan, Lebanon, and Syria] (B)
F. W. T. Craske, B.A., F.K.C. [Gibraltar]   *(Secretary* C)
F. H. Olang' [Mombasa (Asst.)] (B)
H. W. Baines, M.A. [Singapore] (C)

Note.—The Committee worked together on the main topic. *Sub-Committee B* considered the subject "Unity and the Ecumenical Movement", *Sub-Committee C* "Particular Churches", and *Sub-Committee D* "Relations with the Presbyterians". The letters B, C, and D indicate the names of the bishops who served on these Sub-Committees.

INTRODUCTION

"Physician, heal thyself"—such is the challenge which comes with ever increasing urgency to the Church to-day, as the Church seeks, in obedience to Christ, to proclaim the word of reconciliation in the midst of a world torn by divisions and conflicts. To proclaim effectively the Gospel of God's reconciling love to the world, the Church must manifest in its own life the healing and reconciling power of the word it proclaims. The Committee on Church Unity and the Church Universal has been acutely aware of this challenge. Under its constraint we have felt impelled to call upon the Conference to consider the adoption of the following statement on Christian Unity.

A STATEMENT ON CHRISTIAN UNITY

Conscious of the calling of the Church to be one family in Christ and to make known to the whole world in word and deed his Gospel of the Kingdom, we declare our ardent longing for the healing of our divisions, and for the recovery and manifestation to the world of that unity of the Body of Christ for which he prayed and continues to make intercession.

Many prayers have been answered, and much work has been done in recent years by many Christian Communions, including our own. We thank God for this. We record in particular the closer Christian fellowship fostered by the World Council of Churches since its in-auguration ten years ago, the steady growth in strength and unity of the Church of South India, and the proposals now before us from the Churches of North India, Pakistan, and Ceylon. We welcome also the development in varying ways of our relations with the Old Catholics and with the Lutheran Churches in Scandinavia, and the more recent conversations with Presbyterians and Methodists.

Much has been accomplished, but far more remains to be done. The enemies of God are powerful, and the nations and races of the world are divided by strife and fear. In such times the challenge to Christian people to demonstrate unity in Christ is all the more urgent. Because of our desire to further negotiations and conversations with other Churches we feel impelled to put forth in penitence and hope this fresh statement of our convictions.

We believe in One, Holy, Catholic, and Apostolic Church, which takes its origin not in the will of man but in the will of our Lord Jesus Christ. All those who believe in our Lord Jesus Christ and have been baptized in the name of the Holy Trinity are incorporated into the Body of Christ and are members of the Church. Here is a unity already given.

We believe that the mission of the Church is nothing less than the remaking and gathering together of the whole human race by incor-poration into Christ. In obedience to this mission we must continually pray and work for the visible unity of all Christian believers of all races and nations in a living Christian fellowship of faith and sacrament, of love and prayer, witness and service.

The recovery and manifestation of unity, which we seek, is the unity of the whole Church of Christ. This means unity in living Christian fellowship, in obedience to Christ in every department of human life, and plain for all men to see. There can be no limit to the range of such unity. We are working for unity with the non-episcopal Churches in our own countries and elsewhere. We continue to seek for such com-plete harmony of spirit and agreement in doctrine as would bring unity with the Eastern Orthodox Church and other ancient Churches. We must hope and pray for such eventual agreement in faith and order as shall lead to the healing of the breach between ourselves and the Church of Rome.

We therefore recall the words of the Lambeth Conference of 1920 as follows:

We believe that the visible unity of the Church will be found to involve the whole-hearted acceptance of:

The Holy Scriptures, as the record of God's revelation of himself to man, and as being the rule and ultimate standard of faith; and the Creed commonly called Nicene, as the sufficient statement of the Christian faith, and either it or the Apostles' Creed as the Baptismal confession of belief;

The divinely instituted sacraments of Baptism and the Holy Communion as expressing for all the corporate life of the whole fellowship in and with Christ;

A ministry acknowledged by every part of the Church as possessing not only the inward call of the Spirit, but also the commission of Christ and the authority of the whole body.

Loyalty to the age-long tradition of the Church, and to our own experience, compels us to believe that a ministry to be acknowledged by every part of the Church can only be attained through the historic episcopate, though not necessarily in the precise form prevailing in any part of the Anglican Communion. This ministry we believe to have been given to the Church by Divine Providence from primitive Christian times with its traditional functions of pastoral care and oversight, ordination, leadership in worship, and teaching. We fully recognize that there are other forms of ministry than episcopacy in which have been revealed the gracious activity of God in the life of the universal Church. We believe that other Churches have often borne more effective witness, for example, to the status and vocation of the laity as spiritual persons and to the fellowship and discipline of congregational life than has been done in some of the Churches of our communion. It is our longing that all the spiritual gifts and insights by which the particular Churches live to his glory may find their full scope and enrichment in a united Church.

The unity between Christian Churches ought to be a living unity in the love of Christ which is shown in full Christian fellowship and in mutual service, while also, subject to sufficient agreement in faith and order, expressing itself in free interchange of ministries, and fullness of sacramental Communion. Such unity, while marked by the bond of the historic episcopate, should always include congregational fellowship, active participation both of clergy and laity in the mission and government of the Church, and zeal for evangelism.

Such is the vision we set before ourselves and our own people, calling them to regard the recovery and manifestation of the unity of the whole Church of Christ as a matter of the greatest urgency. We call upon our own Church members, under the leadership of the bishop and clergy of the diocese, in full loyalty to their own Church, to join with their fellow Christians in united prayer. And we urge them to do their utmost through national and local Councils of Churches, for common Christian witness and common service to their fellows. Only so can the world see the People of God giving united witness to the Lord Jesus Christ, and feeding, clothing, healing, and visiting the least of his brethren in his Name.

Finally we appeal to all our people to show a spirit of charity in their dealings with other Christians wherever they may be, to respect other Christian Churches, to refrain from harsh or unkind words about them, whether in speech or in writing, and to seek to understand both their life and their doctrine by common study and by personal contacts. Above all, we appeal to them to pray for Christian unity, privately, corporately, and together with members of other Christian communions, that all believers may be united "in the way Christ wills and by the means he chooses", and to remember always that the nearer we draw to Christ, the nearer we draw to one another.

FULL COMMUNION AND INTERCOMMUNION

The Committee has examined the use of the terms "full communion" and "intercommunion" in official documents in recent years. Although since 1931 the terminology used to describe various degrees of inter-Church relationship has been inconsistent and confusing, the most common usage has been that advocated by the Lund Faith and Order Conference in 1952, whereby the term "full communion" has been kept to describe the close relation which exists between Churches of the same denominational or confessional family, such as the Churches of the Anglican Communion, and of the Orthodox, Lutheran, or Reformed "families" of Churches; whereas the term "intercommunion" has been used to describe varying degrees of relation between Churches of one communion with a Church or Churches of another. Thus, for example, various Provinces and Churches of the Anglican Communion enjoy unrestricted *communio in sacris* with the Old Catholic Churches. Such unrestricted *communio in sacris*, involving complete sacramental fellowship and the mutual recognition and acceptance of ministries, has been described as "full intercommunion". It has however been pointed out that, although there may be a logical satisfaction in distinguishing between the "full communion" which exists between Churches which have grown up within the same family, and the "full intercommunion" which has been established with Churches outside the family, there is no distinction so far as spiritual reality is concerned. In each case there is unrestricted *communio in sacris*.

The Committee therefore has concluded that it would be less confusing and indeed more true to reality to use the term "full communion" in all cases where a Province of the Anglican Communion by agreement enters into a relation of unrestricted *communio in sacris*, including the mutual recognition of ministries, with a Church outside our Communion. This would mean, for example, that the relation already existing between Churches of our Communion with the Old Catholic Churches would henceforth be described as that of "full communion", rather than "full intercommunion". The term "intercommunion" could then be used to describe the varying degrees of relation other than full communion, which already exist, or may be established in the future, between Churches of the Anglican family with others outside this family.

WIDER EPISCOPAL FELLOWSHIP

The Committee attaches the greatest importance to the strengthening of the ties that unite our Communion now, and will unite us in the future, to episcopal Churches linked to us in a relation of "full communion" or of "intercommunion". It would therefore recommend the implementation of Resolution 74 of the Lambeth Conference of 1948 which suggested that—"bishops of the Anglican Communion and bishops of other Churches which are, or may be, in communion with them should meet together from time to time as an episcopal conference, advisory in character, for brotherly counsel and encouragement."

The Committee therefore expresses the hope that the Archbishop of Canterbury may within the next five years invite to an episcopal conference representative bishops from each Province of the Anglican Communion and from each episcopal Church with which Churches or Provinces of the Anglican Communion are in "full communion" or in a relation of "intercommunion". Such conferences for mutual discussion and counsel will do much to foster the growth of an ever wider and richer fellowship uniting episcopal Churches within the Catholic Church.

Within the wider fellowship of episcopal Churches, the Committee would emphasize the important part which it believes the Lambeth Conference must continue to play as a bond of unity holding together the various parts of the Anglican Communion. If, however, our Communion is to fulfil what we believe to be its vocation and to be ready to merge its own separate existence in different parts of the world in the wider unity of a Church both Catholic and Reformed, it has to be recognized that as Churches of our Communion believe themselves called by God to carry their Anglican heritage into a united Church, the Lambeth Conference as at present constituted would be deprived in increasing measure of the fellowship of bishops from many parts of the world and of the rich and varied contributions which are at present made by them to our Conference. Moreover, the bishops of those parts of our Communion who join united Churches would be deprived of the inspiration which comes from the enriching experience of sharing in this Conference. There would also be a risk of new united Churches, especially in small geographical areas such as Ceylon, becoming isolated, with the passing of the years, from the main stream of Catholic tradition and the life of the Church Universal.

For these reasons the Committee feels constrained to make a radical recommendation regarding the membership of future Lambeth Conferences, that when any Church belonging to the Anglican Communion decides, with the encouragement and goodwill of the Lambeth Conference, to join a united Church, the bishops, or representative bishops, of the united Church should be invited to attend Lambeth Conferences as members. It is recognized that there will be occasions when matters of Anglican policy are under discussion and when it may be desirable for decisions to rest with those who have jurisdiction in Anglican dioceses.

This recommendation is made in the conviction that its adoption would be for the strengthening of our ties with those Churches to whose life we contribute so much of our heritage.

THE CHURCH OF SOUTH INDIA

The Lambeth Conference at its last session in 1948 left one issue in suspense which is of crucial importance for determining the relationship of the Churches of the Anglican Communion to the Church of South India. It was unable to make one unanimous recommendation in regard to the status of the bishops, presbyters, and deacons consecrated or ordained in the C.S.I. at or after the inauguration of that Church. While a majority held that such bishops, presbyters, and deacons should be acknowledged as true bishops, presbyters, and deacons in the Church of Christ, a substantial minority held that it was not yet possible to pass any definite judgement on their precise status.[1]

Since 1948 seven Churches or Provinces of the Anglican Communion have taken some synodical action in regard to the ministry of the C.S.I. Of these seven Churches two—the Church of the Province of South Africa and the Church of the Province of the West Indies—have accorded recognition only to former Anglican clergy serving in the C.S.I. and have permitted them to exercise their ministry within the Provinces concerned, provided they do so in Anglican churches only. The decisions of the two Churches are not, however, exactly equivalent in their significance. For, whereas the Church of the Province of the West Indies has expressly deferred definite judgement on the status of the clergy of the C.S.I. until the end of the thirty-year interim period, or alternatively, until the constitution of the C.S.I. has been amended in accord with the six points from the Derby Report,[2] the regulations

---

[1] Resolution 54c.
[2] *The Lambeth Conference, 1948*, Part II, p. 44.

governing the relations of the Church of the Province of South Africa with the C.S.I. have been referred to the dioceses for examination and report to the Episcopal Synod for further consideration.

The five other Churches, namely, the Churches of England, Wales, Ireland, the Episcopal Church in Scotland, and the Church of India, Pakistan, Burma, and Ceylon, have, in virtually the same form, acknowledged the bishops and the episcopally ordained presbyters and deacons of the C.S.I. to be true bishops, presbyters, and deacons in the Church of God. Another Church, the Episcopal Church of the U.S.A., has before it, for consideration by the forthcoming session of its General Convention, the unanimous advice of its Joint Commission on Ecumenical Relations that it need no longer postpone a favourable judgement concerning the status of such bishops, presbyters, and deacons.

Pursuant to this basic acknowledgement, all five Churches have issued regulations governing the ministration within their several jurisdictions of the clergy thus recognized and establishing a limited measure of intercommunion with the C.S.I. during the thirty-year interim period. These regulations are in their main provisions closely similar. All five Churches, for instance, permit invitations to preach to be extended, under proper authority, to C.S.I. clergy; four of them permit the bishops and episcopally ordained presbyters of the C.S.I. to celebrate the Holy Communion in Anglican churches conditionally upon their willingness to confine their celebrations to Anglican churches, while sojourning within the territory of each particular Church. Similarly, four of the Churches allow their own bishops and priests to accept the hospitality of the C.S.I. for celebrating Holy Communion within it; and the same four Churches have also provided for the possibility of episcopally ordained clergy of the C.S.I. officiating either temporarily or permanently as ministers of those Churches. The C.I.P.B.C. permits such clergy to celebrate on ecumenical and special occasions, and in pastoral necessity. Former Anglicans may temporarily resume their status for purposes of celebrating. Three of the Churches have included a resolution permitting (while stipulating various provisos) a bishop to authorize the loan of a church within his jurisdiction for the celebration of the C.S.I. Liturgy by a bishop or an episcopally ordained presbyter of that Church. The draft resolutions recommended by the Joint Commission on Ecumenical Relations for adoption by the General Convention of the Episcopal Church of the U.S.A. agree substantially with these regulations made by the other Churches.

No Church or Province of the Anglican Communion is bound by the action of another. Nevertheless the common traditions of faith, order, and worship which unite the Anglican Churches inevitably dispose them to give due weight to each other's actions. The concurrent adoption of a similar pattern of relationship with the C.S.I. by five autonomous Anglican Churches, re-inforced as it is by recommendations made to yet another Church, must therefore be reckoned as a fact of great importance for the whole Communion.

In 1948 the Bishops at Lambeth were fully agreed in recognizing that, so far as regularity and validity can be guaranteed by the form and manner used in consecrating and ordaining, the orders of the C.S.I. were regular and valid. They endorsed the report of the committee of the conference on the Unity of the Church which contains the statement: "The C.S.I. had used for the consecration of its bishops a form and has prepared an ordinal so similar in all essentials to those in use in the Anglican Communion that any suggestion that these forms were in themselves inadequate to convey the authority of the episcopate and the priesthood can be dismissed without question."[3] This consideration has contributed not a little to influence the decision of those Churches which have recognized the bishops and episcopally ordained clergy of the C.S.I. In January 1958 the synod of the C.S.I. adopted and ordered to be used a radically revised ordinal. The revised forms of consecration and ordination have been carefully examined and we have no hesitation in adjudging them to be adequate to secure a regular and valid ministry.

This bare record of factual development in the life of the Church of South India, and in the relation to it of provinces of the Anglican Communion, does scant justice to the really significant aspects of growth in that Church within the last ten years.

The United Report of the two Joint Committees of the Convocations of Canterbury and York, accepted by those Convocations in 1955, contains this passage:

"We cannot doubt that the Church of South India has grown in its inner unity and cohesion, and in its sacramental life. There has been a growing appreciation of the office of the bishop in the Church of God, as a bond of continuity and unity; a continuous spread of liturgical worship, as expressed for example in the Services issued by the Synod for Holy Communion, Baptism, and Confirmation; and a growing use of the rite of Confirmation administered by the bishop. In this last matter there is evidence that an institution which is not made obligatory in the Constitution of the Church of South India has been winning its way in circles where it had been unfamiliar, in virtue of its inherent truth and appeal."

To this may be added the evidence which is forthcoming from many sources of the growing appreciation of the *pastoral* value of the episcopal office. It may well be that the Church in the West may be able to learn from the polity of the Church of South India lessons which would restore to its exercise of episcopacy more of its primitive pastoral character as the office of Father in God.

The Lambeth Conference of 1948 expressed the hope and desire that ignorance and misunderstandings might be dispelled by increasing communication between the Church of South India and our Churches

---

[3] *The Lambeth Conference, 1948,* Part II, p. 47.

and Provinces. This hope and desire have borne fruit. The visits of delegations and of individuals have contributed greatly to the knowledge on which such a judgement as that quoted above is based.

The Committee believes that we can indeed thank God for the grace which he has bestowed upon the bishops, presbyters, and people of the Church of South India in these past ten years, and for the response to that grace shown in the growth of inner coherence and missionary zeal. It believes that with an increased sense of assurance the words used in 1948 can be reiterated: "[We] look forward hopefully and with longing to the day when there shall be full communion between the Church of South India and the Churches of the Anglican Communion."[4]

NANDYAL

Although the breach in Christian fellowship in the Nandyal area in South India deplored by the Lambeth Conference of 1948 has been to some extent healed, it has become clear that the arrangements for the spiritual oversight of the Anglicans in that area cannot have the very temporary character envisaged at that time. The Metropolitan's Commission which visited Nandyal in 1956 was of the opinion that the organization of the area as a diocese might, for pastoral reasons, be necessary before there could be ultimate union between the Nandyal Anglicans and the C.S.I. The Commission also recorded its opinion that such a step should be taken only after consultation with the authorities of the C.S.I., and on the clear understanding that the formation of a diocese of Nandyal within the C.I.P.B.C. should be regarded not as an alternative to ultimate union but rather as providing conditions more favourable to the growth of that ultimate organic union for which all should work and pray.

In view of this the Committee recommends to the Conference that, notwithstanding the recommendation of the Lambeth Conference of 1930, re-affirmed in 1948, that no province of the Anglican Communion should set up dioceses or congregations in the area of the Church of South India, it should be left to the Church of India, Pakistan, Burma, and Ceylon to make the arrangements that seem best for the spiritual oversight of Anglicans in the Nandyal area, after consultation with and with the good will of the Church of South India, bearing in mind that the union of Christians in the Nandyal area is the ultimate aim.

CHURCH UNION IN NORTH INDIA/PAKISTAN AND CEYLON

INTRODUCTORY

It will be recalled that the Committee of the Lambeth Conference of 1948 had before it the *Scheme for Church Union in Ceylon* as then

---

4 Resolution 52c.

drafted, and also the Basis of Negotiation provisionally prepared by a Round Table Conference with a view to Church Union in North India, and that it reviewed both projects in the section of its Report headed "Current Negotiations and Specific Projects in Various Parts of the World", its attitude towards both being one of general encouragement and cautious friendliness.

The Resolutions passed by the Conference as a whole included three (Resolution 56, on "Further Approaches to Reunion", and Resolutions 62, on "Ceylon", and 63, on "North India") which it seems desirable in this connection to quote. They were as follows:

Resolution 56. The Conference calls upon all the Churches of the Anglican Communion to seek earnestly by prayer and by conference the fulfilment of the vision "of a Church, genuinely Catholic, loyal to all truth, and gathering into its fellowship 'all who profess and call themselves Christians', within whose visible unity all the treasures of faith and order, bequeathed as a heritage by the past to the present, shall be possessed in common and made serviceable to the whole body of Christ." It recognizes that "within this unity Christian Communions now separated from one another would retain much that has long been distinctive in their methods of worship and service."

In the hope of setting forward the fulfilment of this vision, the Conference recalls the principles set forth in the *Appeal to All Christian People*, and the relevant Resolutions of the Lambeth Conference of 1920 on the Reunion of Christendom, and records certain counsels and considerations which it believes should guide the Churches of our Communion in future approaches to reunion.

(*a*) The theological issues, especially those concerning the Church and the ministry, should be faced at the outset, and to this end the negotiating Churches should obtain the help of theologians in framing schemes for reunion or intercommunion.

(*b*) The unification of the ministry in a form satisfactory to all the bodies concerned, either at the inauguration of the union or as soon as possible thereafter, is likely to be a prerequisite to success in all future proposals for the reunion of the Churches.

(*c*) The integral connexion between the Church and the ministry should be safeguarded in all proposals for the achievement of intercommunion through the creation of a mutually recognized ministry.

(*d*) The goal in any steps towards a united Church within a given area should always be a Church with which the Anglican Churches could eventually be in full Communion.

(*e*) Because the Anglican Communion is itself a treasured unity with a special vocation, a part of our Communion contemplating a step which would involve its withdrawal from the Anglican family of Churches should consult the Lambeth Conference or the Provinces and member Churches of this family of Churches before final commitment to such a course.

Resolution 62. The Conference has learned with deep interest of the proposed scheme for Church Union in Ceylon, regards it as being, in many respects, among the most promising of the various schemes of its type in different parts of the world, and expresses the hope that, subject to the assent of the Church of India, Burma, and Ceylon,[5] the projected union may, under the blessing of God, in due course be carried into effect.

Resolution 63. The Conference welcomes generally the negotiations informally begun in North India with a view to union, desires to encourage the authorities of the Church of India, Burma, and Ceylon[6] to go forward, and expresses the hope that in the working out of the proposed scheme account may be taken of the lessons to be derived from South India and of the proposals made in Ceylon.

It is gratifying to note that since 1948 the negotiations both in Ceylon and in North India and Pakistan have progressed to a point where a *Scheme* and a *Plan* have been presented to the negotiating Churches for decisive action. The *Scheme of Church Union in Ceylon* and the *Plan of Church Union in North India and Pakistan*, each in the third edition, have been referred by the Church of India, Pakistan, Burma, and Ceylon to the Lambeth Conference for advice and for assurance that if the *Scheme* and the *Plan*, as they will be referred to below, are carried into effect it may be expected that the Churches of the Anglican Communion will be in full communion from the start with the resulting Churches in Ceylon, India, and Pakistan.

The Churches participating in the *Scheme* are:

The Church of India, Pakistan, Burma, and Ceylon,
The Methodist Church in Ceylon,
The Baptist Churches in Ceylon,
The Presbyterian Churches in Ceylon, and
The Jaffna Diocese of the Church of South India (formerly Congregationalist).

The Churches participating in the *Plan* are:

The Council of the Baptist Churches in Northern India,
The Church of the Brethren in India,
The Disciples of Christ,
The Church of India, Pakistan, Burma, and Ceylon,
The Methodist Church (British and Australasian Conferences),
The Methodist Church in Southern Asia (Episcopal), and
The United Church of Northern India (a previous Union of Congregationalists and Presbyterians).

---

[5] Now India, Pakistan, Burma, and Ceylon.   [6] Ditto.

1. GENERAL CONSIDERATIONS

Both the *Scheme* and the *Plan* under consideration constitute a great and significant step towards the healing of divisions and the recovery of the visible unity of the Church Universal according to the will of Christ. What has been achieved is especially impressive in view of the number of the Churches to be brought together, the variety of their polities, and the consequent complexity of the problems involved. We urge that the Conference express gratitude to God for the manifest evidence of the guidance and activity of his Holy Spirit in the negotiations which have led to these most encouraging results.

The Lambeth Conference of 1948 set forth certain principles to guide further progress toward Church unity. It is noted that these principles have been followed:

DOCTRINE. Care has been taken on theological issues; and the doctrinal statements of both the *Scheme* and the *Plan* are unexceptionable. No Anglican need entertain any doubt concerning the orthodoxy of the Faith of the resulting Churches.

Some comment should be made on the fact that in Appendix A. II of the *Plan* a number of sixteenth and seventeenth century Confessions of Faith, reflecting controversies of that period, are listed as "worthy exponents of the Word of God, and as systems of doctrine to be taught in our Churches and seminaries", and that in Section IV of the Constitution it is laid down that "the act of Union will not debar any teacher of the Church of North India/Pakistan from using" such Confessions "for the instruction of the faithful". It is understood that the primary reason for including Appendixes A. I and II is to secure the legal continuity of the united Church with the Churches from which its membership will be derived, and for the safeguarding of property. It is assumed, however, that it will be in the power of the Churches of North India/Pakistan to issue their own statements concerning the faith for the guidance of their teachers and the edification of the faithful, and that the earlier traditional formulas will then be interpreted in the light of the doctrinal standards thus set forth. It is hoped that this task will be taken in hand in due course.

UNIFICATION OF THE MINISTRY. It is an integral purpose of both documents to provide at the outset a "unification of the ministry in a form satisfactory to all the bodies concerned, at the inauguration of the union".[7]

In the *Plan* (p. 53) it is stated that: "The Churches before uniting agreed that the 'Episcopate shall be both constitutional and historic', and that by 'historic' is meant 'the Episcopate which is in historic

---

7 Preface, pp. 52f. of the *Plan*.

continuity with that of the early Church'." It is further stated in the *Plan* that through the Act of Unification of the Ministry the Church of North India and the Church of Pakistan "desire and intend to secure for the former bishops of the Church of India, Pakistan, Burma, and Ceylon and the former bishops of the Methodist Church in Southern Asia authority to minister and discharge the duties of their office throughout the Churches of North India and Pakistan in such a manner that no member thereof may have cause to question their authority, or to entertain any doubt or scruple in recognizing and acknowledging them as bishops in the Church of God". It is also said in the *Plan* (ibid.) that the Church of North India and the Church of Pakistan "intend through this Act and by the grace of God, on the one hand to supply to the former bishops of the Methodist Church in Southern Asia the special link with the Episcopate of the primitive Church which the Anglican Communion claims to have preserved, and on the other hand to enable the former bishops of the Church of India, Pakistan, Burma, and Ceylon to enter into the spiritual heritage of the Episcopal branch of the Methodist Communion".

Both the *Plan* (p. 53) and the *Scheme* (p. 25) also express the intention of securing a ministry "fully accredited in the eyes of all their members, and so far as may be of the Church throughout the world". This intention includes the ministry of presbyters and deacons as well as that of bishops.

Also in the *Scheme*, it is said that "it is the intention of this Church to continue and reverently to use and esteem the threefold ministry of Bishop, Presbyter and Deacon which existed in the undivided Church" (p. 24).

Moreover, it is clearly stated that the intention of the rite is that all may receive through all, whatever each has to contribute and whatever each may need of the fullness of Christ's grace, commission, and authority for the performance of his proper office in the Church Universal within the Churches of North India, of Pakistan, or of Ceylon. From the Anglican point of view, therefore, the rite is intended to convey everything of value in the Anglican ministry, including the tradition of episcopal ordination. Whilst there is no judgement passed on the reality and effectiveness of the various ministries, God is asked to supply whatever each may need. It appears that every minister taking part in such a Unification can humbly submit himself and the sufficiency of all that God has already given him in ordination in his own Church to the judgement of God, and accept from God whatever of grace, commission, and authority he may need. We may surely trust that God will answer the prayers of his people and provide for the resultant Churches a ministry possessed of all the richness of inheritance which the uniting Churches previously treasured in separation. The Committee warmly approves these statements of the aims and intentions of the negotiating Churches.

BAPTISM. Baptists are among the Negotiators, and there is an appreciation of the problems involved where there are two alternative practices in the administration of the same sacrament. The view that Christian Initiation is only completed when the neophytes first receive Holy Communion is theologically sound. It is fully recognized that it is the duty of the Church to care for and nurture neophytes in all stages of initiation. The *Scheme* sets out these responsibilities in § III, 1 (b) (iii) on page 32, and in doing so avoids the ambiguous word "member" in describing those not yet baptized which the *Plan* uses in the corresponding passage in § III, B, 3 (page 3). The committee would earnestly urge the revision of the *Plan* at this point to avoid the use of the word "member" except in connection with the baptized, as in § III, A, 1 (page 2).

It is noted that in India it has not been found possible to accept the suggestion that Baptism should be described as an "effectual sign" rather than simply as a "sign" in Chapter VI, paragraph 2. It is recognized, however, that in the Anglican Catechism Sacraments are described simply as "signs", the phrase "effectual signs" occurring in Anglican formularies only in the 25th Article of Religion. The Committee would prefer "effectual sign", but recognizes that the language of the previous paragraph in which Sacraments are described as "means of grace by which we are united to God and through which God works in us" and the language of paragraph 7 in which Baptism is described as "the outward and visible sign of the regenerating grace of God" adequately covers the doctrine implied in the use of the term "effectual".

As it is of such prime importance that there should be no doubt about the validity of any baptism, the Committee expresses concern over the method of "sprinkling", and trusts that it is only to be used with individuals, and in a manner to ensure that water actually flows on the candidate.

CONFIRMATION. The Committee welcomes the pastoral opportunity given to the bishop at confirmations in the Ceylon *Scheme*, and hopes that the practice of confirmation by a bishop may spread in North India and Pakistan where at first it might not be the practice. Meanwhile it recognizes that in some parts of Christendom it is the custom for presbyters to confirm under the authority of the bishop, and presumes that the bishop's *authorization* (*Plan*, p. 14) would include such authority implicitly, if not explicitly. It is laid down that every service of admission to full communicant membership of the Church shall include "profession of faith before the assembled congregation, prayer for the gift of the Holy Spirit, the laying-on of hands by the bishop or presbyter, and acknowledgement of his attaining the full responsibilities of Church membership". Therefore the type of service contemplated as an alternative to confirmation ("through confirmation by a bishop *or through some such service* conducted by a

B+

bishop or presbyter") could scarcely be regarded in the judgement of Anglicans as different from what they themselves call confirmation.

The Committee hopes that confirmation will be regarded, not only as an admission to communicant status, but primarily as a means whereby the Holy Spirit is given for the strengthening of the candidates for spiritual warfare.

THE EUCHARIST. The Committee warmly welcomes the Eucharistic doctrine in both the *Scheme* and the *Plan*, and looks forward to rich liturgical development such as has marked the early years of the Church of South India.

RELATION TO OTHER CHURCHES. In view of the fact that the resulting Churches intend to be fully episcopal and have as their acknowledged goal the full reunion of Christendom, the declared intention is (to quote the *Plan*) that "after union, full communion and fellowship shall be maintained with each of the several Churches with which any of them is now in communion".

The provisions in question are in fact an inevitable corollary of "the nature of the Union whereby the Church ... is formed",[8] which is, *inter alia*, that it should "maintain fellowship with all those branches of the Church of Christ with which the Churches from which it has been formed have severally enjoyed such fellowship".[9] Yet the permission for non-episcopally ordained ministers to celebrate the Holy Communion is contrary to the practice of the Anglican Communion.[10] The question arises whether this permission is so serious a departure from Anglican practice as to make it necessary for Anglicans to withdraw from the negotiations; or, if they do not withdraw, to make it impossible for the resulting Churches to be in full communion with the Anglican Churches.

The Committee is of the opinion that this permission need not have these unhappy consequences. The Committee considers that the other negotiating Churches have gone as far as they possibly can (given the nature and purpose of the proposed union as described above) to meet Anglican difficulties. For example, Clause (iv) on p. 29 of the *Scheme* requires that any "ordained minister of any Church which is in full communion ... with any of the uniting Churches shall, if he be accepted for service in the Church of Lanka as one of its ministers, be received by the Church of Lanka" in the same way as, at the time of the inauguration of the Union, all its ministers were brought into a unified ministry. This means that the permission is necessarily limited to occasional visiting ministers of the uniting Churches only. The permission is clearly not intended to cover any widespread and general practice within the Churches. Secondly, in the *Scheme* it is explicitly laid down in connection with these permissions that the "conscience of

---

[8] *Scheme*, p. 29.
[9] *Scheme*, p. 6.
[10] There are, however, precedents in the post-Reformation Anglican practice both at home and overseas, for the occasional toleration of such anomalies.

the congregation" should be respected. This conscience clause does justice to the statement in the section on "Faith and Order"[11] that "No one particular theological interpretation of episcopacy shall be demanded from any minister or member of the Church of Lanka". The conscience clause protects those who interpret episcopacy as being essential to the structure of the Church and in consequence judge non-episcopal ministries to be invalid. In the *Plan* this matter is to be governed by constitutional provisions which include respect for the consciences of congregations.[12]

The Committee is clear that this permission for occasional visiting non-episcopally ordained ministers to celebrate the Holy Communion cannot reasonably be held to throw doubt upon the clearly expressed intention of the Churches to maintain the ministry of bishop, presbyter, and deacon—to quote the statement of intention from the *Scheme*: "to continue and reverently to use and esteem the threefold ministry of Bishop, Presbyter and Deacon which existed in the undivided Church" (p. 24). The Committee recognizes that these anomalies are occasioned by the present divisions of Christendom and that such anomalies are bound to continue until reunion progresses further in other parts of the world.

While, therefore, this permission is a serious departure from Anglican practice nevertheless the Committee believes that if such permission were given, the Churches of the Anglican Communion should not, on that account, have any hesitation in accepting the ministry of the resulting Churches as fully accredited and in historic continuity with that of the undivided Church.

THE ORDAINED MINISTRY. Careful consideration was given to the ordained Ministry.

The Committee is glad to observe the insertion in the Third Revised Edition of the *Plan* of the word "one" in the phrase "any one particular theological interpretation of episcopacy" as a useful clarification of meaning.

The Committee notes with approval the clear and full definition of the functions of bishops in Chapter IX, paragraph 6.

The Committee notes that in the Ceylon Scheme[13] there is a clear statement that "a minister who for any reason has ceased to exercise his ministry shall not be re-ordained on beginning again to exercise that ministry". The Committee greatly hopes that such a provision may be included also in the *Plan* for North India and Pakistan, since it safeguards what is for Anglicans a very important principle.

The Committee approves the provision made in Chapter IX of the *Plan*, paragraphs 13 and 14, for the administration of the Sacraments

---

[11] P. 19.
[12] *Plan*, p. 5.
[13] P. 16.

in special circumstances; and expresses its warm appreciation of the provision for life-long deacons contained in Chapter IX, paragraph 18.

The Committee considered the footnote on page 17 of the *Plan* stating that "the question of the admission of women to the ordained ministry is left for the consideration of the Synod of the Church". Clearly any autonomous Church can if it so desires consider this question, and therefore the proposed Churches of North India and of Pakistan would inevitably have freedom to raise the matter in their own Synods if they so desired. The admission of women to an Order of Deaconesses would raise no difficulty. If, however, the Churches of North India or Pakistan were to decide to ordain women to the presbyterate this would raise a grave problem for the Anglican Communion, the constituent Churches of which might well find themselves unable to recognize the ministry of a woman so ordained.

2. THE SERVICES FOR THE UNIFICATION OF THE MINISTRY

The Committee has noted the *desire* and *intention* of the Negotiating Committees to provide a ministry "fully accredited in the eyes of all their members, and so far as may be of the Church throughout the world", and is deeply concerned that the actual methods proposed by the Negotiating Committees should not fail to carry out that intention adequately.

The Services by which unification is to be achieved have a crucial importance. The Lambeth Conference of 1948 strongly recommended that unification at or near the start should be a part of every future scheme of union. The Services proposed in the *Plan* and the *Scheme* are the first to be put forward to achieve such initial unification. For Anglicans future advance in reunion schemes depends greatly upon whether the services proposed can be considered sufficient and satisfactory for their purpose. It is necessary therefore to examine them carefully to see that the liturgical function and form is appropriate and is expressed in sufficiently clear phraseology.

All the negotiating Churches are agreed as to the functions which are to be fulfilled through the liturgical forms proposed. They are three:

1. Negatively, the liturgical form must be such as to raise no question as to the relative sufficiency, reality, or effectiveness of the various ministries which are brought to be unified.

2. Positively, the liturgical form must be one appropriate to the essential function of seeking from God through prayer and laying-on of hands a continuance and increase of spiritual gifts already received and possessed by each Minister, for the work of the Office and Order of Ministry in the Church of God to which he is now freshly called in the United Church.

3. In order that the intention of removing all ground for doubts or scruples may be fulfilled, the liturgical form must also be appropriate for its function of seeking from God that he will "endue each according to his need" with whatever of grace, gifts, character or authority may in the sight of God be needed for the Office and Order of Ministry referred to. Thus every Church may be satisfied that all of its inheritance has been faithfully conveyed to and shared by the ministry of the United Church.

It is clearly the earnest desire of all the negotiating Churches equally that these three functions may be fulfilled to the satisfaction of all, in order that the United Church may rejoice in a ministry possessed of the richness of all the Uniting Churches.

The Committee is happy to find that the first two of the three functions are abundantly fulfilled. It is its duty to examine with special care what is provided for the discharge of the third function, since the Anglican Communion as well as the negotiating Churches themselves would wish to be assured that no room for doubt or scruple is left here.

The form taken by the services for the unification of the ministries is as follows: Preface; Prayer; Laying-on of hands with Formula invoking the Holy Spirit.

In Anglican Ordinals, the Prayer in this position, while referring generally to ministries given by Christ to his Church, does not name the particular ministry which is being conferred. The Laying-on of hands is associated with the subsequent Formula in which the particular office or Order (Bishop/Priest in the Church of God) is explicitly named. The Committee appreciates the fact that the order of the *Plan* or *Scheme* is that of our own existing rites, and notes that the wording of the proposed Formula adds an element essential to this particular and unique form of unification of ministries. The Committee desires to make only two general comments before turning to consider the services of the *Plan* and the *Scheme* separately.

1. Wherever it is possible, it is desirable that in the Prayer (as well as in the Formula) the specific office or Order of Ministry in view should be named. Thereby an extra degree of precision and clarification is achieved.

2. In the Prayer and in the Formula reference is naturally made both to ministry in the Church of God and to ministry in the particular Church (North India, Pakistan or Ceylon). It avoids confusion of thought, if these two ministries are kept in their suitable order throughout.

   There is the grace and authority of ministry in the Church of God, which each brings and which is to be continued and enriched by means of the Prayer, the laying-on of hands, and the Formula. All this is properly in the sphere of the Universal Church and takes precedence over all else. There is also the conferring of authority and jurisdiction within the local Church. There is nothing to prevent the universal and the local significance being closely associated provided that they are placed in their appropriate order in such a way as this:

"For the exercise of the office (of Bishop/Presbyter) in the Church of God according to the constitution of the Church of . . ."

or, more simply:

"in the Church of God and within the Church of . . ."

With these two clarifications the Committee considers that in general the services would fully satisfy the third function which is to be required of the liturgical form.

We now turn to the services proposed in the *Plan* and the *Scheme* respectively.

CHURCH OF NORTH INDIA/PAKISTAN
The Bringing Together of the Episcopates

The Committee strongly recommends that the unification of the Ministry as far as concerns the bishops should be completed in a single act, and suggests that if this is done representative ministers from all the uniting Churches should take part in the laying-on of hands. Would it be not only acceptable to the negotiating Churches but actually an increase of the significance of this episcopal unification if presbyteral representatives of all the uniting Churches thus took part in the laying-on of hands upon the bishops, sharing both in the prayers for the Holy Spirit, and in the conferring of authority to exercise the office of a bishop in the united Church?

The service should begin with the reading of the Preface followed by the Presentation of Bishops in a form similar to that on page 8 of the *Services Proposed for Use at The Inauguration.*

The Committee suggests also that the formula at the laying-on of hands should be conformed to the formula accompanying the laying-on of hands in the Representative Act of Unification of the Ministry (*Plan*, p. 57, para. 18).

The Committee further recommends that the prayer on pages 5 and 6 be modified along these lines (*Plan*, p. 54):

O Almighty Father, Everlasting God . . . making perfect His Church; Continue, we beseech Thee, Thy blessing already granted to these Thy servants called this day to a fresh dedication to Thy service as Bishops and Chief Pastors of the Church Universal; and on all of them pour out Thy Holy Spirit to enrich each according to his need with grace and authority for the exercise of the office of a Bishop in the Church of God according to the constitution of the Church of North India/Pakistan, that they may ever be ready, &c.

The Representative Act of Unification of the Ministry

Liturgical function and form. The proposals of the *Plan* at this point are undoubtedly confusing, and the Committee finds it extremely awkward that the bishops whose episcopates have already been brought together in the previous Act should again be involved in the course of the same service in an Act which provides practically an identical prayer.

It is to be remembered first that the Churches have already been united in the first part of the service whereby the separate inheritances of the uniting Churches have come together in a single stream of Church life.

Then secondly the episcopates have been united with a specific mention of the office and ministry which is being so unified, in such a form as to remove all doubt or scruple.

The third step is entitled a representative act of unification of the ministry. The whole ministry of each Church had its part in the unifying of the Churches; the episcopate has been unified and commissioned by the joint action of bishops and presbyters, on the assumption that the suggestion made above has been accepted. What remains is to unify the presbyterate so as to complete the union in such a way as to bring spiritual enrichment to all and to remove at this level also all doubt or scruple. The unification at this level must be by laying-on of hands (including both episcopal and presbyteral hands) together with a prayer before it and with a formula accompanying it. In the prayer or in the formula or in both, the office and ministry to which the laying-on of hands is related must be mentioned, that is to say in this context the presbyterate. As the service stands, it is in fact very difficult to name this office in the prayer in such a way that it will not appear to include the bishops taking part in the representative act, while it would involve some element of confusion and even of insincerity to let it be taken indifferently as covering bishops and presbyters. It might look like mere repetition. That is why the Committee recommends that the unification of bishops should be completed in a single act. If the Committee's suggestions are adopted the presentation of the representatives of the ministry would not include bishops.

The Prayer would then be said by one of the bishops, and together with him representative ministers from each of the Churches now united should lay their hands on three ministers chosen beforehand, none of whom should be a bishop, using the form of words which the Committee has recommended for the unification of the episcopate. The bishop, together with the three chosen ministers, should lay hands on each of the representative ministers from each Church (except the bishops) using the same formula.

An alternative suggestion. While the Committee prefers the suggestion just made, it offers the following alternative suggestion:

The bishops should stand aside from the general statement to be made by all the other representatives of the Churches and from the prayer which precedes the laying-on of hands, seeing that in their case these have been already used, but not from the laying-on of hands.

The laying-on of hands should be by the three chosen ministers (one of them being a bishop) and should be accompanied by the formula on page 9 (*Plan*, p. 57, para. 18), with the omission, when hands are being laid on a bishop, of the words ... "mayst thou receive ... within this Church; and ..."

In addition, for the reason stated on page 37, the prayer (pp. 8–9) should be modified in some such way as follows:

Continue thy blessing already given and upon all thy servants called this day to a fresh dedication to thy service pour out thy Holy Spirit and endue each according to his need with grace and authority for the exercise of the ministry of a presbyter in the Church Universal within this Church of North India/Pakistan.

CHURCH OF LANKA

Order of Service for the Unification of the Ministry

For the reason given above (p. 37), the Committee strongly recommends that in the Prayer for the Ministry (*Scheme*, pp. 26–27) for the words "presbyter in this Church of Lanka within the Church Universal" should be substituted the words "presbyter in the Church Universal according to the Constitution of the Church of Lanka" (or, more simply, "in the Church Universal and within the Church of Lanka"). A similar order of phrases should consistently be used in any formula which may follow. It may be noted that the suggested order of phrases is already used under item 13 in the Order of Service (p. 24).

RELATIONS BETWEEN ANGLICAN AND PRESBYTERIAN CHURCHES

1

A Report bearing the title *Relations Between Anglican and Presbyterian Churches* was published simultaneously in Scotland and England in 1957[14] as the outcome of a prolonged series of conversations between representatives of the Churches of England and Scotland, the Episcopal Church in Scotland, and the Presbyterian Church of England. The Convocations of Canterbury and York, in May 1957, commended the document for study by the Church, but deferred further discussion of it until after the Lambeth Conference of 1958. The General Assembly of the Church of Scotland, in May 1957, also deferred any immediate action upon the Report, which was referred for study and consideration to the presbyteries throughout Scotland, pending a further consideration of its

[14] S.P.C.K.

implications at the General Assembly of 1958. In the words of a sentence written by the Archbishop of Canterbury at the end of a Foreword contributed by him, the Report "considers not the relations between the Church of England and the Church of Scotland, but the more fundamental and fruitful subject of the relations between the Episcopalian and the Presbyterian systems of Church Order".

In the Report itself those taking part in the conversations themselves renounced, and expressed the belief that "the Churches concerned should renounce, the method of selecting and measuring such faults and errors in the past history of the Churches now conferring as might be judged to be responsible for our present divisions. These matters have been investigated frequently, and complete agreement on them is not to be expected at this stage in history. It is acknowledged that mistakes have been made on both sides, and that over the generations attitudes tending to bitterness and strife have been not infrequent, but the time has come when the voice of mutual recrimination should be silent."

In the context of the Ecumenical Movement, of the revived interest in Biblical theology which has been a notable feature of the last few decades, and of an atmosphere of assured friendship, a new approach had become possible. A number of important "Biblical and doctrinal considerations concerning the Church and its ministry" were able to be formulated in an agreed statement. The Anglicans recognized that Presbyterians certainly hold a firm, clear, and positive doctrine alike of the Church and of its Ministry, and that many of the functions ascribed to the Ministry are under both systems in essentials the same. In neither Church is the local church or the individual minister left without "oversight" (*episcopé*). "In the Presbyterian Churches" (to quote the words of the Report) "the ministers of the Word and Sacraments exercise a corporate episcopate, collectively through the presbytery, along with the lay elders associated with them . . . In the Anglican Churches there is the distinctive office of the bishop, the essence of" which "lies in the coalescence of certain functions in a single person". The Anglican representatives were, however, "anxious to emphasize that the bishop's office is rightly exercised only within the context of the corporate life of the whole Church", at the same time admitting that this principle "has been too often obscured in practice". The Anglicans who took part in the conversations recognized that many of the functions which in Anglicanism are exercised by the bishop are in Presbyterianism exercised through the corporate oversight of the presbytery. It was also noted that in many Anglican provinces there is a similar sharing of many of these functions with the other clergy and with the laity. Nevertheless, the Anglicans expressed their belief that the more directly pastoral functions of *episcopé* can be better exercised by a permanent "Father in God" than by a presbytery presided over by a Chairman or Moderator holding only a brief temporary office. There

B*

was further the question of the effective linking of the local ministry with the ministry of episcopal Churches in different parts of the world which have preserved, and which highly value, continuity with the ministry of pre-Reformation times through ordination by bishops standing in the historic episcopal succession.

It was found in the conversations that "on the Presbyterian side there was a willingness to consider the functions of a bishop, as they are recognized by the Anglican Communion, so long as the office was duly integrated with the presbytery and the whole Church", and on the Anglican side there was a corresponding willingness "to consider the complementing and strengthening of the episcopate in Anglican Churches by ensuring the corporate functioning of *episcopé* through developments within the existing order corresponding to the sacral courts of the Church as found within the Presbyterian order". It was suggested, in short, that the Presbyterian Churches might be prepared to consider the acceptance of the "historic episcopate" on the understanding that the bishop would function strictly as a presiding "Bishop-in-Presbytery", and that the Anglican Churches on their side should be encouraged to consider the development of a form of order in which ministry and laity should be closely linked together in decisions concerned with the government and doctrine of the Church at all levels. This would mean, for example, that in the Church of England a lay element, such as already exists in the Church Assembly, should be introduced also into the Convocations of Canterbury and York in association with the existing Houses of Bishops and Clergy: and that consideration should be given to the possibility of the development in Anglican Churches of an office corresponding to that of the lay "elder" in Presbyterianism.

2

In May 1958, further attention was given to the Report by the General Assembly of the Church of Scotland, and it was referred to the presbyteries throughout Scotland, this time for their official consideration. At the same time, in a Report made to the General Assembly by its Inter-Church Relations Committee, six points which had given rise to special difficulty among members of the Church of Scotland were set out. The Lambeth Committee on Church Unity and the Church Universal has considered these six points and makes the following observations regarding them.

1. The Report on *Relations between Anglican and Presbyterian Churches* itself envisaged that "the rite of admission to full membership, or confirmation", would in a reconstituted Church of Scotland "still be administered by each parochial minister, but the rite might come to be shared by the bishop and parish minister acting together". The Report to the General Assembly, commenting on this, represented that "the responsibility of the Kirk Session in this context must not be

overlooked. Admission to Holy Communion is given by resolution of the Kirk Session as responsible for the 'Godly discipline' of the congregation." This Committee on the other hand must stress the importance for Anglicans of episcopal confirmation. Nevertheless the Committee considers that Anglicanism has something to learn from the Presbyterian practice, the association of the lay communicants of the parish with the incumbent in the reception of new communicants being in itself worthy of consideration. On the other hand, some members of the Committee were uncertain how this would work in an Anglican context, and were apprehensive about the safeguarding of the incumbent's final responsibility as the minister to whom has been committed the exercise of the cure of souls.

The Committee, however, is strongly of the opinion that the existing practice of the Anglican Communion in the matter of the administration of confirmation and the admission of persons to Holy Communion ought not to be regarded as something which must necessarily be imposed in all its details upon every branch of the Church. On the contrary, the Committee considers that this is a matter which might well become the subject of further conversations with Presbyterian Churches.

2. The Committee is agreed that the relation of bishops to the final authority of the General Assembly needs clarification. We understand the historic suspicion by Presbyterians of any authoritarianism on the part of bishops, a suspicion which, in fact, is shared by many Anglicans; and, so far as the General Assembly is concerned, we would express the hope that the problem may be solved by allowing in all matters of doctrine separate votes in the Assembly by bishops, by presbyters, and by elders, so that any decision should require concurrence by all three groups. With this safeguard no one group could impose its will on the other two and any one of the three could veto proposals of the other two.

3. The Committee is agreed that the lay eldership as it exists in the Church of Scotland ought to be considered seriously by the Anglican Communion. We see no objection in principle to this but are indeed rather attracted to the idea. We know, however, that in Anglican Churches as yet there is little knowledge or understanding of the nature of this office and suggest that it requires further serious study on the part of Anglicans.

4. It is the Committee's opinion that the Anglican Churches ought to be ready to recognize the Presbyterian Churches as true parts of the One, Holy, Catholic, and Apostolic Church, and that the spiritual effectiveness of their ministerial orders ought not to be implicitly or explicitly questioned. We believe also that it might be possible, as is suggested in the Report of the Inter-Church Relations Committee, to reach eventual agreement as to some method of unifying their ministries

similar to the proposals for the Churches in North India and Ceylon, with a view to securing a ministry fully accredited in the eyes of all the members of the Churches on either side.

5. The Committee shares the conviction that the goal of all our efforts towards unity must be nothing short of organic unity. As regards the situation in Great Britain, it also agrees that relations between the Church of Scotland and the Episcopal Church in Scotland should be settled by negotiations between these two Churches before relations between the Church of England and the Presbyterian Churches are carried further.

6. The Committee notes that each Church has its own rules for admission to Holy Communion. The Church of Scotland requires baptism and approval by the Kirk Session. The Anglican Churches require baptism and episcopal confirmation. We appreciate the strength of the Presbyterian desire for immediate intercommunion as the sequel of the expression of a solemn resolve on the part of the Churches concerned to seek unity and reconciliation with one another. It must, however, be recognized as a fact that Anglicans conscientiously hold that the celebrant of the Eucharist should have been ordained by a bishop standing in the historic succession, and generally believe it to be their duty to bear witness to this principle by receiving Holy Communion only from those who have thus been ordained. The existence of this conviction as a view held among Anglicans clearly makes it in practice impossible to envisage the establishment of fully reciprocal intercommunion at any stage short of the adoption of episcopacy by the Churches of Presbyterian Order, and the satisfactory unification of the Presbyterian and Anglican ministries. The Committee believes, however, that such a solemn resolve as has been suggested would have the effect of making it possible to regularize, as a general practice, the admission of Presbyterians to communion at Anglican altars. It expresses the sincere hope that the Churches in England and Scotland may in due course be led to enter upon such a solemn resolve. The Church of England has recently agreed to admit communicants of the Church of Scotland to communion at altars of the Church of England when they are cut off by distance from their own Church or in special personal circumstances. The Committee would hope, however, that after such a solemn resolve, followed by decisive action, these restrictions would be removed.

3

The Committee expresses its thankfulness to Almighty God for the movement of his Spirit which it believes has made possible the initiation and the present outcome of the conversations between the four Anglican and Presbyterian Churches. It recognizes that the Report entitled *Relations between Anglican and Presbyterian Churches* envisages what must inevitably be long-term policy. Full time must be allowed to permit the Churches concerned thoroughly to study the implications of what is proposed, and only then, after prayer and full consideration, to make up their minds; but the doctrine of the one Church is the emphatic teaching of the New Testament. Our Lord's prayer for the unity of his Church in John 17 is an imperative and continuing challenge to a divided Church and a judgement on all our divisions. Moreover, in view of the Church's mission to the world, the present state both of the world and of Christendom makes Church unity a matter of present urgency. The Committee welcomes the suggestion that a special day of prayer should be appointed for the furtherance of Christian unity, and draws attention to the Universal Week of Prayer for Christian Unity now widely observed in January of each year. It believes, however, that apart from such special occasions there should be a continual movement of prayer, study, and instruction throughout our Churches with regard to these proposals. Local conferences for the study of these matters at the congregational level should be encouraged.

The Committee realizes that in those parts of the Church where schemes for organic reunion have reached an advanced stage the local position has gone much further than anything which is at present proposed regarding the relationship of Anglicans and Presbyterians in the older parts of Christendom. It believes that what is proposed in the Report entitled *Relations between Anglican and Presbyterian Churches* is a promising method of approach to the problem where schemes of immediate unity are not in prospect. It would emphasize that organic unity must at all times and in all cases be the ultimate goal.

THE METHODIST CHURCH

Conversations have been proceeding in the United States between representatives of the Protestant Episcopal Church and representatives of the Methodist Church since 1942. From 1948 onwards the agreed basis of discussion has been the exploration of possibilities of intercommunion as an approach to organic union, arising directly out of the Archbishop of Canterbury's Cambridge sermon in 1946. Similar conversations, with the Archbishop of Canterbury's sermon also as their starting point, have gone on between representatives of the Church of England, at the request of the Convocations of Canterbury and York, and representatives of the Methodist Church in England, appointed at the request of the Methodist Conference, following upon a series of meetings between representatives of the Archbishop of Canterbury and representatives of the Evangelical Free Churches of England of which a Report was published in 1950 under the title *Church Relations in England*. In both cases the proposals under consideration are proposals, not for organic union, or for corporate union involving constitutional schemes, but for intercommunion between Churches in the same area on the basis of provision for parallel but mutually acceptable episcopates. In the words of the Report of the Committee on Unity to the Lambeth Conference 1948, "The Churches concerned would remain distinct Churches, though carrying on along parallel lines episcopal oversight and episcopal ordination. They would live side by side, but with many of the barriers which now separate them removed."[15] In neither case has the stage of definite recommendations to the Churches concerned as yet been reached.

An Interim Statement, published in July 1958 and entitled *Conversations between the Church of England and the Methodist Church*,[16] without in any way prejudicing the question whether and if so how episcopacy could be taken into the Methodist Church, offers a great deal of valuable material which the two committees hope will be studied by members of the Church of England and members of the Methodist Church (when possible together, as well as separately).

A particularly important chapter in the Interim Statement is that drawn up in agreement by two of those taking part in the conversations, both well-known Church historians, Dr Norman Sykes (Anglican) and Professor Gordon Rupp (Methodist), on the "Special Situation of the Methodist Church in relation to the Church of England, and the circumstances of the Breach". This chapter lays special emphasis on such factors as the employment of lay preachers by John Wesley, and the principle of itineracy as opposed to the static ministry of the established Church. The two authors give good grounds for deprecating the pressing of attention on the single episode of Wesley's presbyteral ordinations, away from the context of the contemporary Church of England.

There is a chapter written by the members of the Church of England committee on "The Anglican Inheritance and Episcopacy", which incidentally throws light on the meaning attached by Anglicans to "the historic episcopate", and emphasizes the fact that "in the Church, the household of God, the Bishop should represent in his own appointed area the principle of Fatherhood". A Methodist statement follows entitled "Some Marks of Methodism and its Approach to Episcopacy": and the Marks to which attention is particularly called are Scriptural Holiness, the Doctrine of Assurance, the Methodist Hymn Book, the place that laymen occupy in the government of the Church, and the itinerant ministry. The Methodist Statement adds some very pertinent observations on the significance of the Bishop, "as the father of Christ's flock, the *pastor pastorum* who builds up the life of the Churches, maintains faith and order, and represents the unity and universality of the Church". But it says also plainly that "the one fatal objection to Church reunion would be any requirement of the reordination of its ministers, which would in fact be a denial of Methodism's place in the Catholic Church . . . A way forward to that Union of Christendom to which we believe God is calling us now, whose Will is our peace, may lie not through negative judgements on each other's

---

[15] *The Lambeth Conference, 1948*, Part II, p. 53.
[16] S.P.C.K. and The Epworth Press.

order, but through a positive and creative Act of Unification of Ministries in which each could find an enlargement and self-fulfilment."

It is to be observed that there is much "common ground" between the Methodists and the Anglicans, set out in the English Interim Statement, "an existing unity in Christian faith and purpose", which is also assumed in the account of the American negotiations. In both series of discussions there is still a great deal to be considered, concerning the theological as well as the practical issues involved. And if the Methodists are challenged with regard to the acceptance of the historic episcopate the Anglicans are also challenged in regard to the place they give, or might give, to the participation of the laity, to the doctrine of Scriptural Holiness, and to evangelism, amongst other factors. It is true that (in the language of the Archbishop of Canterbury's Cambridge sermon) the function of the Church of England as the nodal point of the Anglican Communion is safeguarded by this proposal of parallel Churches. But a permanent condition of parallel episcopal Churches existing side by side in the same area would, in the Committee's opinion, be most unsatisfactory. Intercommunion without living fellowship is not enough. But the Committee would welcome the continuing of the conversations and negotiations on the express understanding (*a*) that organic union is accepted as the ultimate aim, and that this aim is kept clearly in view, and (*b*) that after the establishment of intercommunion a steady process of assimilation is going on all the time, as part of the present step toward organic union, that there should be a genuine sharing of spiritual life, each Church receiving enrichment from the other Church, and that their bishops, presbyters, and laity, should meet together regularly in a representative assembly for counsel and prayer.

OTHER APPROACHES TO UNITY

1. WEST AFRICA

The Committee heard with great interest of the continuing conversations on reunion within the Province of West Africa, and in particular that the proposed Scheme of Union for Nigeria and the Cameroons is being considered by the dioceses of the Province and by the Methodist and Presbyterian Churches in Nigeria and the Cameroons. The Committee is strongly of the opinion that the Province of West Africa should be advised to give further consideration to the Ceylon Scheme of reunion as a model for union in Nigeria and the Cameroons, in order to maintain from the outset the full communion which the Province desires.

The Committee also felt that the Ceylon or North India/Pakistan statements concerning the faith of the Church should be recommended as the model for any Reunion Scheme in West Africa.

2. THE JERUSALEM ARCHBISHOPRIC

All advances toward Christian unity are of deep concern to the Archbishopric in Jerusalem and the Anglican Bishoprics of the Middle East, and they are happy to make a report of steps taken within the area.

In Iran discussions have taken place in the past between Anglicans and Presbyterians, although these talks have for the present been suspended. In the Sudan conversations have been taking place between Anglicans and Presbyterians working in the area, and a report on the preliminary discussions has been issued. In Egypt a Fellowship of Unity has brought together both Eastern and Western Churches in common worship, and a Liaison Committee has worked particularly on questions affecting religious liberty. The Arabic-speaking evangelical communities, including Anglicans and Presbyterians, held a conference in Beirut in 1956 to discuss plans for union from which a continuation committee has been making a study of union schemes. In Jerusalem itself the Church has for long had a responsibility for strengthening relationships with the Eastern Churches and it is hoped that conversations with the Armenian Church may soon take place there.

The Episcopal Synod, conscious of the urgency of the matter and recognizing the far-reaching effects of any action taken, decided that no bishop should act in isolation and that before any union scheme is undertaken the Synod should be informed and consulted.

RELATIONS WITH PARTICULAR CHURCHES

1. THE ROMAN CATHOLIC CHURCH

Although the Roman Catholic Church retains its conviction that the only goal of re-union must be submission to the Papacy, there are some welcome signs of an increasing recognition by the Roman authorities of the importance of the Ecumenical Movement. In the instruction *On the Ecumenical Movement* issued by the Holy Office in December 1949 a carefully guarded permission is given to Roman Catholics to engage in theological discussions with other Christians, and unrestricted permission is given for mixed gatherings which have as their purpose "to take counsel together concerning joint action in the defence of the fundamental principles of Christianity and the natural law" or "to deal with the rebuilding of the social order and similar questions". The same instruction allows such meetings to be opened or closed with the common recitation of the Lord's Prayer or some other approved prayer. In spite of the negative character of much of the contents of this document, its official recognition of the Ecumenical Movement as an important element in the Christian world, the permission to Roman Catholics to have some relations with it, the permission for discussions to take place, and the permission for common prayer to be used at such meetings, are all to be welcomed as solid gains. It is to be hoped that Roman Catholic Ordinaries will take generous advantage of this easing of restrictions in the areas under their control.

In order to produce useful results, discussions with Roman Catholics of specifically theological questions should continue to be undertaken by representatives of similar standing and equipment on both sides.

The observance of the Universal Week of Prayer for Christian Unity (18 to 25 January) becomes wider every year in England, on the Continent of Europe, and in some other parts of the world, with much official Roman Catholic approval. The form of this prayer which is most to be welcomed, and is in fact widespread, is that initiated by the late Abbé Couturier, that the unity of Christians may be achieved as our Lord wills and by the means that he wills. The simultaneous observances of this Week by Roman Catholics and by many members of other Churches are a valuable contribution to the efforts towards unity.

It is recognized that there will be occasions when Anglicans must adopt a critical attitude towards Roman Catholic utterances or policies when issues, such as those concerning the meaning and application of the principle of religious freedom, or the valid claims of Anglicanism, are at stake. Nevertheless we feel certain that Anglicans for their part, while striving at all times for the promotion of truth, frankness, and just dealing between Christians, will wish to do all in their power to secure understanding with Roman Catholics, as part of their efforts to promote peace and unity among all Christian people.

The main hope of advance in the immediate future must lie in the fostering of contacts at the personal and unofficial levels wherever opportunity occurs. Co-operation in conferences and discussions designed to promote scholarship in certain fields, for example that of patristic study, is sometimes possible and is of great value.

2. THE EASTERN ORTHODOX CHURCH

The visit of Orthodox delegations to the present Lambeth Conference, and the informal discussions for which it has provided an opportunity, have given grounds for hope that further conferences of the kind which took place in 1931 may before long be arranged between groups of theologians widely representative of the Orthodox Churches and the Churches of the Anglican Communion.

The Lambeth Conference of 1948 coincided with the celebration in Moscow of the 500th anniversary of the autocephaly of the Russian Orthodox Church, which was attended by representatives from some other Orthodox Churches. As a result of this gathering of Orthodox leaders, a statement on the subject of Anglican doctrine and Anglican orders was issued in Moscow which gave expression to certain difficulties felt by the Orthodox Church, but was at the same time friendly in its general tone.

Since that time, however, efforts initiated by the Archbishop of Canterbury to improve relations with Orthodox Churches have had the happy result of bringing about the renewal of direct contacts between the Church of England and the Russian Orthodox Church. In July 1956 at the invitation of the Patriarch of Moscow and All Russia an Anglo-Russian Theological Conference was held in Moscow lasting a fortnight. The leader of the Church of England delegation was the Archbishop of York. An account of the conference has been published. Those participating in it judged the discussions to be useful and it was felt that the cordiality of the reception of the Anglican delegation by the Russian Church leaders, as well as their deep interest in the subjects of the conversations, showed that a new and substantial link had been forged between the two Churches.

No other advances in formal relations with the Orthodox Church can be recorded. It is pleasant to note the good relations which exist between Anglican and Orthodox Christians, for example, in the United States, in Canada, as well as on the Continent of Europe, and to record gratitude for numerous acts of pastoral and personal kindness to Anglicans resident in Europe on the part of the Orthodox clergy and people.

The movements of population since the War have brought Orthodox congregations into contact with Anglicans in various parts of the world and this fact continues to be of great importance for the promotion of understanding and friendly relations between the two groups of Churches.

3. OTHER EASTERN CHURCHES

In general, relations remain friendly between Anglicans and members of these Churches but there is little to record in the way of advance in official contacts since 1948.

The Armenian Church

In the course of his visits to his communities throughout the world the Supreme Catholicos of All the Armenians came to England from Etchmiadzin in 1956, and was received by the Archbishop of Canterbury. Conversations of a preliminary kind were planned to take place between representatives of the Church of England and representatives of the Armenian Church at Easter 1958 in Jerusalem. Unhappily difficulties experienced in some parts by the Armenian Church have led to the postponement of these conversations. Meanwhile there is evidence from other parts of the world of continuing friendly relations between Anglican and Armenian Christians.

The Church of the East, or The Assyrian Church

The reduction in number of British forces in Iraq since 1945 has posed some difficult questions for large numbers of Assyrians who had been employed by the Royal Air Force in the civil cantonment at the aerodrome of Habbaniyeh. Since the establishment of Archbishop Benson's Mission to the Assyrians in 1866 Anglican interest has been unflagging in this small but historic Church, the Patriarch of which, Mar Eshai Shimun XXIII, lives in California. It is therefore a matter of much satisfaction that the Iraqi authorities took constructive steps to afford to the Assyrians, who were displaced, opportunities for settling and working elsewhere.

The Syrian Orthodox Church

The death of the Syrian Orthodox Patriarch of Antioch, Mar Ignatius Ephrem I, took place in 1957. He was succeeded by Mar Jacob of Beirut, who became Mar Ignatius Jacob III. The Committee welcomes the evident desire of the new Patriarch for Christian fellowship with other Churches and assures him of its sympathetic attitude towards his Church.

It is of great interest that a conference took place in August 1957 between representatives of the Church of India, Pakistan, Burma, and Ceylon and representatives of the Syrian Orthodox (Malankara Jacobite) Church. It is understood that the report of this conference has not yet been considered by the Episcopal Synod of the Church of India, Pakistan, Burma, and Ceylon. It is to be hoped that it may be found possible to carry forward these conversations. At the same time in response to request for advice the Committee would like to make two recommendations. The first recommendation is that the principle laid down by the last Lambeth Conference,[17] should not be overlooked, namely that in all such negotiations the relations between the Anglican Communion and all the Eastern Churches should be borne in mind and that nothing should be done which is likely to prejudice those wider relationships. The second recommendation arises from the fact that Syrian Orthodox communities exist in other Churches, Provinces, and Dioceses of the Anglican Communion, e.g., that of the Archbishopric in Jerusalem. It is to be hoped that before proceeding to any further stage of conversations with the Syrian Orthodox Church, the Church of India, Pakistan, Burma, and Ceylon will take these other Churches, Provinces, and Dioceses into consultation and carefully consider any representations and advice which they may wish to offer on the subject of relations between Anglicans and Syrian Christians.

It is desirable that in any further official conversations with the Syrian Orthodox Church, these other Provinces and Dioceses should be officially represented.

---

[17] *The Lambeth Conference, 1948*, Part II, p. 72.

The Mar Thoma Syrian Church

The Lambeth Conference of 1948 noted the action taken by the Church of India, Burma, and Ceylon in 1937 in establishing a measure of limited and partial intercommunion with the Mar Thoma Syrian Church of Malabar. The Committee on Foreign Relations of the Church of India, Pakistan, Burma, and Ceylon has now stated that discussions are being held with a view to the revision and extension of this agreement between the two Churches. Mar Thoma Christians are now widely dispersed not only throughout India but also in other lands, and are often isolated from the corporate life and ministrations of their own Church. The Committee welcomes the desire of the Church of India, Pakistan, Burma, and Ceylon, when asked, to meet the pastoral needs of these dispersed fellow Christians. While generally commending the terms of the proposed revised agreements it is aware that other parts of our Communion are directly concerned with this problem, e.g. in East Africa and Malaya. It strongly recommends that the Church of India, Pakistan, Burma, and Ceylon, before reaching any final agreement with the authorities of the Mar Thoma Church in India, should take the other Churches, Provinces, and Dioceses into consultation, so that if possible, a common agreement may be reached by all the authorities concerned, especially since the agreement which is under consideration would include the terms of admission to the corporate life and ministrations of each Church of members of the other. The Committee also feels it to be most important that no Church of the Anglican Communion should take any action in respect of the Mar Thoma Syrian Church which would hinder or make more difficult an eventual reconciliation between all Christians of the Syrian tradition or which would prejudice the progress towards closer relations between our Churches and the Syrian Church generally.

The Coptic and Ethiopian Churches

Attempts continue to be made to secure closer fellowship with the Coptic and Ethiopian Churches, but no formal steps have been taken in regard to these Churches since the last Lambeth Conference.

4. THE OLD CATHOLIC CHURCHES

The year 1957 saw the 25th anniversary of the establishment of full intercommunion between the Church of England and the Old Catholic Churches. It is to be noted with great satisfaction that the Bonn agreement has now been adopted by nearly all the other Churches and Provinces of the Anglican Communion.

In the United States of America and in Canada the Polish National Catholic Church of America, one of the family of Old Catholic Churches in communion with the See of Utrecht, has several hundred thousands of members, and its day-to-day relations with the Anglicans are a matter of importance. A joint committee has been set up in the United States and Canada. It meets annually and takes practical action for the mutual benefit of the Churches concerned.

Old Catholic bishops continue to take part in Anglican consecrations in England, Canada, and the United States from time to time. Anglican Bishops as official representatives attended International Old Catholic Congresses in Germany in 1953 and in Switzerland in 1957.

Furthermore, at an ordination held recently in the Diocese of Western New York in the United States, the Polish National Catholic Bishop of Buffalo, acting at the specific request of the Bishop of Western New York in his absence, was the officiating Bishop, using the Prayer Book of the Protestant Episcopal Church of the U.S.A.

In the Netherlands, where a recent census revealed that sixty per cent of those regularly attending worship in Anglican churches are of Dutch nationality, the inadequacy of ministrations offered solely in the English language has been increasingly felt. In January 1958 the sole surviving priest of the Catholic Apostolic (Irvingite) Church in the Netherlands died, and all the members of his congregations, most of whom can only speak Dutch, began to make regular use of the worship of the Anglican churches and to seek Anglican Sacraments. A small Old Catholic/Anglican conference was called in April 1958 in Utrecht to discuss what should be done. That conference made certain recommendations to the authorities in the two Churches regarding reception of and ministration to the Catholic Apostolics, including the recommendation that, should the occasional use of the Dutch language be found unavoidable in Anglican worship in the Netherlands, subject to episcopal approval Old Catholic clergy be invited to minister from time to time in Anglican churches using the Dutch language but using the Church of England Prayer Book. It was also suggested that Anglican clergy might be invited to celebrate from time to time in Old Catholic churches using the English language but using the liturgy of the Old Catholic Church.

The Committee welcomes this proposed arrangement as a happy instance of co-operation between the Anglican and the Old Catholic Churches in dealing with a complex and delicate problem.

5. LUTHERAN CHURCHES

Relations with the Lutheran Churches of Scandinavia remain cordial, and some further action was taken by several Anglican Churches in relation to the Churches of Scandinavia.

As requested in Resolution 72 of the Lambeth Conference of 1948, the Archbishop of Canterbury appointed a committee to confer with the representatives of the Churches of Denmark, Norway, and Iceland. The present position in regard to the discussions is that the Archbishop of Canterbury is in correspondence with the Bishops of Oslo and

Copenhagen in order to continue contacts by correspondence in matters of mutual interest.

The decisions of various Churches of the Anglican Communion in regard to the Churches of Scandinavia and the Baltic, are summarized below in tabular form. The Church of England in 1954 for the first time took action following the relevant Resolutions of the 1920 Lambeth Conference by passing resolutions in the Convocations of Canterbury and York, formally recognizing the admission of communicant members of the Swedish Church to Communion in the Church of England.

Church of Sweden

Lambeth Conference 1920 (Resolution 24)
,,   ,,   1930 (Resolution 37)
,,   ,,   1948 (Resolution 69)

Church of England:

  Formal recognition of admission to communion therein of Swedish Communicants.

Church of Province of South Africa:

  Joint consecration of Swedish Bishop (1949).

Episcopal Church in Scotland:

  Lambeth Conference Resolutions adopted as defining relationship.

Church of India, Pakistan, Burma, and Ceylon:

  Admission to Communion therein of Swedish Communicants.

  Acceptance of Swedish clergy to give addresses in churches.

Churches of Denmark, Norway, and Iceland

Lambeth Conference 1948 (Resolution 72)

Church of England:

  Admission of Communicants in special circumstances.

Church of Finland

Lambeth Conference 1948 (Resolution 70)

Church of England:

  Admission of Communicants in special circumstances and encouragement to join in consecration of Finnish Bishops.

Episcopal Church in Scotland:
> Report referred to in Resolution 70 accepted
> with approval.

Churches in Latvia and Estonia
Lambeth Conference 1948 (Resolution 71)

Church of England: As Finland.

Episcopal Church in Scotland:
> Recommendations accepted with approval.

In the last two or three years the present heads of the Lutheran Churches of Latvia and Estonia (now part of the U.S.S.R.) have been able to travel abroad, and to make new contacts with Christians outside the Soviet Union. It is therefore possible that opportunities may come to re-establish the friendly relations which existed before the second World War with the Christians of those Churches in their homelands.

Friendly contacts of numerous kinds have been maintained with the Lutheran Churches of Germany, and many unofficial conferences have been held between Anglican and German Lutheran Christians, both theological and practical, and much consultation and co-operation in Inter-Church Aid and in refugee service. No official action has been taken which affects the formal relations of the Anglican Churches with the Lutheran Churches of Germany.

In 1957 delegates of the Church of India, Pakistan, Burma, and Ceylon, met four representatives of the Tamil Evangelical Lutheran Church with a view to drawing up terms of relationship between the two Churches. On receipt of their representatives' report, the Committee on Foreign Relations of the Church of India, Pakistan, Burma, and Ceylon agreed to continue to maintain contacts with the Tamil Evangelical Lutheran Church to secure closer understanding, and recommended that conversations should be continued in order to clarify on both sides the doctrinal positions, customs, and usages, which require further examination. To these ends the Committee on Foreign Relations of the Church of India, Pakistan, Burma, and Ceylon appointed a group to conduct such conversations and to report in due course.

6. REFORMED CHURCHES

In 1958 a theological conference was held between representatives appointed by the Archbishop of Canterbury and representatives of the Netherlands Reformed Church. The request for these discussions came officially from the Netherlands Reformed Church and constitutes a new development in relations between the Anglican Communion and particular Churches so far as the Continent of Europe is concerned. These new contacts may have their own contribution to make to the whole relationship between Anglican and Calvinist Churches, which is closely affected by the present contacts between Anglicans and Presbyterians in England and Scotland, to which reference is made elsewhere in this report.

There are constant informal contacts between members of the Church of England and Christians of the Reformed Churches, especially those in France and Switzerland, and a series of unofficial theological conferences has recently started with members of the Reformed Church of France.

7. THE SPANISH REFORMED EPISCOPAL CHURCH AND THE LUSITANIAN CHURCH OF PORTUGAL

Brief reference was made to these two Churches in the Report of the Lambeth Conference of 1948,[18] which asked that further information should be available concerning their doctrine and discipline. The Archbishop of Armagh was invited to cause an inquiry to be made.

As a result of this inquiry the doctrine and discipline of these Churches have been found to be entirely satisfactory.

The Spanish Reformed Episcopal Church

Since the formation of this Church in 1871 and in the following years, Anglican Orders have been transmitted to it through the bishops of the Church of Ireland, but from the beginning it has been an indigenous Church. Since the death of Bishop Cabrera in 1916, it has had no Spanish Bishop. On 29 April 1956 Santos M. Molina was consecrated in Madrid by the Bishop of Meath, assisted by the Bishops of Minnesota and Northern Indiana, as Bishop of the Spanish Reformed Episcopal Church, and his leadership has already brought great encouragement to his people. This Church hopes that Churches of the Anglican Communion will now enter into agreement with it, similar to that with the Old Catholic Churches.

The Lusitanian Church

This Church, whose official title is "The Lusitanian Church, Catholic, Apostolic, Evangelical", claims to be a restoration (in 1880) of a former Church which had seceded from the Church of Rome, and was led in its restoration by Portuguese priests and laymen who refused to accept the dogma of the infallibility of the Pope. Like the Spanish Reformed Episcopal Church, the Lusitanian Church has received much help from the Church of Ireland, and its position is analogous to the Churches of the Old Catholic Communion. The Reverend A. F. Fiandor was

---

[18] *The Lambeth Conference, 1948*, Part II, p. 77, and Resolution 77.

consecrated Bishop for the Lusitanian Church on 22 June 1958 by the Bishop of South-Western Brazil, assisted by the Bishop of Meath and Bishop Nash of the Episcopal Church of the United States of America.

As the Spanish Reformed Church Liturgy has been greatly influenced by Anglican and Mozarabic sources, so the Book of Common Prayer of the Lusitanian Churches owes much to Anglican and Portuguese influence, traces of the latter being found in the Liturgy of the Braga Church. The Lusitanian Church wishes to continue as an indigenous and autonomous episcopal Church, and hopes that it may have the same relationships to the Churches of the Anglican Communion as have the Old Catholic Churches.

The Committee suggests that the bishops of these two Churches be invited to any conference arranged in accordance with the recommendation of Resolution 74 of the Lambeth Conference of 1948, "for brotherly counsel and encouragement".

7. THE PHILIPPINE INDEPENDENT CHURCH

The Philippine Independent Church has had close relations with the Protestant Episcopal Church in the United States of America ever since the consecration of three bishops by bishops of the Protestant Episcopal Church of the United States of America in 1948, and there is every hope that these relations will become closer in the years to come. It continues to show vigorous growth and is quite independent in its Church life and polity. The position of St Andrew's Theological Seminary in Manila is most important as it is in this Seminary of the Protestant Episcopal Church of the U.S.A. that young men of the Philippine Independent Church are and will be trained. A revised draft of a Book of Common Prayer has been completed and was to be submitted to the 1957 meeting of the General Assembly of the Philippine Independent Church as the Supreme Council of Bishops for approval and authorization.

A word of thanks is due to the sometime Bishop of the Philippines, the Right Reverend Dr Norman Binsted, for his statesmanship in bringing about what may well prove to be a model for effective co-operation in the field of inter-Church relations.

THE ECUMENICAL MOVEMENT AND THE WORLD COUNCIL OF CHURCHES

Of necessity in this report special attention is given to particular schemes of union and to important "conversations" directly involving parts or provinces of our Anglican Communion. Important and critical as are these particular projects of union, the Committee would stress also the wider movement within which they are set. This is commonly spoken of in our time as "the Ecumenical Movement". The name is new. The basic reality is as old as the Church. From the beginning Christian people have known themselves called to pray and to struggle for unity and fellowship among themselves. What we now name the Ecumenical Movement is the fresh tide in this drawing together of the separated companies of God's people which has marked the past fifty years. Unions between hitherto divided Churches, concordats for official intercommunion, conversations between Churches, meetings for prayer, evangelism, and healing which draw together Christians of different Communions, Councils for co-operation in missions and evangelism and education and social service, are all rightly seen as expressions of this movement of the Spirit of God among us. The whole is pervaded and largely motivated by a fresh recognition of the place of the Church and its mission in Christian faith and life.

The most dramatic and widely recognized expression of this movement is the World Council of Churches, which came into being in 1948 since the meeting of the last Lambeth Conference. The World Council has drawn together in shared counsel and service more diverse groups within the world-wide Christian community than any other organization which all the centuries have known. This is a cause for thanksgiving even as it is a matter for regret that the Church of Rome and other Christian bodies have not yet been ready to share in its membership.

The World Council of Churches keeps all its member Churches mindful of the universal dimension of the Christian fellowship and mission. It has encouraged and made possible a continuing and fruitful conversation between theologians and responsible leaders of the many Churches concerning our common Scriptures, questions of faith and order, our one mission, the content and methods of evangelism, the vocation of the laity, the needs and problems which our troubled world presents to us all. It has sponsored an interchange of theological students between Churches and countries, which can mean much for the future leadership of the Churches. In conjunction with the International Missionary Council it has provided in the Commission of the Churches on International Affairs a most competent instrument for the concern of the Churches in the area of international relations. It has established a distinguished centre of ecumenical study at Bossey, in Switzerland. It has provided the channel for a vast measure of aid to Christian brethren in distress and of relief to the refugees and the dispossessed.

In these ways the World Council makes real aspects of unity which may be lost sight of in the consideration of organic unions of particular Churches and in the achievement of formal intercommunion. Communication and community are intimately related to communion. Unity has a moral dimension in shared obedience to the demands of God's justice and mercy. Intercommunion and even union will bear little fruit without the love that bears one another's burdens and seeks deep mutual understanding. Wherever intercommunion may be established between us and another Communion, we should seek to follow it up by provisions for continuing counsel and sharing, in order that the sacramental relationship may be clothed with more substance. Likewise, in encouraging the emergence of new national Churches, serious thought must be given to ways by which they may be guarded against isolation from the worldwide Christian community.

In order to clarify the position of the World Council of Churches, certain portions of the statement of the Central Committee at the Toronto meeting in 1950 are included in this report. It is entitled "The Church, the Churches, and the World Council of Churches", and the following crucial paragraphs may correct misapprehensions found in some sections of our own communion.

1. The World Council of Churches is not and must never become a super-Church.

2. The purpose of the World Council of Churches is not to negotiate unions between Churches, which can only be done by the Churches themselves acting on their own initiative, but to bring the Churches into living contact with each other and to promote the study and discussion of the issues of Church unity.

3. The World Council cannot and should not be based on any one particular conception of the Church. It does not prejudge the ecclesiological problem.

4. Membership in the World Council of Churches does not imply that a Church treats its own conception of the Church as merely relative.

5. Membership in the World Council does not imply the acceptance of a specific doctrine concerning the nature of Church unity.

The assumptions underlying the World Council of Churches:

1. That member Churches of the Council believe that conversation, co-operation, and common witness of the Churches must be based on the common recognition that Christ is the Divine Head of the Body.

2. The member Churches of the World Council believe on the basis of the New Testament that the Church of Christ is one.

3. The member Churches recognize that the membership of the Church of Christ is more inclusive than the membership of their own Church body. They seek, therefore, to enter into living contact with those outside their own ranks who confess the lordship of Christ.

4. The member Churches of the World Council consider the relationship of other Churches to the Holy Catholic Church which the Creeds profess as a subject for mutual consideration. Nevertheless, membership does not imply that each Church must regard the other member Churches as Churches in the true and full sense of the word.

5. The member Churches of the World Council recognize in other Churches elements of the true Church. They consider that this mutual recognition obliges them to enter into a serious conversation with each other in the hope that these elements of truth will lead to the recognition of the full truth and to unity based on the full truth.

6. The member Churches of the Council are willing to consult together in seeking to learn of the Lord Jesus Christ what witness he would have them bear to the world in his name.

7. A further practical implication of common membership in the World Council is that the member Churches should recognize their solidarity with each other, render assistance to each other in case of need, and refrain from such actions as are incompatible with brotherly relationships.

8. The member Churches enter into spiritual relationships through which they seek to learn from each other and to give help to each other in order that the Body of Christ may be built up and that the life of the Churches may be renewed.

It is a joy to record the facts that at the Second Assembly of the World Council (Evanston, 1954) the Churches of the Anglican Communion in Australia, Canada, India, Pakistan, Burma, and Ceylon, Japan, New Zealand, South Africa, West Africa, England, Scotland, Wales, Ireland, the United States, and the West Indies were strongly represented, and that from the beginning representatives of our communion have had abundant opportunity to exercise leadership as officers, as members of the Central Committee, and as members of the staff.

The Committee urges all the provinces and Churches of the Anglican Communion to take a just share in the financial support of the World Council and to make provision for the expenses of their representatives who are serving on the Central Committee and important Commissions and Departments.

It has often been observed that one of the most serious weaknesses of the ecumenical movement is that it draws the divided Churches together "at the top", but fails to draw them together equally at the local level, where actual congregations of Christ's flock live and worship side by side. The Committee believes it to be the duty of every bishop to take the lead in promoting this work in his own diocese. It calls upon all our clergy and people to break out of the isolation and introversion of much of our Church life, and to seek, by every means at national and local level, to establish brotherly relationships and contacts and to share perplexities and burdens, that we may be one with our Christian brethren of other traditions in Christ's mission to the world.

FALKNER CHELMSFORD
Chairman

3. Progress in the Anglican Communion

MEMBERS OF THE COMMITTEE

A. MISSIONARY APPEAL AND STRATEGY

ENGLAND

N. B. Hudson, D.S.O., M.C., D.D. [Ely]
C. A. Martin, D.D., LL.D. [Liverpool]
   (*Joint Vice-Ch.*)
W. L. Anderson, D.S.C., D.D.
 [Salisbury]
W. H. Baddeley, D.S.O., M.C., D.D.,
 S.T.D. [Blackburn]
F. D. Coggan, D.D. [Bradford]
C. R. Claxton, M.A. [Warrington
 (Suffr.)] (*Joint Secretary*)
C. E. Stuart, M.A.

SCOTLAND

K. C. H. Warner, D.S.O., D.D.
 [Edinburgh]

UNITED STATES

A. H. Blankingship, C.B.E. (Hon.),
 D.D. [Cuba]
W. H. Gray, D.D. [Connecticut]
   (*Chairman*)
E. H. Jones, D.D. [West Texas]
C. A. Voegeli, S.T.D. [Haiti and the
 Dominican Republic]
H. S. Kennedy, D.D. [Honolulu]
F. L. Barry, D.D. [Albany]
C. A. Mason, D.D. [Dallas]
H. W. B. Donegan, D.D. [New York]
N. M. Burroughs, D.D. [Ohio]
E. M. Krischke, D.D. [Southern
 Brazil]
G. V. Smith, S.T.D. [Iowa]
J. S. Higgins, D.D. [Rhode Island]
A. M. Lewis, D.D. [Salina]
J. B. Bentley, D.D.
H. L. Doll, D.D. [Maryland (Coadj.)]

CANADA

R. H. Waterman, D.D. [Nova Scotia]
I. A. Norris, D.D. [Brandon]
D. B. Marsh, D.D. [The Arctic]
S. C. Steer, D.D. [Saskatoon]
   (*Joint Secretary*)
G. P. Gower, D.D. [New Westminster]
T. Greenwood, D.D. [Yukon]
K. C. Evans, D.D. [Ontario]
H. G. Watts, D.D. [Caledonia]

INDIA, PAKISTAN, BURMA, AND CEYLON

J. W. Sadiq, M.A., B.D. [Nagpur]

AUSTRALIA

J. Frewer, C.B.E., TH.D. [North-West
 Australia]
P. N. W. Strong, C.M.G., TH.D. [New
 Guinea]
G. F. Cranswick, TH.D. [Tasmania]
W. J. Hudson, TH.D. [Carpentaria]
I. W. A. Shevill, TH.D. [North
 Queensland]

NEW ZEALAND

L. S. Kempthorne, C.B.E., D.D.
 [Polynesia]

SOUTH AFRICA

J. A. A. Maund, M.C., B.A.
 [Basutoland]
J. D. Vincent, M.C., M.A.
 [Damaraland]

WEST INDIES

A. J. Knight, C.M.G., LL.B., D.D.
 [Guiana]
G. H. Brooks, M.A. [British
 Honduras]

JAPAN
P. K. Ueda, D.D. [Hokkaido]

WEST AFRICA
A. W. Howells, O.B.E., M.A., B.D. [Lagos]

CENTRAL AFRICA
W. J. Hughes, D.D. [Matabeleland]
(*Joint Vice-Ch.*)

EXTRA-PROVINCIAL
W. J. Thompson, C.B.E., M.A. [Iran]
L. C. Usher-Wilson, M.A. [Upper Nile]
W. S. Baker, M.A. [Zanzibar]
A. Stanway, M.A., TH.L., [Central Tanganyika]
J. Marcel [Madagascar (Asst.)]
J. C. S. Daly, M.A. [Korea]
N. E. Cornwall, C.B.E., M.A. [Borneo]

B. THE BOOK OF COMMON PRAYER

ENGLAND
C. M. Chavasse, O.B.E. (Mil.), M.C., T.D., D.D. [Rochester]
W. M. Askwith, K.C.M.G., D.D. [Gloucester]
E. R. Morgan, D.D. [Truro]
D. C. Dunlop, M.A.

WALES
J. J. A. Thomas, D.D. [Swansea and Brecon]

IRELAND
G. O. Simms, D.D. [Dublin]
(*Chairman*)
C. J. Tyndall, D.D. [Kilmore and Elphin and Ardagh]
H. A. Stanistreet, D.D. [Killaloe, Kilfenora, Clonfert, and Kilmacduagh]

SCOTLAND
F. H. Moncreiff, M.A. [Glasgow and Galloway]

UNITED STATES
M. E. Peabody, D.D. [Central New York]
O. L. Loring, D.D. [Maine]
J. P. DeWolfe, D.D. [Long Island]
O. J. Hart, D.D. [Pennsylvania]

W. W. Horstick, D.D. [Eau Claire]
E. R. Welles, D.D. [West Missouri]
A. C. Lichtenberger, D.D. [Missouri]
(*Vice-Chairman*)
R. M. Hatch, D.D. [Western Massachusetts]

CANADA
H. E. Sexton, D.D. [British Columbia]
H. H. Clark, D.D. [Edmonton]

INDIA, PAKISTAN, BURMA, AND CEYLON
C. J. G. Robinson, M.A. [Lucknow]
V. G. Shearburn, C.R., M.A. [Rangoon]
J. Aung Hla [Rangoon (Asst.)]

AUSTRALIA
R. W. H. Moline, M.C., D.D. [Perth]
J. A. G. Housden, B.A. [Rockhampton]
R. E. Richards, M.A. [Bendigo]
T. T. Reed, D.LITT. [Adelaide]
M. A. Loane, M.A. [Sydney (Coadj.)]

SOUTH AFRICA
G. P. L. Turner, L.TH. [St Helena]
J. Hunter, M.A. [George]

WEST AFRICA
E. D. Martinson, C.B.E. [Accra (Asst.)]

CENTRAL AFRICA
F. O. Thorne, C.B.E., M.C., D.D. [Nyasaland]

EXTRA-PROVINCIAL
L. W. Brown, D.D. [Uganda]
          (*Secretary*)
P. J. Brazier, M.A. [Uganda (Asst.)]
G. Miles [Madagascar (Asst.)]

C. MINISTRIES AND MANPOWER

ENGLAND
H. C. Montgomery Campbell, M.C., D.D. [London]
H. W. Bradfield, D.D. [Bath and Wells]   (*Chairman*)
T. Longworth, D.D. [Hereford]
L. M. Charles-Edwards, D.D. [Worcester]
F. R. Barry, D.S.O., D.D. [Southwell]

IRELAND
R. C. H. G. Elliott, D.D. [Connor]

SCOTLAND
E. F. Easson, B.SC., M.A. [Aberdeen and Orkney]

UNITED STATES
H. H. Kellogg, D.D. [Minnesota]
J. G. Saucedo, D.D. [Mexico]

CANADA
W. E. Bagnall, D.D. [Niagara]
C. C. Robinson, D.D. [Moosonee]
W. A. Townshend, D.D. [Huron (Suffr.)]

INDIA, PAKISTAN, BURMA, AND CEYLON
R. W. Bryan [Barrackpore]

AUSTRALIA
T. M. Armour, B.A. [Wangaratta]
K. J. Clements, B.A. [Grafton]

NEW ZEALAND
W. J. Simkin, L.TH.(Dur.) [Auckland]

SOUTH AFRICA
J. Boys, M.A. [Kimberley and Kuruman]   (*Secretary*)
T. G. V. Inman, D.D. [Natal]
J. L. Schuster, M.A. [St John's]

WEST INDIES
F. N. Chamberlain, C.B., O.B.E., M.A., F.K.C. [Trinidad and Tobago]

EXTRA-PROVINCIAL
L. J. Beecher, M.A., B.SC., A.R.C.S. [Mombasa]   (*Vice-Chairman*)
R. P.-C. Koh, D.D. [Singapore (Asst.)]

PREFACE

The primary concern of this Committee has been with *progress* in the Anglican Communion. The three sub-committees—

3A—Missionary Appeal and Strategy
3B—The Book of Common Prayer
3C—Ministries and Manpower—

have worked under the conviction that stagnation spells death, a conviction corroborated all too often by the records of history.

The Anglican Communion is faced in this mid-twentieth century with problems of great complexity for which no easy answers from past decades will prove adequate. But it is conscious also of the sufficiency of its Lord to meet the needs of this new age, of the power of the Spirit whose vitality is seen on every hand, and of the peculiar mission which it knows has been committed to it by God himself.

Only when the Church is a worshipping and a praying Church will it be a progressive Church. The forms of its worship must, therefore, be a first care in the pastoral concern of the Church for her people. For this reason the highest importance is attached to the report of sub-committee B, which had the task of considering the Book of Common Prayer.

It is emphasized in this report that the work of evangelism is the duty and privilege of every member of Christ. But if the laity are to take their full share in the spiritual warfare of the Church, an adequate, well-trained, and alert priesthood is of paramount importance. Hence the urgency of the report of sub-committee C.

We are strongly opposed to any spirit of defeatism in regard to the missionary work of the Church. The Lord of the Church is the Living God, Creator, Redeemer, Life-Giver. Through the Body of Christ that living God is at work all over the world. Within the Anglican Communion older Churches and younger are joining in a great partnership of obedience and advance.

"Now God be thanked Who has matched us with His hour."[1]

---

[1] " Peace," by Rupert Brooke.

A. MISSIONARY APPEAL AND STRATEGY

1. MISSIONARY APPEAL

The basis of the Christian missionary appeal is the fact that God has spoken and still speaks to men. He who spoke "at sundry times and in divers manners in times past unto the fathers by the prophets", spoke to men supremely in his Son. Jesus of Nazareth is the very Word of God. In that Word alone, incarnate, crucified, risen, ascended, alive for evermore, history has meaning, as in him alone it will reach its consummation.

The mighty acts of God focused in the incarnation, the crucifixion, the resurrection, the ascension, the descent of the Spirit—these facts of history constitute the groundwork of all missionary appeal and endeavour. From them, from the very character of the God who loves and who therefore speaks and whose words *are* acts, from them and not from any theories or feelings, springs the missionary motive. Jesus came not simply to preach a message of brotherhood and goodwill, but *to be to men what God has to say to them.* There is no Gospel apart from him. "He came, not so much to preach the Gospel, as that there might be a Gospel to preach." In the words of Origen, he was himself the Kingdom.

But the utterance of the divine word did not cease with the ascension of the Lord. At Pentecost, the Church of the old covenant, which had failed its Lord, was re-constituted and empowered in order that it might be the continuation of the divine mission, the expression of the divine love and yearning for the souls of men. The members of the Church, themselves very ordinary men and women, looked back to the mighty acts of God (to them so recent) and gave utterance to them with conviction and enthusiasm. As they watched the power of the risen Christ operative in his Church by his Spirit, they said: "This is that which was spoken of by the prophets." They had found the Messiah, and the Messiah had laid hold on them. The universality of the Gospel was a subject not for debate but for proclamation. They would have agreed totally with the dictum of William Temple that "if the Gospel is true for anyone, anywhere, it is true for all men everywhere, and the Church is his Church exactly in so far as it is carrying out its missionary task".

Theirs was a word of reconciliation—reconciliation of sinful men to God and hence of antagonistic men to one another. Men saw in these followers of the Way, in these members of the redeemed community, the Holy Spirit of God released, the very life of God radiated. They spoke indeed—spoke with a freedom and power which surprised no one more than themselves. But they *lived* Christ with a holiness and a zest which were self-authenticating. Their words and their lives constituted the continuation of the words and life of the Incarnate

C+

Lord. No wonder that the Church spread like wild-fire throughout the Graeco-Roman world.

We turn from the first century to the twentieth. The need of the world for the Christian Gospel is profound. On the most generous estimate only one third of the world's population has been evangelized. As a contemporary missionary thinker puts it: "Christ has a Kingdom. That Kingdom is to be proclaimed to the uttermost parts of the earth. It is not being proclaimed to the uttermost parts of the earth. Therefore *Dieu a besoin des hommes*, God has need of men",[1] men who in the words of St Paul, will "beseech you, in Christ's stead, be ye reconciled to God". This task, however, cannot be relegated to the specialist, to the "professional missionary". The Willingen Missionary Conference of 1952 affirmed: "There is no participation in Christ without participation in his mission to the world. . . . God sends forth his Church to carry out his work to the end of the earth, to all nations and to the end of time."[2] The mission of the Church cannot mean less than *the whole Church bringing the whole Gospel to the whole world*. To think of missionary activity (whether to the islands of the far seas or to the unevangelized masses of Great Britain or America) as a kind of "optional extra" to be undertaken by those who are enthusiastic for that kind of thing, is to make complete nonsense of the Gospel. God gave his only-begotten Son, and he gave him to be a missionary. Christ has but one Church, his Body, and through that Church in its totality he gives himself to men. "If Christ is what Christ is, He must be uttered. . . . We present Christ for the sole, sufficient reason that He deserves to be presented."[3]

FIVE MAJOR ISSUES

It is the duty of the Church to be faithful to the theological principles upon which its work of evangelism is based. It is its duty also, to note that the conditions under which its work is attempted are not chosen by the Church but given by circumstances of time and place. Conditions have changed greatly since our last Conference. There are five things of which the Church must take account, in particular:

Nationalism. Nationalism represents a major fact in present conditions. It is an urge towards nationhood. It is a process in the evolution of peoples, and it has significance as, under God, each national group makes its particular contribution of character and service to the family of nations. It becomes sinister when in an excessive desire for its own preservation and purposes it begins to disclose a hatred of anything outside itself. The Church must recognize the legitimate aspirations of peoples and by its life and witness seek to sanctify them.

---

[1] S. Neill, *The Unfinished Task*, p. 221.
[2] *Missions under the Cross*, p. 190.
[3] K. Cragg, *The Call of the Minaret*, pp. 334, 335.

Distrust. The distrust among the peoples of the world cannot be neglected. Its root is fear: fear of the strong by the strong, and of the strong by the weak; fear of total loss through war; fear that legitimate aspirations will be denied; fear of the loss of "rights". There is much evidence available, that such fears are not without foundation.

Industrialism. In the newly developing countries, industrialism creates a major problem. In Europe at the time of the industrial revolution the Church failed to meet the challenge. It must not fail again. In Africa, Asia, and elsewhere the rapid process of industrialization means the break-up of the old life undisturbed for centuries. It means the rise of a new urban society, which in turn creates fresh problems in family and home life. It creates increasing demands for education and technical knowledge. It creates stronger and legitimate desires for a fair share of production. It creates new tensions between man and man and between race and race. It throws into sharp relief the Church's duty to press on with its gospel of reconciliation.

The resurgence of some non-Christian religions. This is an important fact in the given set of conditions. In the Middle East and in Asia and to some extent in parts of Africa, the revival may develop into a crusade. It is difficult to gauge accurately the spiritual content of this resurgence, or to say how far it is being used as a means to further national aspirations, or as a protest against Christianity, wrongly believed to be peculiarly western. The Church has a duty to make it plain that the Christian faith is not something used in a struggle of east against west, but that it is God's answer to the needs of all men everywhere: not Christ *versus* Mohammed or Buddha, but Christ the Saviour of the world.

"Christian Deviations." The importance of presenting the *whole* Gospel to men is evident in the growth of those religious bodies which flourish through over-emphasis on some particular aspect of the Faith such as Adventism and "Divine Healing". The missionary enthusiasm of these groups is a rebuke and a challenge to the Anglican Communion. To counter these distortions there is need of clear teaching on eschatology and the healing mission of the Church, aspects of the Faith too often neglected in the thinking and teaching of the Church.

THE MISSIONARY AND MISSIONARY SOCIETIES

In the fellowship of the Church as a world society, there will always be needed a sharing of leadership and financial support from land to land, as we bear one another's burdens and so fulfil the law of Christ. Certain areas still need workers from other sections of our Communion, especially for purposes of theological training and the sharing of special skills. The lands from which they go can profit from the experience of the growing life manifested in the lands to which their aid has been given.

For such sharing of life from land to land, men and women are needed, both for life-long service and for specific tasks for specific terms. They will go as servants, not masters, expecting to work under the leadership of the Church where they serve. They will go as representatives, not of any particular country, but of the Church. They will learn from the heritage of the land to which they go and share that of the land from which they come, and so help in the building of Christ's Kingdom into which there will be brought the glory and the honour of all peoples.

The sending of men and women from one land to another has in England been the function of the missionary societies, but in some other lands other means have been used. Although the Committee appreciates that this is a domestic matter of the Church of England, it nevertheless thinks that the following points are relevant:

1. The mission of the Church is a mission of the whole Church to the whole world.
2. Missionary societies came into existence to recall the Church of England to a task which had been neglected: indeed, many Provinces of the Anglican Communion would not have come into being, had it not been for their work. They have done and are doing a missionary task as handmaids of the Church.
3. Any plan by which the societies would be drawn into even closer co-operation should be welcomed.

WORLD COUNCIL OF CHURCHES AND INTERNATIONAL MISSIONARY COUNCIL

A full account of the World Council of Churches and its setting in the Ecumenical Movement is dealt with in the Report of the Committee on Unity and the Church Universal. This Committee would draw attention to the far-reaching implications of the proposals by which that Council may be integrated with the International Missionary Council, and expresses the hope that a solution satisfactory to both Councils may be achieved.

---

2. STRATEGY

In its statement on the nature, growth, and function of the Anglican Communion, the Report of the Lambeth Conference of 1948 drew attention to the need for increased opportunities of consultation between the various parts of the Communion. That Conference noted that, as far back as 1867 when the Church overseas was beginning to comprehend its larger destiny in the New World, the Lambeth Conference itself was the outcome of the demand for closer contact and increased opportunities for fellowship one with another.

Since that time an unprecedented expansion has taken place and we look upon the truly inspiring structure of a Communion, the spiritual home of many races and peoples, using the historic forms of worship locally adapted, where necessary, to special needs.

In recent years it has become evident that this Communion, which has been characterized by a spontaneity of growth, is destined for greater and perhaps more dangerous responsibility. Despite the crises of nearly half a century it can bring to the modern world conflict a tempered wisdom and a spiritual stability which can reinforce the hopes and aspirations of the human race in its pilgrimage.

It is obvious, however, that it will not fulfil this task unless it takes cognizance of some of its weaknesses. Dispersed throughout the world and working under every conceivable condition, its growth tends to a fragmentation of its efforts and a failure to reap the full benefit of its resources. It needs to be reminded in all its parts that no one lives to himself, and that as a body with a common life the whole is always something greater than the sum of those parts. In the context of the modern world with its pressures, competing systems, rival philosophics, and expanding frontiers of knowledge, the need for consultation is of paramount importance.

If the responsibilities of a world-wide Communion are to be grasped and its resources mobilized, fuller expression must be given to four vital principles of corporate life—co-ordination, co-operation, consolidation, cohesion.

The present difficulties of securing information and maintaining liaison must be overcome. If there is to be effective co-ordination of effort, means must be found of securing a consensus of opinion and of communicating advice to the proper authority.

It is necessary to guard against the setting up of a department with its dangers of bureaucracy. At the same time some instrument is necessary whereby a more frequent exchange of ideas and information may permit the better exercise of statesmanship in Church affairs and a greater efficiency in the use of its resources.

An Anglican Communion Advisory Council on Missionary Strategy was set up as a result of Resolutions 80 and 81 of the Lambeth Conference of 1948. The report of the Conference contains a section (page 89) setting forth the kind of questions which might be referred to such an Advisory Council.

The Committee is of the opinion that this Advisory Council should continue and that it can become even more effective in promoting the work and welfare of the Anglican Communion if the following recommendations are adopted.

RECOMMENDATIONS

1. The Committee recommends that a full-time secretary of the Advisory Council on Missionary Strategy should be appointed by the Archbishop of Canterbury with the approval of the Advisory Council.

This officer would collect and disseminate information, keep open lines of communication and make contact when necessary with responsible authority.

2. The Committee recommends that the Council should consist of:

   (a) The Archbishop of Canterbury as *ex officio* Chairman of the Council and one representative of the Church of England appointed by him.

   (b) The Primates or Presiding Bishops of National Churches or their representatives, clerical or lay.

   (c) The Metropolitans of the remaining provinces or their representatives, clerical or lay.

   (d) Such representatives from the extra-provincial dioceses under the jurisdiction of the Archbishop of Canterbury as may be appointed by him, clerical or lay.

The Committee believes that such a membership, drawn from the whole Anglican Communion, is yet flexible enough to permit adequate attendance of competent personnel whenever a meeting is necessary. The inclusion of the laity would enable the Council to draw upon the largely untapped spiritual resources and knowledge of many outstanding Churchmen.

3. The Committee recommends that the Chairman should summon the Council or any part thereof to meet when and where in his judgement it may be necessary, provision being made for a meeting to be summoned on request if circumstances should so require.

A plenary meeting of the Council should be held whenever the Lambeth Conference or the Anglican Congress meets.

4. The Committee suggests the following terms of reference for the Council:

   (a) The purpose of the Council is to enable the whole Anglican Communion to deal effectively with matters of world-wide strategy and the welfare of the whole Communion.

   It may advise on such matters as:

   (i) questions of policy and the opening of new areas of missionary activity;

   (ii) the advantages of grouping dioceses and developing a common life prior to the formation of a new province;

   (iii) the increase of workers and strengthening of the position in areas where the Churches face increasing opposition or other difficulties;

   (iv) the fostering of vocations in the service of the Church;

   (v) closer co-operation between missionary societies;

   (vi) the preparation and dissemination of information.

   (b) The Council is advisory and cannot settle policy. Recommendations of the Council are to be referred in the first instance to the

Chairman, who will bring them to the notice of the Primates, Presiding Bishops, Metropolitans, and Bishops of extra-provincial dioceses for information and action and for communication to diocesan bishops.

(c) It is not within the province of the Council to deal with matters concerning relations with other Churches or concerning re-union between Churches. It may, however, draw attention to questions in these fields which in its opinion need investigation and may recommend that they be referred to the appropriate body.

(d) The Council may settle its own procedure.

5. The Committee recommends that the cost of carrying out this plan should be borne by the whole Anglican Communion in such proportion among its parts as the Advisory Council shall decide.

6. The Committee recommends that in view of the urgency of this matter immediate steps should be taken to secure the necessary funds.

7. The Committee recommends that a meeting of the Advisory Council to appoint the new secretary be held within one year of the Lambeth Conference.

If the foregoing proposals are accepted by the Conference, the following subjects are among those which will need careful consideration by the Advisory Council. These subjects are mentioned as being of special urgency, arising as they do from the great missionary tasks on which the Anglican Communion is already engaged.

1. African Townships

Bishops in Africa have reported the serious problem for the Church which new African townships have created. The process of industrialization brings with it an increasing demand for African labour. Thousands of African men come to the towns for employment. Old tribal ties are soon lost, family life breaks up, and all the difficulties of an industrial revolution are thrown into relief. In many dioceses the resources for new Churches and for men to serve them are beyond the capacity of the local Church. This is an urgent problem demanding immediate attention.

2. South America

The Committee believes that so far as the Anglican Communion is concerned, South America is "the neglected continent", while it is equally a continent of increasing importance in the world to-day.

Jurisdictional boundaries and responsibilities need to be studied. In a few areas the Church is well established, but in most of the continent very little is being done. The little-known and uncivilized tribes of the interior call for pioneer evangelistic work. Vast masses owe no definite allegiance to the Roman Catholic Church and are a prey to materialism or to distorted forms of the Christian faith.

South America offers a challenge and opportunity to the Anglican Communion as a great field for evangelistic work. There is no reason why it should not strengthen and extend its work in the continent. There is every reason why it should assume larger responsibilities there.

3. Chinese Dispersion

Millions of Chinese have left their homeland. In particular, Hong Kong, Malaya, Singapore, and Taiwan have been affected by this dispersion. This constitutes a problem for the Church and calls for a careful survey.

4. New Guinea

A unique opportunity exists in the Highlands of Northern New Guinea, discovered and opened out only in the last fifteen years. Here the white man is drawing out the rich resources of these mountain valleys, where there are thousands of primitive people hitherto untouched by the Gospel. The Australian Church realizes that it is more important to put into these valleys the riches of the Gospel than to take from them material wealth. New Guinea presents an opportunity that perhaps exists in few places in the world, of building up a Christian civilization. If this opportunity is to be taken additional help is needed.

5. The Middle East and the Archbishopric in Jerusalem

This is an area of rapid social change, of violent national feeling and desire for self-expression on the part of its newly awakened peoples. Here is the centre of the Moslem World with its great challenge to the Church.

The Committee welcomes the action of the Archbishop of Canterbury in the creation in 1957 of an Archbishopric in Jerusalem with metropolitical jurisdiction in the dioceses of the Middle East.

6. New Provinces

The Lambeth Conference of 1948 considered this question and noted that discussions were taking place for the formation of provinces in East, Central, and West Africa, and in the Pacific. Since then, the Provinces of West Africa and Central Africa have been formed and the Jerusalem Archbishopric constituted. In South-East Asia and in the South-West Pacific, Regional Councils have been formed, containing among their members dioceses which are already linked with other provinces. It has also been reported that discussions are taking place for the formation of two provinces in East Africa.

7. Missionary Dioceses

Attention has been called to the fact that opportunities before the Church in certain areas make necessary the creation of new dioceses.

The Committee considers that full information should be obtained in each case and suitable courses of action be proposed.

8. Restrictions of Religious Freedom

In some parts of the world where the Anglican Communion is at work, there are serious restrictions of religious freedom imposed by a government or by a Church. The Committee, in recording its strong disapproval of such restrictions, expresses the hope that this matter will receive continuing attention from the Advisory Council.

9. Possible Conflicts with Governments

There are occasions when the policy of governments raises moral issues of such seriousness that active steps must be taken by the Church to uphold the Divine Law. When this occurs, there must be an effort to create informed Christian opinion and active support for that opinion throughout the Anglican Communion. It is, however, important that systematic prayer on behalf of governments be made by members of the Church. This is a primary duty which must be brought home to members of the Church. The Committee would also urge that where conflicts arise the Church should remember that it is its duty "to be the Church" and not to rely in any way on government approval or aid.

OPINIONS

The Committee was asked to express its opinion on the following matters:

1.	Anglican Congress,	3. Migration.
2.	Colonial Churches.	4. Ministry to Seamen.

1. Anglican Congress

The Committee notes that the Anglican Congress of 1954 was received with thankfulness throughout the Anglican Communion. It is agreed that another Congress should be held.

2. Colonial Churches

In certain dioceses "Colonial churches" exist, the congregations being European and ministered to by European priests. Such clergy hold the bishop's licence yet the congregation is not integrated into the life of the diocese. Since the bishop is the bishop of all parishes in his diocese, the Committee requests that provinces initiate or continue action to put this recognition of the bishop's position into full effect.

3. Migration

The Committee calls the attention of the Conference to the relation between the constant movement of persons from one country to another and the maintenance and growth of the Church.

c*

Viewed from the Christian standpoint, there are various categories of migrants:

(*a*) Those coming from "Christian" countries to countries where Christians are a small proportion of the population.

(*b*) Those coming to "Christian" countries from Asia, Africa, and other predominantly non-Christian lands, who come as Christians expecting a Christian welcome and atmosphere.

(*c*) Non-Christians coming to such countries, who will be drawn to or repelled from the Church by their experiences during their stay.

The Committee makes the following recommendations:

1. For the past four years valuable work has been done in Great Britain by the organization known as "Oversea Service", which "has been providing training courses to help people who are going to overseas posts in commerce, government, or welfare organizations to adapt themselves to their new environment".[4] The Committee recommends that every encouragement be given to organizations of this kind and that consideration be given to the setting up of similar facilities in other countries.

2. Every effort should be made to commend promptly Church people who are going overseas to the bishop of the diocese to which they go.

3. A Christian welcome to Asians, Africans, West Indians, and others when they come to "Christian" countries is likely to be ensured only if it is regarded as a work of every parish or district into which such persons come to live.

4. Ministry to Seamen

The Anglican Congress at Minneapolis, 1954, resolved that "the Church should explore possibilities of greater co-operation within our Communion in such special ministries as the care of the seamen". The Committee draws attention to many problems which have arisen in the development of the work of the Missions to Seamen and other Anglican Societies serving seamen.

---

3. EVANGELISM

Evangelism is *encounter*; it is *confronting* a person with the Person of Jesus Christ. The outcome of the encounter cannot be foretold. This may issue in acceptance or in rejection of the Person and claims of Christ. But evangelism cannot be said to have taken place without such confrontation. It is the aim of the Church in its evangelistic task so to present Christ to the world that his purity may rebuke men's sinfulness, his power elicit their cry for help, his love draw out their full response in worship and service.

---

4 Article in *The New Commonwealth*, December 1957.

The evangelist thus finds himself in the position of the speaker described by St Augustine: "So ought the speaker to fulfil his task that he teaches, attracts, turns." That is to say, the evangelist aims at the conversion of the whole man to discipleship of Christ and to worship and service in his Church—mind (teaching), emotions (attraction), and will (turning).

The state of our world, with its fears, frustrations, and prejudices, is such that evangelism is the Church's greatest responsibility and privilege. People to-day need more than a philosophy or a moral code; they must have a power to enable them to live victoriously in such a world. This power comes *only* to mankind through Christ and his Church.

This evangelistic task is of great urgency in the vast unevangelized areas of the world and among the masses of people living in professedly Christian countries who rarely enter a church. This is a challenge which brooks no refusal and no delay. But the nominal Church member also, to whom Christianity is little more than a moral code, must be "confronted" with Jesus Christ. As a living theology must be thought out anew for every age, so it is with evangelism. Each generation must be evangelized; the task will not be complete "till he come".

While personal evangelism is primary, the ultimate aim of Christianity is not only the "saving of souls" but also the bringing in of a new order "wherein dwelleth righteousness", a new and better civilization here in this world. The Church claims for Christ the *whole* of man's life, and proclaims good news to nations and communities as well as to individuals.

Evangelism is not to be thought of as the task of a select few. Baptism and confirmation constitute "the ordination of the laity" for the task of evangelism. It is for every Christian to do what Andrew did for his brother—to say, "We have found the Messiah", and to bring him to Jesus.

This is the Church's prime objective, and in this task it must use every means available for the education of its members. Some of these means must now be considered.

CHRISTIAN COMMUNICATION

Although the Anglican Communion has penetrated into every continent, new possibilities of Christian communication now appear which offer fresh scope for the presentation of the Gospel. Television, radio, films, religious drama, and the secular and religious press provide an opportunity for the whole Church if imaginatively employed.

Through such means contacts can now be made with vast numbers. Television and radio can reach people behind doors ordinarily closed to the proclamation of the Gospel. More use can be made of the cinema.

Religious drama, an important medium of communication in the past, is proving its value once again as an effective means of religious education.

The secular press should be used more effectively and the techniques of modern journalism be employed more widely in the Church Press.

We suggest that each province should set up its own information centre where material is collected, assessed, and distributed.

STEWARDSHIP

Stewardship is the regarding of ourselves and our possessions as a trust from God to be utilized in his service according to his will. A parish without a sense of stewardship has within it the seeds of decay. A man who refuses to be a steward of his time, talents, and money is unworthy of being in the Father's House. Therefore it is primary that all clergy and lay leaders practise and teach stewardship as an integral part of Christian life and worship.

Not only do we have full biblical warrant for practising stewardship; we have further the scriptural injunction to give a tenth of our possessions for God's work. Tithing, however, is not an end in itself. Sacrificial giving of our financial resources begins only when all our parochial and diocesan obligations have been met. It is only when we give with no possibility of receiving material return that we can be said to be giving sacrificially.

CHRISTIAN LITERATURE

Every year millions of people are learning to read. What shall they read? The means of influencing mass opinion are being exploited by political and commercial bodies. The Church also should make the fullest possible use of literature in its approach to the minds and souls of men. There is urgent need for newspapers, magazines, books, pamphlets in simple and popular idiom, designed to commend Christianity to those outside the Church. Such literature should supply a Christian commentary on life in general and current events in particular. Some Christian communions are already providing literature on a scale commensurate with its importance. By comparison, experiments within missionary areas of the Anglican Communion appear lamentably unimpressive.

The supply of Bibles, Prayer Books, and Hymn Books does not fully meet the demand. In many areas the training of ordinands must in future be done in their mother-tongue; priests should have text-books in the idiom, and if possible written by nationals in the actual vernacular, in which they have to preach. What is true of literature for the clergy is true of books for instructing and equipping the laity to understand the faith of the Church to which they belong. This is done in some parts of the world by Bible correspondence courses.

4. CONCLUSION

The nature of the work entrusted to this Committee has necessarily involved it in the consideration of many big problems and much detail of strategy. That is as it should be, for the follower of the Incarnate Lord is only a true disciple when his theology is related to life at every point. But as we draw our work to a close we wish to give expression to three underlying convictions.

1. *God reigns.* The eternal God is the God who makes himself known to men in history. He has not abdicated. His Kingdom has arrived with the coming of his Son and, wherever the Church advances, it is operative in the hearts of men. So, to a world obsessed by fear we say: "Lift up your hearts. God reigns. Fear not."

2. *God calls.* The God who has made himself known to men as Father, Son, and Holy Spirit, as Creator, Redeemer, and Sanctifier, has committed to his Church the Gospel of salvation. The Father sent the Son to be the Saviour of the whole of man, the whole of society, and the whole of the world. Man finds his destiny only when he links his life to the fulfilling of God's purpose for the world. Each member of Christ must honestly ask of God the question: "Lord, what wilt thou have me to do?"

3. *God sends.* The Christian Church has spread throughout the world. Yet the missionary task in many parts has only begun. Its greatest need is for men and women, with a sense of venture, of mission, of total dedication; men and women who have heard the voice of the Lord Jesus saying to them: "As the Father has sent me, even so I send you"; men and women who know the joy of worship, service, and sacrifice in the overmastering compulsion to evangelize.

We call upon each baptized and confirmed member of the Anglican Communion, and especially the young people, to hear anew the word of God: "Whom shall I send, and who will go for us?" and to respond: "Here I am! Send me."

B. THE BOOK OF COMMON PRAYER

INTRODUCTION

The subject with which this sub-committee is charged, the Book of Common Prayer, is fundamental to all the subjects which the Conference is considering, for the Prayer Book is the public expression of the worship of God in the Anglican Communion, and it is on the worship of God, creation's secret force, that all human activity depends. It is only in worship that all the Church can learn the will of God and receive wisdom and power to do it. Our Lord called his first disciples that they might be with him and that he might send them forth to preach (Mark 3.13); that is the order of priority for his disciples and for the Church in every age and land.

Worship then is the first concern of the Church, and it must be the worship of the whole Church, priests and people together bringing to God every human interest and activity and problem and conflict to be taken into his will and used for his purposes.

It is with this end in view that the sub-committee has approached its task of considering the Prayer Books of the Anglican Communion, and their continuing suitability as the instrument of the worship of the Church in the world as it is to-day.

THE PLACE OF THE BOOK OF COMMON PRAYER OF 1662 IN THE ANGLICAN COMMUNION

When in the past, there has been discussion on the place of the Book of Common Prayer in the life of the Anglican Communion, the underlying assumption, and often the declared principle, has been that the Prayer Book of 1662 should remain as the basic pattern, and, indeed, as a bond of unity in doctrine and in worship for our Communion as a whole. Even in the changed situation of to-day, this Prayer Book has the power of winning a deep loyalty and affection. This loyalty, however, may easily be overstated; it has always been more evident in some parts of our Communion than in others. But we may be glad that at previous Lambeth Conferences there was no premature advice to go beyond 1662 at a time when the principles which should govern extensive liturgical revision could not clearly be established or win general acceptance.

Yet now it seems clear that no Prayer Book, not even that of 1662, can be kept unchanged for ever, as a safeguard of established doctrine. As Article XXXIV declares, "every particular or national Church hath authority to ordain, change, and abolish, ceremonies or rites of the Church ordained only by man's authority, so that all things be done to edifying". That, in fact, is what has been happening. A number of new Prayer Books has appeared in our Communion, and in practically every case there has been a revision, more or less adventurous, of the 1662 Service of Holy Communion.

We have entered a period of liturgical change, with all the advantages and disadvantages of such a time. We may see in the different Prayer Books of the Anglican Communion a variety which enriches our worship of God. Yet we must recognize the dangers in this development. It is hard on the people of the Church in that they are sometimes bewildered by the variety of use and custom they find. Moreover, this variety, if it is not carefully watched, may make more difficult that unity in worship and in faith which we are all determined to preserve.

THE BOOK OF COMMON PRAYER AS A BOND BETWEEN ANGLICANS, TOGETHER WITH SUGGESTIONS AS TO PRINCIPLES OF PRAYER BOOK REVISION

Committee IV of the 1948 Conference reported,[1] "We consider that the time has come to examine those 'features in the Book of Common Prayer which are essential to the safeguarding of the unity of the Anglican Communion' ".

This statement appears to rest upon the conviction that the Anglican Communion owes its unity to the Prayer Book. But our unity exists because we are a federation of Provinces and Dioceses of the One, Holy, Catholic, and Apostolic Church, each being served and governed by a Catholic and Apostolic Ministry, and each believing the Catholic faith. These are the fundamental reasons for our unity.

At a less profound level we experience a unity based on the consciousness of having a common history and deriving from a common root. Of this history, the Prayer Book in its various forms is probably the most powerful symbol. The use of its forms for sacrament and worship enables us to live the life of the Catholic Church. But the special character and quality of these forms, and the theological and liturgical principles upon which they are based, impart to Anglican worship everywhere a distinct ecclesiastical culture. This common culture undoubtedly aids the widely separated provinces and dioceses of our Communion in their task of living and worshipping in godly union and concord with each other. Only in this secondary sense can the Book of Common Prayer be said to possess "features which are essential to the safeguarding of the unity of the Anglican Communion".

Should we not do better to ask what are the features of the various Prayer Books of the Anglican Communion which are most effective in maintaining the traditional doctrinal emphasis of our worship, and in preserving that ecclesiastical culture which has hitherto informed our common life and witness?

A true and discerning answer to this question would supply a number of principles which would greatly assist provinces and dioceses in the future revision of their Prayer Books.

---

[1] *The Lambeth Conference, 1948*, Part II, p. 86, quoting Resolution 37 of the Lambeth Conference of 1920.

A further question might well be put. It was Cranmer's aim to lift worship in England out of the liturgical decadence of the late medieval Church in western Christendom, and to recover as much as possible of the character of the worship of what he called the "Primitive Church". In this he achieved notable success, but there was not available in his day the historical material necessary for the full accomplishment of his aim. Since that time, and indeed since 1662, valuable evidence has been brought to light, by the use of which what he began may be further developed. Therefore we might ask what elements in the Book of Common Prayer are due to the sixteenth and seventeenth century misunderstanding of what is "primitive" in public worship, and what elements need to be substituted or added in order to make Prayer Book services truer to the ideal towards which Cranmer was feeling his way.

Features in the Books of Common Prayer which are essential to the safeguarding of the unity of the Anglican Communion

1. Use of the Canonical Scriptures.
2. Use of the Apostles' and Nicene Creeds.
3. Orders of Holy Baptism with water and the threefold Name.
4. Orders of Confirmation by the Bishop, by prayer with the laying-on of hands.
5. Orders of Holy Communion, with use of bread and wine and explicit intention to obey our Lord's command.
6. Forms of episcopal Ordination to each of the three Holy Orders by prayer with the laying-on of hands.

Features in the Books of Common Prayer which are most effective in maintaining the traditional doctrinal emphasis of the worship and witness of the Anglican Communion

1. Forms of worship in the vernacular.
2. Wholly *common* prayer; avoiding official private prayers of the celebrant while the people are otherwise engaged; avoiding prayer which cannot be heard by the congregation, and providing for the audible response of the congregation, and for communicants at every celebration.
3. Services easy for the people to follow and therefore with a restrained use of seasonal variations.
4. The importance of both Word and Sacrament in worship is recognized, a due balance being kept between them. This involves provision for the regular celebration of the Holy Communion and the extensive use of Holy Scripture in the Offices and Holy Communion. Similarly in many Prayer Books Baptism is required to be administered in the course of Morning or Evening Prayer, thus providing a setting of psalms and lessons for the sacramental act.

5. The use of one of the historic Creeds, recited by all, at the principal popular services of Mattins, Holy Communion, and Evensong.
6. The reading of the Old Testament, as well as of the New, in lessons of approximately equal length at the Offices of Mattins and Evensong.
7. The use of the Psalms as the normal vehicle of common praise and meditation.
8. The honouring of the Saints without invocation.

Suggested modifications or additions for the further recovery of other elements of the worship of the Primitive Church

1. Exhortations have a legitimate function in the liturgy but they should be shorter and fewer.
2. The present corporate expressions of penitence need to be modified both in length and language.
3. More extensive provision of litanies, with shorter clauses, for corporate intercession, thanksgiving, and adoration; with the discouragement of long strings of collects or other prayers for this purpose.
4. The recovery of the "People's Prayers" at the Eucharist by breaking up the Prayer for the Church into sections, each followed by congregational response, or into a litany with short clauses.
5. The Offertory, with which the people should be definitely associated, to be more closely connected with the Prayer of Consecration.
6. The events for which thanksgiving is made in the Consecration Prayer are not to be confined to Calvary but include thanksgiving for all the principal "mighty works of God", especially the resurrection and the ascension of our Lord, and his return in glory.

THE HOLY COMMUNION SERVICE

We turn now to a consideration of the service of Holy Communion. There are reasons for hoping that it is now possible to work towards a liturgy which will win its way throughout the Anglican Communion. The Committee would not suggest a return to those rigid and legalistic ideas of uniformity which prevailed for some centuries. It recognizes that even in the Sacrament of Unity there is a place for variations of rite to meet local situations and needs. What is urged is the possibility of a basic pattern for the service of Holy Communion which will commend itself to all provinces.

It is for this reason that there appears to be a need for a Committee representative of all parts of our Communion, which would be asked to work towards the production of an outline of the structure of the Holy Communion service. There would, of course, be difficulties in giving effect to this suggestion, but it is thought that they could be overcome. It would mean that the revising authorities in the different provinces would have the opportunity of seeing their work in relation to the whole Anglican Communion.

In the Committee's judgement it is regrettable that there should be any necessity for alternative rites within a single province, but it recognizes that circumstances sometimes make this inevitable, at least for a period. It considers, however, that a province may find it advisable to test new liturgical work for limited periods under the control of the Ordinary.

The Scriptures, Sermon, and needs of Catechumens

From the earliest times the Holy Communion has been preceded by a separable service of which the primary content was the reading of the Old and New Testaments, the singing of psalms, and the preaching of a sermon. To this were added intercessions, before which the cate-chumens were dismissed. Later the Nicene Creed was inserted as the congregation's response to the Ministry of the Word. Before the reading of the Scriptures there came to be an introductory section including eventually the *Kyries, Gloria in Excelsis*, and Collect.

From 1549 in England the reading of the Old Testament was omitted and the psalms were reduced to one, used as an Introit. This dis-appeared in 1552, so that (except for the Decalogue) at the present time the Old Testament is seldom read or sung at the Eucharist. Like-wise from 1552 the *Gloria in Excelsis* was postponed till the end of the Communion Service proper, thus depriving the catechumens of any act of direct adoration of Almighty God. The growing custom in many parts of the Anglican Communion of making the Parish Communion the principal Sunday service, and the consequent displacement or neglect of Mattins, is having the result that a generation is growing up which rarely hears the Old Testament in church or sings the Psalms.

We therefore suggest that when revision of the Prayer Book is con-templated or in progress, careful consideration should be given to the following points:

1. A lesson from the Old Testament might form part of the delivery of God's Word in the Ante-Communion at the principal Eucharist on Sundays. Such lessons should be chosen with a view to their correspondence with the Epistle or Gospel. The Ten Commandments or the Summary of the Law might be used as Old Testament lessons.

2, The three lessons might be separated by psalms or portions of psalms, chosen if possible so that they may underline or develop the theme of the lessons (e.g., if Ezekiel 36.24–8 were the Old Testament lesson, the psalm following it might be Psalm 107.1–8). Where desired, a further psalm or portion thereof might be sung during the entry of the ministers.

3. The function of the preacher as the interpreter of God's Word might be better emphasized if the sermon at the principal Sunday Eucharist immediately followed the reading of the three lessons, with the Nicene Creed succeeding it as the response of faith to the whole Ministry of the Word.
4. Where catechumens are habitually present at the Ante-Communion the note of adoration should be sounded, since for them this is their entire Sunday service. The restoration of *Gloria in Excelsis* to its original position would meet this need, and this has already been done in some churches of the Anglican Communion. Alternatively, *Te Deum* might be sung before the Collect, while *Gloria in Excelsis* is retained before the Blessing.

The Eucharistic Sacrifice

Dr Massey Shepherd in his address to the Anglican Congress at Minneapolis in 1954 reminded his hearers that basically there are two Eucharistic liturgies in the Anglican Communion which stem respectively from the Prayer Books of 1549 and 1552, and then commented: "Our Communion, with its two types of liturgy, expressive of two approaches to the problem [of the Eucharistic Sacrifice] may be able to hold its various facets in tension. Sooner or later, however, it must be resolved."[2]

The Committee believe that as the result of new knowledge gained from biblical and liturgical studies the time has come to claim that controversies about the Eucharistic Sacrifice can be laid aside, the tensions surrounding this doctrine transcended, and the way prepared for the making of a liturgy in God's good time which will in its essential structure win its way throughout the whole Anglican Communion. It records with thanksgiving both the labours of biblical and liturgical scholars, and also the unity of spirit in which we have been enabled to learn from them.

If the redeeming work of Christ is limited to the Cross as a past act in time, we can only be thought of as entering into this wholly past action either by remembering it or by repeating it. This partly explains the quarrel at the time of the Reformation. But we are now in a different climate of thought.

It is commonly acknowledged that what Christ accomplished on the Cross can properly be described as a sacrifice. It is enough to recall the two sacrificial sayings of our Lord himself, "My life a ransom for many" and "This is my blood of the covenant which is shed for many", and the phrases in the Epistle to the Hebrews (10.10,12) "The offering of the body of Jesus Christ once for all", and "when Christ had offered for all time a single sacrifice for sins, he sat down at the right hand of God."

---

[2] *Anglican Congress, 1954*, Eng. ed., p. 82.

This sacrifice is an act of willing obedience, "Lo, I am come to do thy will, O God" (Hebrews 10.7; Phil. 2.8), and inasmuch as Christ is not only perfect and representative man but also the eternal Son of God, "this act of will is not only the one perfect response of humanity to the will of God but also it is the will of God going out to man in yearning love".[3] "The new man, the Adam who is Christ, fulfils in the Cross the thanksgiving of man to God. In Christ the fulness of God giving himself to man meets with the fulness of man offering himself to God."[4]

The sacrifice of Christ as the offering of willing obedience included not only his death on the Cross but all that contributed to it, of which it was the culmination. The finished work of Calvary is consummated in the resurrection and ascension.

This sacrifice is once and for all, but though it cannot be repeated, it is not merely a past fact; it is not only an event in history, but the revelation of eternal truth. He is the Lamb slain from the foundation of the world, now seated at the right hand of God after the power of an endless life. The fact revealed in time past has to be continually translated into the present by the operation of the Spirit. "He will take what is mine and declare it to you" (John 16.14).

Christ's sacrificial work on the Cross was *for* us; he died as our Redeemer. He who once died and is now alive for ever more is also *in* us; he dwells in our hearts by faith. And in virtue of this union, we are now identified with him both in his death and passion, and in his resurrection life and glory. There is but one Body, of which he is the Head and we are the members; and we are made one with each other because we are one in him.

In our baptism we were united with him by the likeness of his death (Rom 6.5) and in the Eucharist we abide in him as we eat his Body and drink his Blood (John 6.56). So we come to the Father in and through Jesus our great High Priest. We have nothing to offer that we have not first received, but we offer our praise and thanksgiving for Christ's sacrifice for us and so present it again, and ourselves in him, before the Father. We are partakers of the sacrifice of Christ (1 Cor. 10.16), and this is shown forth by our sacrifice of praise to God continually through Christ (Heb. 13.15), and by our life of service and suffering for his sake in the world (Phil. 3.9,10). We ourselves, incorporate in the mystical body of Christ, are the sacrifice we offer. Christ with us offers us in himself to God.

Accordingly the Committee endorses the words of Dr A. G. Hebert, S.S.M.: "The eucharistic Sacrifice, that storm-centre of controversy, is finding in our day a truly evangelical expression from the 'catholic' side, when it is insisted that the sacrificial action is not any sort of

---

[3] C. F. D. Moule, *The Sacrifice of Christ*, p. 26.
[4] Bouyer, *Life and Liturgy*, p. 131.

re-immolation of Christ, nor a sacrifice additional to His one Sacrifice, but a participation in it. The true celebrant is Christ the High-Priest, and the Christian people are assembled as members of His Body to present before God His Sacrifice, and to be themselves offered up in Sacrifice through their union with Him. This, however, involves a repudiation of certain mediaeval developments, notably the habitual celebration of the Eucharist without the Communion of the people; or the notion that the offering of the Eucharist is the concern of the individual priest rather than of the assembled church; and, above all, any idea that in the Eucharist we offer a sacrifice to propitiate God. We offer it only because He has offered the one Sacrifice, once for all, in which we need to participate."[5]

Epiclesis

Whether or not an invocation of the Holy Spirit upon the worshippers or upon the elements or both is to be included in the Prayer of Consecration, it is to be remembered that the Holy Spirit informs and vivifies the whole Rite and that the so-called Collect for Purity has in consequence a profound theological significance.

Consecration

We desire to draw attention to a conception of consecration which is scriptural and primitive and goes behind subsequent controversies with respect to the moment and formula of consecration. This is associated with the Jewish origin and meaning of *eucharistia* and may be called consecration through thanksgiving. "To bless anything and to pronounce a thanksgiving over it are not two actions but one."[6]

"Everything created by God is good, and nothing is to be rejected if it is received with thanksgiving; for then it is consecrated by the word of God and prayer" (1 Tim. 4.4,5).

Thanksgiving unveils the glory and generosity of the Creator and the original meaning and purpose of creation. It releases man's response to what has been done for him in redemption and sets free the love implanted in him.

"The Word of God accepted by the People of God and coming back to God from the lips of those giving thanks, actually sanctifies the creatures over which it is pronounced."[7]

CHRISTIAN INITIATION

While much thought has recently been given to the theology of Christian Initiation, the stage has not yet been reached where the new knowledge can be assimilated and fresh conclusions can be put forward

[5] *Ways of Worship*, S.C.M., 1951 (New York: Harper and Brothers).
[6] Bouyer, op. cit., p. 120.
[7] Bouyer, op. cit., p. 119.

that would be generally accepted. Meanwhile practical problems are demanding more than tentative solutions, and it is to be hoped that an opportunity may be given for a full consideration of the theology of Christian Initiation at the next Lambeth Conference.

The Committee draws attention to the Report of Committee V (B), "Baptism and Confirmation", of the 1948 Lambeth Conference [8] and the corresponding Resolutions 100–112.[9] It also commends the study of *Baptism and Confirmation To-day*,[10] the work of the Joint Committees of the Convocations of Canterbury and York, which deals with many of the issues raised at the 1948 Conference. It is gratifying to learn that the Church of England Liturgical Commission, set up in 1954, is producing new forms of services for Christian Initiation in all its stages.[11] *Prayer Book Studies I*, of the Standing Liturgical Commission of the Protestant Episcopal Church in the United States of America,[12] and the Church in Wales's *Revised Services for Experimental Use: Holy Baptism and Confirmation*, are also recommended for study.

The first Prayer Book Services of Initiation assumed that those to be baptized would be infants, the children of Christian parents. Until 1662 no provision whatsoever was made for the baptism of adults, the form of baptism then being only an adaptation of the service for the baptism of infants. The Church, however, is charged with preaching the Gospel and with baptizing those whom God calls into its fellowship. The Church therefore should be as much concerned with the baptism of adults as with that of infants. This points to the need of a revised service for adult baptism which should not merely be an adaptation of the service of infant baptism "but should be closely related to the Confirmation Service and should be based on primitive patterns of Christian Initiation, which culminate in first Communion".[13]

The Committee suggests that in any baptismal service the following elements need to find liturgical expression:

1. The Ministry of the Word declaring the teaching of Scripture concerning baptism, e.g. Matt. 28.19; John 3.5; Acts 2.38; Rom. 6.3,4; 1 Cor. 12.13; Col. 2.12.

2. A renunciation of the former way of life, the putting off of the old man (Col. 3.8–10).

3. A profession of faith in Christ with the reciting of the baptismal creed.

4. The promises:

>to hold fast to the Christian faith;
>to obey God's commandments;
>to bear witness to Christ.

[8] Part II, pp. 106–18.
[9] Part I, pp. 50–2.
[10] S.P.C.K., 1955.
[11] *Prayer Book Revision in the Church of England*, S.P.C.K. 1957, pp. 25–6.
[12] Church Pension Fund, New York, 1950.
[13] *Prayer Book Revision in the Church of England*, pp. 25–6.

5. Blessing of the Water, with a thanksgiving for Christ's baptism and the benefits of his redeeming work and prayer for the fruits of baptism in those to be baptized, which might well be expressed in litany form.

6. Baptism with water in the threefold Name, thereby uniting the baptized person to Christ (John 15.1–8).

7. The signing with the Cross as a sign that we have been bought with a price, that we belong to Christ (1 Peter 1.18,19).

8. The reception of the baptized person into the fellowship of the Church (Gal. 3.26–8).

9. Thanksgiving for having been sealed by the Holy Spirit for ever unto the day of redemption (Eph. 4.30; cf. 2 Cor. 1.21,22 and Eph. 1.13,14). [This is the reason why, according to the universal doctrine of Christendom, baptism cannot be repeated.]

10. Prayer for growth in the Christian life.

11. An Exhortation to the congregation reminding them that the newly baptized person has been brought into the life of the family of God and is to be encouraged by its fellowship, supported by its prayers, and strengthened by its example.

12. An Exhortation to the baptized person to live the new life in the power of the Holy Spirit (Col. 3.1).

The Committee endorses the recommendation of the 1948 Lambeth Report concerning witnesses and sponsors (Resolution 106).

"Some too would welcome the revival of some of the traditional ceremonies where desired, in order that people may learn through the eye as well as by the ear".[14]

While recognizing that pastoral conditions vary greatly in different parts of the world, the Committee is of the opinion that, when advisable, adult baptism should be combined with confirmation and first communion so that the three stages may be seen to be one process of initiation. It is in this way that the balance and proportion between baptism, confirmation, and first communion will be restored. Once more the Committee repeats the suggestion of "the provision without delay of an Order of Service combining Adult Baptism and Confirmation"[15] where this has not already been done.

THE ORDINAL

Any consideration of Anglican Ordinals at this time is inevitably bound up with current reunion schemes. The matter arises definitely in connection with the proposals for the unification of ministries in North India, Pakistan, and Ceylon. It would seem therefore that this

---

[14] *Prayer Book Revision in the Church of England*, p. 25.
[15] *The Lambeth Conference, 1948*, Part II, p. 107.

Committee may best serve at the present time by drawing out such fundamental principles as are to be seen in the Ordinals in use among us.

The essential ministry of the Word and Sacraments is the ministry of Christ himself. In the Body of Christ, the Church, this ministry must be present and operating. Thus the heart of the matter is the relation between Christ and the visible Church. Here we may recall Archbishop Temple's words: "The authority by which I act (i.e. in consecrating and ordaining) is his, transmitted to me through the apostles and those to whom they committed it: I hold it neither from the Church nor apart from the Church, but from Christ in the Church."[16] The whole ministry, not only that of bishops, priests, and deacons, but also the exercise of every gift for the work of ministry (Eph. 4.7–12) is a function of Christ in his Body, the Church. Christ himself acts through the Spirit in and through his members.

One element in this whole gift of ministry may be called *episcopé*. This is Christ's own oversight and direction of his members, as Head of the Body. He co-ordinates and rules all so that they may as one body fulfil the will of God. So within the Church on earth every expression or enactment of true *episcopé*—oversight directed to the fulfilling of God's will—is the act of Christ, and is derived from him. Ordination is an act of Christ, working through his *episcopé* in the Church, bestowing grace to fulfil various functions in the Church—to exercise *episcopé* as a pastor (1 Peter 5.2–4), to proclaim the Gospel, to fulfil the priestly ministry of the Body (1 Peter 2.5).

In ordination certain requirements must be met, as they are in fact met in our Anglican Ordinals. The individual must affirm that he believes himself called of God to the ministry, and the Church must be satisfied of the reality of his call and his fitness for the work. Then the Church also calls, and the body of the faithful assents to the ordination. Ordination must be performed by those who have received and are acknowledged to have received, authority to exercise *episcopé* in the Body, and to admit others to share in that ministry. This acknowledgement by the Body of the authority of the ordaining member means that his own ordination to the ministry of *episcopé* must be recognized and accepted. From this arises the principle of continuity by succession, which appears to be indispensable, at least from the human point of view. This is not to say that God cannot dispense with the succession if he wishes, as indeed he did when the Aaronic priesthood was superseded by the appointment of the High Priest of our Confession (Heb. 7.11–28). We must also recognize that the divisions in the Body make it difficult to discern the *episcopé* of Christ in its fullness, for in this, as in all things, Christ's fullness will

---

16 W. Temple: Presidential Address to Convocation of Canterbury, 25 May 1943. Quoted by E. L. Mascall, *The Recovery of Unity*, p. 188.

not be seen until all his members are united in love and truth in the one Body.

Where is this *episcopé* of Christ to be found in the Church we know? Where is the authority for ordination? We believe that our "Orders of Ministers in Christ's Church; Bishops, Priests, and Deacons"[17] are within the *episcopé* of Christ, and that we have his authority for ordaining. When we say that episcopacy is essential in any reunion scheme we are not offering to others one feature of Church life in isolation, but rather saying that we cannot enter into the fullness of Christ's life in the Church without the recognized embodiment of this element of his ministry. No doubt all the divided members have retained, by God's grace, some element of *episcopé*. We do not dispute that. We are concerned to bring others to share the gift we ourselves have been given, that with them we may ever grow in the fullness of his Body.

It is a consequence of this view of ordination that it should always be administered when the faithful are assembled for the Eucharist. When we come to the liturgical pattern of the rite of ordination, study of the early rites has made clear the fact that in them the prayer which was offered at the laying-on of hands defined the meaning, for that particular service, of the ancient scriptural gesture of blessing. The bishop, as God's agent in the local Church, and also as that Church's representative, offered the prayer asking for the sending of the Spirit upon the candidate to make him bishop, priest, or deacon, as the case might be.

While this was the primitive practice, in the West the prayer came, after a time, to be regarded as "solemnity" only. For the definition of the meaning or "form" of the rite, the emphasis was laid on the delivery of instruments and laying-on of hands accompanied by an imperative formula, for priests, and in laying-on of hands, with imperative formulas, for bishops and deacons.

Our ordinal is the heir of this Western development. The intention of our rites is clear, but at present it is chiefly expressed in the imperative formula which is used at the laying-on of hands. This formula uses words taken from St John's Gospel, and thus safeguards the underlying doctrine that ordination is the act of Christ himself, working through his Body, the Church.

The Committee recognizes that liturgical considerations, based on our increased knowledge of primitive practice, may suggest some revision of our ordinals. In the Ordination Prayer, for example, after thanksgiving for the Lord Christ, the eternal Bishop, Priest, and Deacon, and for the gifts of ministry he has given to the Church, there could be, in the prayer for those to be ordained, mention of the specific ministry to be given to them. After the laying-on of hands

---

[17] Preface to the Ordinal.

there might also be a declaration, in the manner of the Eastern Church, that *N.* is now ordained to such and such a ministry in the Church of God. However, the Committee would plead for a wise conservatism in any revision of the ordinal.

THE LECTIONARY

It was Cranmer's objective to provide for the systematic reading of the Bible at the daily services of the Church in the course of the year. The lectionary in the Prayer Book of 1549, therefore, assigned the greater part of the Old Testament to be read straight through the days of the civil year, with the exception of Isaiah which was read in Advent; the New Testament, with the omission of the Book of Revelation, was read through three times. In general this method of assigning lessons for both Sundays and weekdays on the basis of the civil calendar was used in all Anglican lectionaries until the present century.

In recent years, however, throughout the Church, lectionaries have been constructed on new lines, and out of this work of revision certain principles for the making of a lectionary have emerged.

1. The course of lessons should be based on the ecclesiastical rather than on the civil year.
2. Separate courses should be provided for Sundays and for weekdays.
3. The Sunday series should be complete in itself and cover as comprehensively as possible the most important passages of Scripture. This can best be done by extending the Sunday course over a period of two years or more.
4. The Apocryphal books of the Old Testament should be given their due place in the Lectionary.
5. The proper readings for the Eucharist could well be reconsidered so that there should be a recognizable common theme proclaimed throughout.

THE PSALTER

It is high time that a revised translation of the Psalter should be undertaken, such as is already in use in the Church of Ireland or such as is suggested in the Draft Prayer Book of the Canadian Church. There can be no spiritual benefit in repeating phrases which mean nothing. Archaisms in the Psalter as in other parts of the Prayer Book need attention. Such a revision might go some way towards reinstating the Psalter in the affection of clergy and people and checking the present tendency to abbreviate the singing of the Psalms without authorization, or to substitute hymns for them.

THE OCCASIONAL SERVICES

One of the characteristic features of all the Anglican Prayer Books is their emphasis on pastoral care, and it is always pastoral necessity that is the chief cause of demands for their revision. This must be particularly in mind when changes and additions to the occasional offices are considered. There are to-day new modes of thought and new ways of living, and all of them bring new needs. The Church is also now concerned with people in many parts of the world. If it is eager to provide the pastoral help which men require, it must always be alert to examine its forms of worship realistically; if it fails to do so they will become more and more out of touch with human realities. Individuals will be driven to make changes which may be unauthorized and unwise.

A few general and obvious points only can be touched on here.

It would be in line with the growing understanding of the meaning of the Church and of the place of individual members within it if some of the occasional offices were more closely associated with a celebration of the Holy Communion, This applies particularly to the Marriage Service, but also the Service of Thanksgiving after Childbirth and the Burial Service.

It is very important that the Church should be known to be concerned with the affairs of the daily lives of men and women, and wide in its human sympathies. Factories as well as churches call for the blessing of the Church, and the services of the Church should be showing the relevance of its worship and teaching to ordinary things. There is often need for services of a special character in connection with industry, the arts, and science which would relate these activities to God as harvest festivals do for agriculture. A form of service adaptable to such needs as they arise, together with a wider selection of suitable prayers, would be useful.

It may be that to avoid overloading Prayer Books with services which may be of use only rarely or locally a book of supplementary services should be produced.

The present Dean of York in his book *After the Third Collect* writes: "Since the first war the 'Special Service' has come to play a larger part in the Christian life of this country. It is not always appropriate or possible on such occasions to use the Eucharist or the Daily Office with particular intention, desirable though this may be. Yet it is important to maintain Prayer Book standards of order and dignity, whether in structure or content." There is a case for providing some guidance about the principles that should be followed in drawing up special services.

THE MINISTRY TO THE SICK

In most revisions of the Prayer Book certain erroneous assumptions have been removed, such as that God deliberately inflicts all sickness and that sickness is invariably a punishment for sin.

It is of course true that God allows suffering, and that his overruling Providence can use suffering to awake the careless and to make saints; but sickness, like temptation, is our natural heritage in a dis-ordered world. Likewise, sickness is often the natural consequence of sin or is psychosomatic, but it is cruel and false to brand every sufferer as a sinner.[18] At the same time it behoves us to remember that much suffering and sickness is due to the sin either of other persons, or of society in general. Recent revisions have not only removed erroneous doctrine, but have divided up and recast the Ministry to the Sick into different portions such as "Exhortation to Faith and Prayer", "Exhor-tation to Repentance", together with suggestions as to suitable psalms and lections.

In any future revision, seeing that every case of sickness requires its own treatment, the following outline is suggested:

(*a*) The title, "Visitation of the Sick", should be altered to the "Ministry to the Sick", and be introduced by rubrics and directives bidding the priest (i) to minister to the whole person, whose soul and mind are involved as well as his sick body; (ii) to build up the hope and faith of the sufferer; (iii) to help him to put his affairs in order, and to be in love and charity with all men; and (iv) to move him to make his peace with Almighty God.

(*b*) The following elements should be included in this section of the Prayer Book:

    (i) Passages of Scripture for reading and meditation.
    (ii) A form for the Laying-on of Hands.
    (iii) A form for Anointing.
    (iv) A form for the Communion of the Sick.
    (v) A form for Confession and Absolution of the Sick.
    (vi) A Commendation of the Dying.
    (vii) Various prayers and short litanies appropriate to different types of suffering.

PRAYERS FOR THE DEPARTED

Every priest in the Anglican Communion at his ordination solemnly promises that he will teach nothing as required of necessity to eternal salvation but that which he shall be persuaded may be concluded and proved by Scripture. Although Scripture has often been quoted both for and against the practice of prayers for the departed, the evidence from this source does not amount to conclusive proof in either direc-tion. It may be partly for this reason that the Book of Common Prayer (1662) makes no clear provision for prayers for the departed; and we are well aware that some loyal Anglicans prefer to restrict themselves in this respect to what that Prayer Book specifically authorizes.

The teaching of Scripture and the formularies of our Church will not allow us to condone practices and prayers for the departed which

---

18 See the Book of Job and the Fourth Gospel.

reflect those false doctrines of Purgatory and Pardons which were condemned by the Church at the Reformation. But there is an unresolved
difference among members of the Anglican Communion on the subject
of prayers for the departed which are expressions of the love that
unites members of Christ's mystical Body in the Communion of Saints.

The more conservative Evangelical tradition has been content to
think of the faithful departed as having immediately entered into "joy
and felicity". Any ideas of growth, purification, or spiritual progress
after death have been viewed with misgiving and have indeed sometimes been held to imperil the reality and fullness of the Christian's
assurance which is based on the doctrine of justification by faith.

On the other hand the vast majority of people in the Anglican Communion, while rejecting the crudities of the medieval conceptions of
purgatory, are quite sure that the fact of death does not remove the
need for and the appropriateness of praying for the departed that God
will fulfil his perfect will in them; and that such prayer is both natural
and right.

There is evidently need for a fresh study from the Bible of the whole
question, together with the elucidation and criticism of traditional
liturgical forms of prayer for the departed. Meanwhile, in view of the
fact that our Church formularies deliberately leave room for both
these points of view, with varying degrees of emphasis and varying
forms of expression, it may be wise, in future Prayer Book revision, to
provide that prayer for the departed be permissive, and also to provide
alternative forms of thankful commemoration.

CONCLUSION

Much has been said here about revising the services of the Church,
and suggestions have been offered as to ways in which revisions might
be carried out. But it must not be thought that the Committee is therefore advising the Conference to *urge* all parts of our Communion to
embark on revisions, or that it is recommending that revisions should
be carried out all at once on a maximum scale.

Many Churches of the Anglican Communion are in fact already
engaged upon revisions, and the Committee has here offered advice
upon the lines on which such revisions might best run, and the ends
which revisers might keep in view.

It must be remembered that, at any rate in some Churches, the
greater part of the laity is opposed to change in services except on the
most modest scale, and any attempt to make rapid or revolutionary
revisions would in some places cause widespread dismay and resent-
ment.

But revision is nevertheless proceeding, and the movement cannot
now be halted. The Committee's aim has been to try to indicate the
direction which this movement should take when it has begun. We
are not the only branch of Christendom to have set about this task.

Both in the Roman Catholic Church and in the Evangelical Churches
a similar movement is in progress. And because this Liturgical Movement has already begun to draw Christians closer to one another in
thought and ways of worship, we cannot wish that our own Communion should stand aside.

THE COMMEMORATION OF SAINTS AND HEROES IN THE ANGLICAN COMMUNION

In 1937 the Bishop of Nyasaland referred to his Metropolitan (Archbishop Lang of Canterbury) a proposal which amounted to a request
to include in the Liturgical Kalendar of the diocese the name of
Archdeacon William Percival Johnson, a priest of the diocese then not
long dead. The Archbishop replied that he had no kind of objection,
provided that no use of the term "beatification" and no use of the title
"blessed" were formally made, as these words had no authorization in
the Anglican Church. It was eventually agreed that the proposal should
be referred to the Consultative Committee of the Lambeth Conference
with a view to placing it on the Agenda of the Conference due to be
held in 1940. War postponed this Conference till 1948, when the matter
was referred to the Metropolitans. As a result of this the Archbishop
of Canterbury undertook to appoint a Commission to report upon the
whole question of the Commemoration of Saints and Heroes of the
Faith in the Anglican Communion. The Report of this Commission was
issued in 1957[19] and the subject appeared upon the (Draft) Agenda for
1958 as "Recognition of Local Saints and Servants of God".

The first point to be considered, then, is whether the Prayer Book
Kalendar is to be regarded as a finished work or whether there exist
some means by which the Kalendar can rightly be modified both by
expansion and by withdrawal. In England for instance no saint later
than Richard of Chichester (who died in 1253) may properly be
honoured, or, if the 1928 alternatives are regarded as authoritative, no
saint later than Catherine of Siena (who died in 1380). Similar situations exist in other parts of the Anglican Communion. As a missionary
bishop has well pointed out, "the gap of centuries that divides even the
latest of the saints we commemorate in our Kalendar from the present
day is a real obstacle in the way of presenting sanctity as a permanent
possibility of the Christian life".[20] If it be replied that additions to the
Kalendar may be made, but only of already accredited saints, this is
tantamount to saying that though the Pope and the Eastern Churches
and the synods of the Church in the West before the eleventh century
have, or had, power formally to recognize saints, the Churches of the
Anglican Communion have no such power.

[19] *The Commemoration of Saints and Heroes of the Faith in the Anglican Communion.* S.P.C.K. (hereinafter referred to as the "Report").
[20] Letter of the Bishop of Nyasaland to Archbishop Lang.

Much of the misgiving created by the proposal to enter new names in a Kalendar comes from the creeping in of the word "canonization". Though originally this word merely signified the placing of a name upon a list, it has in the course of centuries acquired a technical meaning and a claim which Anglicans would repudiate. It carries with it associations with late medieval abuses and unscriptural beliefs which no one wishes to revive. The word "appears to be bound up with a doctrine; namely that there is a distinction between the faithful departed in the intermediate state and the saints who have already attained their goal in heaven, and that the Church on earth can through the agency of the Pope pronounce with certainty that some particular persons belong to the second glorious category".[21] The rejection of this theory of canonization does not, however, mean that all claim to the recognition of saints or to their commemoration in church must be abandoned. Such theories did not emerge in the early accounts of thanksgivings for martyrs, which were the origin of our modern use of saints' days. Similarly the Orthodox Church, in authorizing the commemoration of saints, makes no claim which implies a definitive judgement on their heavenly status such as is now inseparable from the Roman procedure. Two other features of Orthodox practice merit attention: first, the commemoration of a true saint should be spontaneous, springing from the devotion of the people among whom he lived and worked; second, that a bishop or a synod—provincial, national, or general—is the proper authority to control the commemoration.

What then would be involved in any Anglican attempt to bridge the long gap between the last of the medieval saints in our Kalendars and the present day?

First it should be said that for some years past the instinct to honour in the sanctuary new heroes of our faith has been increasingly showing itself in many different parts of the Anglican Communion. A perusal of Chapters 5 and 6 of the Commission's Report will surprise many with its varied wealth of instances of this growth. Nor has such activity resulted in any public invocation of saints or become involved in any unjustified speculations or doctrines about the present state and condition of departed Christians. It has arisen from a desire to give thanks and glory to God that in his servants he has wonderfully revealed new and fresh aspects of his grace and salvation. Interest has not to be created; it is already in existence.

Next comes the question: What moral and spiritual characteristics, what accomplishments, are we to look for when deciding whether some departed Christian can be entered among the saints in a Kalendar? Except for the somewhat overworked definition that a saint is one who does ordinary things extraordinarily well, nothing much can be

---

[21] Report, p. 10.

said about accomplishments. Saints are often people who do not do much that is striking. It is interesting to try to make a list of men and women about whom no really interesting biography has ever been written. Many of these would be found to be people considered saintly by those who had most to do with them. In fact it could well be said that saints are those at whose death the world felt itself the poorer. Nevertheless, of many saints much activity is demanded, up to the proved readiness to lay down life for the love of Christ. Until times within the memory of many now living, martyrdom had seemed the remotest possibility for a Christian in the modern world. Now we know how near it always is, though we also know how persecuting powers, with modern resources and techniques, can make a true martyr look a knave or a fool.

Still it is true that, as the Report says, "in the long view the Church has reserved public veneration only for those whose character was such that it both illuminates, and excites to, holiness. Without in the least losing sight of the New Testament use of the word saint, we are bound to say that sanctity, in the sense we have just described, is no ordinary thing. It is an evidence of the supernatural in human life".[22] We shall find it sometimes in the cloister, sometimes in the inspired teacher and thinker, sometimes in active lives of heroic endurance and devotion, and sometimes also in the quiet and steady influence of otherwise "ordinary people".

To discern the presence of this "heroic sanctity" in those who have finished their earthly course is no light or easy matter, nor at first sight do ecclesiastical synods or assemblies seem best fitted to undertake it. But the Church has from our Lord the power to bind and loose, and the "recognition" of a saint by a Church synod is akin to that more frequent task of the individual bishop—that of recognizing that a candidate for ordination "is truly called according to the will of our Lord Jesus Christ".

Thirdly it is important not to try to be too clever and over-methodical in our Kalendars. There may be a great temptation to try to get a collection of saints representing different countries into the list; or to try to get saints representing each century of the Church's life, or saints representing all sorts of legitimate and desirable human professions and occupations. These temptations should be resisted. "A Kalendar of saints should proceed from the life of the Church rather than from the researches of an historian . . . The insertion of the name of an Edward King or a Bernard Mizeki is more in accordance with Christian tradition than that of a Jeremy Taylor or a William Laud".[23] Additions to Kalendars should be very sparingly made: it is not too limiting to think of the rate of addition as one name in 30 or even 50 years. But some Kalendars, especially the English, could do with much pruning

---

[22] Report, p. 66.
[23] Report, p. 67.

and jettisoning. There are many names which never again could be made to live in the minds of people as probably they once did in some places; they are now mere archæological remains of what at one time may have been living bonds between the seen and the unseen world. Except as providing welcome alternatives to the Epistle and Gospel of the Sunday at week-day celebrations their function to-day is all but spent.

Doubts are sometimes expressed about the wisdom of entering in the Kalendar the names of departed Christians whom some living Christians still remember when alive. It is certainly rash to make too speedy a judgement, and time should be left for the events of the life concerned to fall into proportion; time also for controversial passions to cool.

Objections to someone we knew being ranked among the saints may sometimes be due to an unconscious desire to forget that we are all called to be saints ourselves.

Who is to decide whether or no a name, or names, should be added to the Kalendar? In early days the initiative for recognizing and honouring saints lay with local congregations, but abuses and difficulties soon crept in, and these had to be settled by bishops in diocesan or provincial synods. By the eleventh century it is plain that no saint could hope for very wide recognition unless his cult had been approved by some synodical authority, whether diocesan or provincial. At first, in the West, the Pope was only brought in to provide enhanced prestige for the cause of some saint, but by the end of the twelfth century the exclusive right of the Pope to declare who were saints and to authorize their commemorations was hardening into absolute law. In the East, as we have seen, the procedure is far more fluid, and though from time to time authority for recognition of saints has been given by the Oecumenical Patriarch, he has never played the exclusive part which the Pope played in the West. At the same time commemorations have always been inaugurated at the provincial and diocesan levels as well, and some have even grown up without any high ecclesiastical intervention at all.

In the future the ecclesiastical authority thought necessary for the issuing of the local variant of the Book of Common Prayer might also be made responsible for removals from and entries into the Kalendar. The same authority could determine what degree of celebration a recognized saint should have, i.e., whether as a Red Letter Day with special Collect, Epistle, and Gospel, and proper lessons at the Offices, or as a Black Letter Day with proper Collect, Epistle, and Gospel, or as a very simple memorial with a Collect recited at all services after that for the Day.

Nothing much can at this stage be said about procedure for recognition, except that a commission, prepared for a great deal of hard and responsible work, should be entrusted with the researches necessary to establish the suitability of a given candidate. Such a commission would not have the obligation to discover evidence of miracles wrought by the candidate for recognition, since in the ages to which our Communion appeals for authority this element was either absent or optional. It should finally be stressed once more that this kind of commission would not frequently be in session, since it is desirable that our Kalendars should have a few names which are significant and which live in the devotion of the people, rather than many which are unknown.

A word is appended on whether it is desirable to establish a Kalendar common to the whole Anglican Communion. If such a Kalendar were to include recent and local saints it would mean that Anglicans in Polynesia would have to celebrate the memory of, say, Scottish saints who would be as remote and unreal to them as are the names of Agatha or Britius to modern worshippers in the Highlands. If such a Kalendar is to be established it should be a minimum list, and for this purpose the Red Letter Days from the 1662 Prayer Book (which already form the greater part of the Kalendars of the Church of Ireland and of the Protestant Episcopal Church of the U.S.A.) would be the most suitable and practicable.

C. MINISTRIES AND MANPOWER

A. GENERAL INTRODUCTION

It is of little use to discuss the future of the Anglican Communion unless we can guarantee to provide a Ministry sufficient, alike in number and in quality, to serve an expanding mission of the Church. Almost everywhere in the world there is such a shortage of ordained men as restricts and even cripples the Church's existing work, and makes it impossible for the Church to seize new opportunities. The responsibility of fostering ministerial vocations, and so increasing the number of ordinands, falls upon, and must be accepted by, the whole Church.[1] No committee of bishops alone can do it. The present critical situation forces us back on fundamental issues. Political, social, and economic changes of many kinds, and in all parts of the world, may imply that the pattern of the Ministry, which has served the Church for more than a thousand years, now requires to be modified or extended.

Questions about training have been referred to the Committee, but it is impossible to decide how men should be trained without first deciding what they are to be trained for. The aim of theological training must be controlled by a growing understanding of the nature and purpose of the Church itself. All our perspectives will be falsified if we do not see the Ordained Ministry in the only context in which it can have meaning: namely, within the life of the whole Church and in the relation of that Ministry to the priestly office inherent in the Body of Christ in the world. There is also a need for a better theology of the laity, together with an increasing realization of what is meant by Christian vocation throughout the rank and file of the Church's membership. In a real sense the laity—that is the *laos,* the People of God—are the Church. All baptized members of the Body are called to share in its priestly function, the offering of life as a living sacrifice, acceptable to God, through Jesus Christ.

There are signs that this fact is being realized. In all parts of the Anglican Communion dedicated men and women are offering themselves, as part of their Christian witness, in the field of education, in the field of medicine, and in the fields of social welfare, of industry, and of technology. Fifty years ago, quite conceivably, many such men might have offered themselves for the Ministry of the Church, and this may well be part of the reason why the supply of men to the Ministry is at the moment inadequate. After all, the Church's task has to be

---

[1] The following is a selection of the New Testament passages which give the scriptural basis for the general conception of vocation and ministry which underlies this report: Mark 1.16–20; 2.13, 14; 8.34–8; Luke 9.57–62; John 1.37–51; Rom. 12.1; 1 Cor. 7.20, 24; Eph. 1.3–23; 2.11,22; 4.11–16; Col. 3.17—4.1; 2 Thess. 1.11, 12; 2 Tim. 1.6–14; Titus 2.11–14; 1 Pet. 2.1–10; Rev. 1.5, 6; 5.9, 10.

fulfilled in the world. We are commissioned to bring into the Kingdom of Christ the whole of the common life of man. As the supply of the Ordained Ministry falls short of the need, so an ever increasing responsibility must rest upon the laity of the Church in bearing their Christian witness in the world.

B. THE CHURCH'S NEED

The task of the Anglican Communion in the world of to-day may be described as four-fold:

1. To maintain the spiritual life of the Church as a corporate body and of all its members individually;
2. To provide a Christian witness and influence which is both relevant and decisive in the rapidly changing society in which it is set;
3. To proclaim the Gospel to a world which is still very largely unaware of the claim of Christ upon the lives of men, or indifferent to it; and
4. To build bridges of understanding between ourselves and our fellow Christians of other loyalties, both within the ecumenical movement and outside it.

We may no longer think of the task of the Church as purely pastoral or purely missionary, and this places a considerable additional responsibility upon those who are called to the Ordained Ministry. It must be said quite plainly that for this task the present number of men in the Ordained Ministry throughout the Anglican Communion is manifestly insufficient. The number of new men taken into the Ministry year by year is barely enough to replace the loss due to death and retirement. As a result of this insufficiency it is difficult enough to maintain the pastoral work which has already been developed. Posts have to be abandoned; new opportunities cannot be seized. Members of the existing clergy, whilst making heroic efforts to cope with important tasks, find that their work can become largely superficial and are all too often driven to a point of breakdown and frustration. Even more serious than this is the fact that the shortage results in many parts of the world in a lack of balance between the Church's Ministry of the Word and its Ministry of the Sacraments. Whilst provision can be made for the Ministry of teaching and preaching by the use of large numbers of catechists and readers in many areas, it is impossible to make adequate provision for a sacramental Ministry because there are too few priests. Again, the present shortage in the Ministry makes it impossible for the Church in many areas to seize new opportunities and openings which present themselves. This is particularly true in the developing dioceses which no longer receive a steady supply of men from the "sending countries" to the same degree as in the past. It cannot be too clearly said that these dioceses still need. the help of men from outside just as much as, if not more than, they have done in the past. Whilst it is true there must be a clear call to men to offer themselves for the Ministry, there must be an equally clear call to men already ordained to consider service wherever it may be most needed.

At the present time there is a great need in the developing dioceses for men of mature experience, of sound learning, and with gifts of pastoral leadership to undertake special tasks where such gifts are needed: it may be in the foundation of the life of the Church in an area which is rapidly changing in character from rural to industrial; it may be in enabling a diocese to strengthen its own endeavours to recruit and train its own Ministry; it may be in undertaking important administrative responsibility. Other possibilities will readily suggest themselves. The Committee recommends that an appeal should be made to priests of experience to volunteer as members of a kind of "task force" from which men may be drawn to undertake work of special responsibility in any part of the world; it recommends that this possibility be submitted to the appropriate missionary agencies of the Church throughout the Anglican Communion for their consideration.

There is, however, a further problem which the Church must face. It has been put to the Committee as a moral issue. Ought the Church to continue to accept for training more men than it can reasonably afford to pay for, after they have been ordained? It is within our knowledge that, in certain areas of the Church, men are available for the ministry, but cannot be accepted for training because money is not available to pay them subsequently. If the need of men is great, the sources maintaining the Ministry are clearly inadequate. Manpower ought to be measured in terms of opportunity rather than in terms of money, and yet the Church must never allow men to be trained for the Ministry and then fail to maintain them at a reasonable standard of subsistence. Steps ought, therefore, to be taken, throughout the Anglican Communion, to secure more generous and regular giving on the part of the laity to maintain the Ministry, upon which the whole life of the Church fundamentally depends. The Committee is concerned that much of the giving for this purpose is haphazard, unsystematic, and, often enough, not even generous. It desires to call the attention of every Province in the Anglican Communion to this fact, and to invite them to consider how best systematic giving for the maintenance of the Ministry may be established upon the scriptural basis set out in 1 Corinthians 16.1,2: "On the first day of every week, each of you is to put something aside and store it up, as he may prosper".

C. THE SUPPLY OF MEN FOR THE MINISTRY

The Committee has noted with deep thankfulness the fact that very considerable progress has been made throughout the Anglican

Communion in raising up a Ministry indigenous to the area in which it is to be exercised; and even more significantly, that in areas, for many years past described as missionary, the Church is beginning to provide not only its own priestly Ministry but its own episcopal Ministry. It must be part of the strategy of the Anglican Communion to foster in every way possible this process, rather than to rely upon men coming from overseas. This matter is urgent in view of rapidly changing political conditions, which cannot be foreseen, and which have the effect of isolating the Church in a particular area. All our policy both with regard to the raising up of the Ministry and its training must have this ultimate purpose clearly in mind. This is not to suggest for one moment that the Church's Ministry must be built up in watertight compartments; rather it must be our concern to raise up men for the Ministry, whose ministry may come to be exercised anywhere in the Anglican Communion. What is needed to set to work to achieve this?

There is a pressing need to create a real sense of vocation in all men, no matter what their task in life is to be. A Christian's faith and discipleship find expression in the work which he feels called by God to do. It may well be that it is because very few people have any sense of vocation at all that it is difficult for men to feel strongly about a particular vocation to the Ministry of the Christian Church. There is indeed a great gain in the life of society if man's daily work is undertaken in a spirit of obedience to a call from God, and a man is encouraged to offer the work for which he has been created and is fitted, as the one contribution that he can make to the life of the world, without which that life would be poorer.

A clear call to men to offer themselves to the Ministry of the Church must be made against that background. We do not doubt that our Lord is calling men to serve him in the Ministry of the Church. We may well need to pray in order that we may discover his Will and help others to see the direction in which God is calling them. The raising up of men to serve in the Ministry of the Church must be committed to the prayer of the Church in an ever-increasing degree. Methods and schemes of recruitment can never be a substitute for this. It is against that background of prayer that the responsibility for the supply of the Ministry must be laid upon the whole Church, and therefore upon each congregation and each individual Christian. It should be one of the responsibilities of the Christian community to try and see to it that some among its own members are encouraged and helped to realize a vocation and to offer themselves for training for the Church's Ministry. The discovery of possible ordination candidates is no less important than the discovery of candidates for Confirmation. But, though a call may be sounded with great vigour from time to time, there is always the danger that such a call may lose its force. The Committee is of opinion that, although such a call on a large scale is desirable from time to time, yet the Church's work of recruitment is most effectively done as it becomes the concern, not merely of every bishop and every diocese, but of every parish priest. It must be for provinces and dioceses to decide how best such a call may be sounded. It must always be considered locally how best information can be given and what steps can be taken to present the Ministry as what has been described as "the most difficult, the most dangerous, and the most rewarding of trades", and as a way of life which demands the very best that man can give in sacrifice, devotion, and courage. The call of God in and through the Church must be seen to involve sacrifice both in material reward and even in the postponement, or even indefinite deferment, of marriage and the establishment of a home.

One encouraging sign should be noted, namely the number of men of mature years who have achieved some measure of distinction in their professional life and are offering themselves for ordination in the Ministry of the Church. They tend to bring into the ministerial activity of the Church a richness and experience which the Church in its work needs. The Committee does not pretend that this solves all the problems with regard to the Ministry, but the Church may indeed be thankful to have this welcome addition to its life.

D. THE TRAINING OF THE MINISTRY

It is difficult to generalize over so vast an area as the Anglican Communion about the content and method of training for the Ministry, having in mind the wide variety of local conditions and circumstances. In the main, methods must be the responsibility of provinces and dioceses, discharged in and through their own arrangements for theological training. The Committee is persuaded, however, that the development of facilities for theological training is one of the most urgent needs of the Anglican Communion, and particularly in the developing areas. If a Ministry is to be raised up locally, then facilities for training such men must be made available locally, and the Committee's survey of the resources for training in the developing areas shows that, although a good deal of admirable work is being done, these facilities are inadequate. It should be regarded as an urgent priority in the missionary strategy of the Church that the strongest possible support should be provided for the developing areas in this respect. The need is primarily for first-class theological teachers, and, secondly, for adequate buildings, suited to local requirements, in which a priest's training may be developed upon the foundation of a corporate life. So far as the intellectual content of training is concerned, some measure of assistance is available in inter-denominational or united colleges. There is a good deal of common ground in theological teaching which can be covered in such a college, staffed and maintained by constituent religious bodies, and a considerable economy of effort and money can be achieved. The evidence available suggests that united colleges of this kind are an effective influence where they exist, and have gone far to meet the demand of the Churches for a better educated Ministry. Furthermore, it may well be that, in such colleges, bridges of understanding can be built which may lead to a growing unity of mind, which may, in turn, result in a unity of doctrine and spirit. It is, however, important that, where such colleges are used, adequate provision should be made for the maintenance of an Anglican discipline for Anglican students. The chief problems seem to arise from questions of intercommunion and interpretation of the Bible, and these difficulties must be faced from the start by dioceses which make use of such opportunities. Nevertheless, provided adequate provision is made for Anglican worship and discipline, the Committee can see no objection to the use of such opportunities. The Committee is also impressed by the need for theological faculties or departments in connection with newer universities or university colleges throughout the area covered by the Anglican Communion, and desires to recommend that the Church should do everything possible to assist in their foundation and support. They will not only serve to assist the actual processes of training for the ministry, but will also influence the whole temper of Christian life and thought in those universities and provide facilities for research into matters directly connected with the Church's Ministry in a world of rapid social change.

While nothing must be allowed to detract from the culture and discipline of the spiritual life as a primary feature in the training for the ministry, the content of the class-room programme for theological training calls for some measure of reconsideration. In the past it has been almost entirely academic in character, and whilst we must always insist on a high standard of theological education as well as of devotion, the Committee is of the opinion that something more is needed.[2] After all, theological training can never be an end in itself: it must be a means whereby the priesthood may come to be exercised. Not only must a man be taught, but he must be encouraged and helped to deliver to those whom he is to serve that which he himself has received. A strong suggestion is made that there should be greater emphasis upon a pastoral theology as a scientific study. For, after all, it is only in his pastoral dealings with people that a priest can interpret the systematic theology in which he has been trained. The Committee has taken note of the experiments which have been undertaken in the Episcopal Church of the United States along this line, in providing courses of clinical pastoral training, in which doctors and psychiatrists have been found ready to co-operate. The Committee has noted, too,

---

[2] See H. Richard Niebuhr, *The Purpose of The Church and its Ministry*, New York, Harper 1956, p. 134, in which a plea is made for a theological education which leads men and women " to embark on a continuous, ever-incomplete but ever-sustained effort to understand the meanings of their work and of the situation in which they labour ". This, though begun in the theological college, needs to be fostered by post-ordination conferences and courses.

the need for preparing men to face during their ministry the problems which an industrial society inevitably presents.

The Committee recognizes that the period of training must vary in length according to the particular circumstances of the candidate and of the area in which he is to work. It is persuaded, however, that if it is in any way practicable, this should be lengthened and that opportunities should be provided for practical experience of the work of the Ministry during his course.

The training of older men for the Ministry presents its own special problems. A real contribution to this process has been made, for example, in the College for Older Men established in the Diocese of Worcester, and by courses of training for similar men established in the Diocese of Long Island in the United States, and in the Diocese of Huron in Canada. It is found by experience that older men who offer themselves for the Ministry are anxious and concerned that their training should be as complete as possible within the limited time that may be available, and that they are ready to accept a hard demand made upon them. The Committee calls attention to three facilities which may assist these men and possibly others who are preparing to offer themselves as candidates for Holy Orders:

1. The extended provision of pre-ordination courses for those who are at present unable to leave their secular employment.
2. The establishment of evening classes (such, for example, as those formerly provided at King's College, London, England).
3. The use of correspondence courses provided by the Church for those living in rural areas, or unable to attend either pre-ordination courses or evening classes.

No man can be given all the training that he needs in the course of the comparatively short period that he spends at a theological college, and therefore the Committee is persuaded that there should be a much greater emphasis on post-ordination training, whose purpose should be to fill some of the gaps left during the theological college course, and, even more importantly, to help a man lay firm foundations of devotion and reading at the outset of his ministry. As far as developing areas are concerned, there is felt to be a real need for the strengthening of facilities for post-ordination training in an advanced form. It is recognized that for such colleges a reasonably wide area is needed. They are felt to be a rather necessary half-way house between ordinary theological training and special post-ordination training which can be provided at St Augustine's College, Canterbury. At such colleges there would be welcomed men from a number of dioceses or provinces, who would thus be brought into contact with priests from other areas, and their experience deepened and their vision enlarged. This seems to be of real importance in view of the fact that the development of the Ministry is increasingly on an indigenous basis, and should provide a

D*

means whereby standards could be raised progressively in order to ensure that the Ministry is equipped for acceptable service in any part of the world, and that a supply of men competent for leadership in Church and community is available.

Apart from this, post-ordination studies under external direction should be available for the clergy generally. It is noted that in some areas such disciplined study is provided by the Church itself by means of correspondence courses leading to the more advanced examinations of recognized Theological Foundations. Such facilities should be extended and their use by the clergy encouraged.

The Church is indebted to the British and Foreign Bible Society and the S.P.C.K. for the immense help which they have afforded both by provision of text books and also by the translation of both the Bible and the Prayer Book into the vernacular. The Committee expresses the hope that both these societies may feel able to extend this particular facility. It would also welcome any provision which can be made for the building up of theological libraries in the theological colleges in developing areas.

E. THE ORDER OF DEACON

There has been a tendency in recent years to depreciate the place of the Order of deacon in the Ministry of the Church and exalt the offices of reader and catechist. This situation has developed very largely on the grounds of expediency when, from time to time, certain forms of a lay commissioned Ministry have been adopted in various parts of the Church without considering the implications of this development in relation to the ordained Apostolic Ministry which the Church has received. Both readers and catechists have rendered an invaluable service in every part of the Anglican Communion. As a result of this development the fact must be faced that in most areas of the Anglican Communion the traditional functions of a deacon may all, under episcopal authority, be fulfilled by a reader or by a catechist. In the Ordinal, it is clear that a deacon is a "dedicated man". He is required to devote the whole of his life to his calling, and the Ordinal pre-supposes that there is a distinctive place which he occupies within the three-fold Ministry of the Church. As a result of the development of responsibilities of readers and catechists, we have arrived at a position where we must either say that there is no place for a deacon in the life of the Church of to-day, or, alternatively, we must set to work to give the office and function of a deacon its distinctive place, not only in the worship, but in the witness of the Church. This is more fundamental than any request for the setting up of a "permanent diaconate". The Committee realizes, of course, that there can be no drastic or even immediate change in the present situation, but is of opinion that each province in the Anglican Communion should be invited to consider whether it will be wise to recover the diaconate as a distinctive Order in the Church. It may well be right that some of the ministries which have hitherto been undertaken by commissioned laymen should, in course of time, come to be exercised within the diaconate. There would, of course, be involved considerable practical difficulties. Provision would have to be made within the Ordinal for the exercise of the diaconate by those who are not called to devote their whole time to the exercise of that particular ministry. Furthermore, in certain areas there would be legal, canonical, and constitutional difficulties to be overcome. It may be admitted that the existence of a substantial number of lay ministries tends to cause some measure of confusion, and that the time has come to clarify the whole structure of lay ministries in relation to the Order of deacon.

F. SUPPLEMENTARY MINISTRIES

The Committee has been asked to consider a suggestion that, wherever such a step seemed desirable, it should be permissible for men to be ordained to the priesthood, whilst continuing to earn their own living and to exercise their own secular responsibilities. The matter has been advanced from a number of a points of view. There are those who would argue that such a step has become almost essential in order to preserve an adequate Ministry of the Sacraments, especially where there is an inadequate supply of priests for the task. There are others who suggest that the ordination of such men to the priesthood will provide a valuable reinforcement to hard-pressed and over-worked clergy. Others would put it to us in terms of the Church's task and opportunity, from the point of view that they might well bring home more effectively the relevance of the Church and its faith to the ordinary working life of men and women. Others again would suggest it as a return to a primitive practice in the Church and as an attempt in these modern days, to give expression to the New Testament conception of the "*ecclesia*".

The Committee has given long and careful consideration to this problem. It has noted the fact that it was considered at some length by the Lambeth Conference of 1930, as a result of which a very guarded resolution was passed to the effect that the Conference, while declaring that ordination to the priesthood involved full and life-long service, not to be made subservient to any other interests, saw no insuperable objection to the ordination, with Provincial sanction and under proper safeguards, of such "supplementary priests" without their being required to give up their present occupation. It is significant that there has been no development as a result of this resolution, except in the Diocese of Hong Kong, where the number of such supplementary clergy is equal to the number of full-time clergy,[3] and in the Church of India, Pakistan, Burma, and Ceylon, which has incorporated

---

[3] See Appendix 1 below, pp. 110–11.

in its constitution and canons a permission based upon resolution 65 of the Lambeth Conference of 1930.[4] The fact must be faced that the absence of any significant development as a result of this resolution seems to indicate very little demand throughout the Anglican Communion for a facility of this sort. It further seems that within a period of twenty-eight years there has been insufficient experience in practice to afford any guidance as to whether it is a desirable development in the life of the Church on a large scale.

The Committee desires to emphasize that in the view of competent theologians there is no theological principle which forbids a suitable man from being ordained priest while continuing in his lay occupation. The difficulties which arise from the conception of a supplementary ministry are administrative rather than theological, practical rather than spiritual. Whilst calling attention to Resolution 65 of the Lambeth Conference of 1930,[5] the Committee would now wish to go further, and is also of the opinion that where conditions make it desirable, and in particular where political emergency threatens, provinces of the Anglican Communion should be encouraged to make provision upon these lines. The Committee, however, wishes to state its view quite clearly that such a supplementary ministry must never be regarded as a permanent substitute for the fully-trained and full-time priesthood which is essential to the continuing life of the Church.

APPENDIX 1 : MEMORANDUM ON "AUXILIARY PRIESTS"

(Submitted by the Bishop of Hong Kong)

1. *Ordained Lay Readers.* I use this name in English to explain more readily what our auxiliary priesthood is. Our Chinese name is more appropriate, but untranslatable, being a mixture of "auxiliary" and "honorary" without suggesting, as "auxiliary" does, a lower grade of ordination.

2. These clergy are ordained under the following Canon of the Chinese Church.[6]

Canon XIX (a)

Of Ordination in Special Cases

1. If a candidate for deacon's orders be over thirty-two years of age, and have adequate means of his own for his support, and have been assisting without pay in the work of the Church for not less than three years, he may be dispensed from all examinations except:

(1) The Bible in general.

(2) Two or three specially selected portions of the Old and New Testaments.

(3) The Contents and Use of the Book of Common Prayer.

---

4 See Appendix 2, below, pp. 111–12.
5 See Appendix 3, below, p. 112.
6 From C.H.S.K.H. Canons, passed 1934, reprinted 1948.

2. Such a candidate may be ordained deacon provided that:

(1) He is not to receive a salary for his work.

(2) He may not receive a letter of transfer to another diocese except on the written request of the Bishop of that Diocese.

(3) He may not minister within the bounds of any parish or mission unless he is licensed thereto by the Bishop, and requested to do so by the priest-in-charge.

(4) The method of procedure for the ordination shall be in accordance with Canon XVIII (Of the Ordination of Deacons).

3. A deacon so ordained after serving two full years as Deacon may, under conditions similar to those laid down under Section 2 of this Canon, be advanced to the Priesthood as provided in Canon XIX, except that the subjects for examination shall only be the Office and Work of a Priest, and two or three selected portions of the Old and New Testaments.

3. Having no endowments and being a city diocese in a city in which the cost of land for building new churches is almost prohibitive, we have to have larger parishes than are ideal. We have, however, deliberately refused to strengthen these parishes by a second priest (even where the membership is over 1000) at the cost of developing new parishes. The auxiliary priests therefore assist in the administration of the Sacraments in the large parishes and the priest has paid secretaries to handle routine work. In our small country area each of our four embryo parishes has a city-dwelling auxiliary priest in charge of the sacramental life of the parish. We have at present no resident priests in the country.

4. It is noticeable that of our auxiliary clergy, nine are University graduates: and of the other three, one is a non-graduate school-master and two are exceptional: (*a*) one being organizing secretary of the Chinese Christian Literature Society with more than a graduate knowledge of English and Chinese; (*b*) the other is a man of most unusual pastoral gifts. As a middle-grade employee in Government Medical Service, he is completely free after office hours. He and his wife give all their spare time to the care of a church and school for fisher-folk and farmers twenty miles away from the city.

APPPENDIX 2: EXTRACTS FROM CHAPTER XVI OF THE CONSTITUTION, CANONS, AND RULES OF THE CHURCH OF INDIA, PAKISTAN, BURMA, AND CEYLON

Canon VII. Notwithstanding any Canon to the contrary made heretofore and subject to the provisions of Rule 20 below, a Bishop may in special circumstances and with the special approval of the Metropolitan admit to Holy Orders men of mature age and assured position who will continue to earn their own living in other callings than those specified in Canon I of this Chapter.

Rule 20. If a candidate for Deacon's Orders be over the age of 39 years and have adequate means for his own support, and have been assisting in the work of the Church for not less than three years, he may be ordained Deacon provided that:

- (*a*) the bishop is satisfied as to his knowledge of the Bible and the the Book of Common Prayer by a test approved by himself and his Examining Chaplains
- (*b*) he is not to receive any salary for his ministerial work;
- (*c*) he may not receive a letter of transfer to another diocese except on the written request of the Bishop of that diocese.
- (*d*) he may not minister within the bounds of any parish or mission, except he is licensed thereto by the Bishop and requested to do so by the priest in charge;
- (*e*) the method of procedure for the ordination shall be in accordance with Chapter XVI, Rules 1, 2, 5, 6, 8, and 10.

Rule 21. A deacon so ordained, after serving as deacon for a period to be determined by the Bishop, may under the relevant Canons and Rules of Chapter XVI and subject to the conditions laid down in Rule 20 (*b*), (*c*), and (*d*) and provided he passes a test approved by the Bishop and his Examining Chaplains, be advanced to the Priesthood.

APPENDIX 3: RESOLUTION 65 OF THE LAMBETH CONFERENCE OF 1930

The Conference, for reasons given in the Report of its Committee on the ministry, cannot recommend a widespread adoption of the proposal that men of mature age and assured position might be called by authority, and, if willing, ordained to the priesthood without being required to give up their present occupation. But, while declaring that ordination to the priesthood involves full and lifelong service, not to be made subservient to any other interests, it sees no insuperable objections to the ordination, with provincial sanction and under proper safeguards, where the need is great, of such *Auxiliary Priests*.

G. READERS, CATECHISTS, SUB-DEACONS, AND OTHER LAY WORKERS

There is wide difference in nomenclature used in various parts of the Anglican Communion to describe its lay workers holding office under licence. The Committee records the Church's appreciation of the devoted service, often given voluntarily, of these many lay workers.

For convenience, all such lay workers will be referred to as "readers", whether stipendiary or voluntary.

The Committee surveyed the methods employed for training, examining, admitting, and licensing readers in the several provinces and extra-provincial areas of the Anglican Communion, taking particular note of the work of the Central Readers' Board of the Church of England in encouraging, training, and examining readers, and of the report of the Joint Committee of the Convocations of Canterbury and York on the Work and Status of Readers.

The Committee gave attention to the following points.

(a) The nature of the office of reader.

The work of a reader should be described as that of an office, not of an order. The service of admission is to an office, and that office is not deemed to possess any character of indelibility. The Committee recommends that initial admission to membership of that office be by the bishop or his duly appointed deputy, and that in the event of discontinuity of service it should be in the discretion of the diocesan bishop in whose diocese the reader is now to be licensed, to require his re-admission to the office of reader.

(b) Training, Examination, and Licensing.

The Committee urges upon all parts of our Communion the importance of adequate training and examination before admission and licensing to the office of reader. Advantage is already being taken by certain dioceses in other provinces of our Communion of the facilities offered by the Central Readers' Board of the Church of England for the examination and certification of readers.

(c) Authority to assist in the administration of the Holy Communion.

In directing attention to the facility afforded in the latter part of Resolution 65 of the Lambeth Conference of 1930 for the authorizing by a bishop of certain readers to assist in the administration of the Holy Communion,[7] the Committee emphasizes that this should be done only to meet pressing needs and that this authority should be given explicitly in writing, and should be renewable only in the discretion of the bishop.

Religious Orders and Communities

The Committee wishes to record its appreciation of the devoted work already being done in many parts of the Anglican Communion both by men and by women in religious Orders and in Communities. It wishes to see this conception of vocation extended to embrace a wider range of churchmanship in our Communion. It is persuaded that there are many tasks in education, in social and moral welfare, and in other spheres which can be committed to such Orders and Communities. The Committee commends to clergy the desirability of encouraging

---

[7] "Further, in order to meet the present pressing need, the Conference would not question the action of any Bishop who, with the sanction of the National, Regional or Provincial Church concerned, shall authorize such licensed Readers as he shall approve, to administer the chalice at the request of the parish priest". (*The Lambeth Conference, 1930.* p. 60).

among young people a sense of vocation to such service, and urges upon the Church as a whole the necessity for the financial support of Orders and Communities.

The Ministry of Women

The work of women in conjunction with the Ministry of the Church is clearly of importance in its own right, as well as being an instrument of pastoral and evangelistic opportunity. Throughout the Anglican Communion, women are offering themselves for that work, and are being adequately trained for this purpose. The Committee regrets that there is, in some quarters, a reluctance to use the help which they can give, and desires to urge a greater employment of such trained workers, especially in areas where pioneer work has to be done.

There is a growing number of women who take theological degrees and diplomas in the universities, often after having graduated in other faculties, with a view to becoming specialists in religious instruction in State schools. Others undertake specialized training in order that they may fulfil a vocation in the social welfare services of the State, where a Christian witness is no less important than in voluntary agencies. These developments ought to be encouraged, and the extension of facilities for such training is desirable throughout the Anglican Communion.

The Committee has considered, in the light of present circumstances, the Resolutions on the Order of Deaconesses (numbered 67–70) of Lambeth Conference, 1930. The Committee has nothing to add by way of further recommendation.

H. THE WITNESS OF THE LAITY

The task before the Church throughout the world presents a sharp challenge to the laity. By laity in this context we mean all those who are seeking to fulfil the membership of the Church which is theirs by baptism. This membership involves not only worship but witness, and the very fact of baptism involves a share of responsibility for the Church's task. It is no exaggeration to say that the Church's task in every part of the world is a missionary one. Everywhere a clear lead is needed as to what the laity can do to fulfil the task of the Church and as to what is required of them.

It is a source of weakness that we have tended to indulge in a process of fragmentation of the laity, and to think of the laity in terms of men, women, youth, and children, with subdivisions of all four. Furthermore, the very existence of a large number of Church societies, admirable as many of them are, has tended to obscure the one-ness of the laity and, where they exist as an end in themselves rather than as means to the fulfilment of the Church's task, they can very easily distract their members from a clear conception of their responsibility as members of the Church. This general process of fragmentation may have developed from the breakdown of family worship. There is also the splitting up of the Christian family by providing for several celebrations of the Holy Communion on one day and indeed special or "corporate" celebrations for particular groups. The New Testament knows no such divisions. There the mission of the whole Church is to be the Body of Christ, and, through all its members, to show forth Christ to the world.

Ministry and laity are one. There may be a difference in function but there is no difference in essence. Each, minister and layman, has a responsible share in the task of the Church to fulfil, each in his own way and in fulfilment of his own gifts. There could be a revolution in the life of the Church if this truth could be rediscovered.[8] Both in the thickly-populated town areas and in scattered rural districts many a priest is faced with a task which he cannot possibly fulfil in its ministerial, pastoral, and evangelistic demands. But if he realizes that within his worshipping community Sunday by Sunday he has a number of potential pastors and evangelists to work with him, then the task is one which is within sight of fulfilment to the profit of all concerned.

The first step needs to be the recovery of the Christian home. To all those who receive the Church's blessing in marriage there comes a challenge to create a home in which family prayer is given its rightful place, where family worship engenders a spiritual cohesion, where children are brought by the example and teaching of their parents to know the truth as it is in Jesus, and where a Christian discipline springing from love supplies the family with its true freedom. But it is possible to go further and try to see such homes as centres of evangelization and fellowship for every street or for every village. Let each home become a centre for prayer, for discussion, for preparation for the Holy Communion at church on Sunday, and for rediscovery of the truth of the Bible. Let it become a place where the sinner and the helpless may make their distress known and may be led to take the first step on the road to recovery and restoration to fellowship. The Committee believes that many of the laity are prepared to become agents of evangelism, of fellowship, and of reconciliation if they are shown the way; and that every Christian household can become a point of contact between the Church and those who know not Christ as Lord, but who may be won to hear his call, to be made captive by his love, and to share in his service. Such a development must find its inspiration in the family worship of the Church and its fulfilment in the integration of each "house-church" in the fullness of the life of the whole Christian body.

But the laity must bear their witness too in places where they work,

---

[8] Much valuable work is being done in this respect by the Department of the Laity, World Council of Churches.

particularly at a time when the context of a man's life tends to be where he works rather than where he lives. What is needed there? First, men and women who are known to be distinctively and unashamedly Christian, who bear their witness by the integrity of their lives, by the responsibility of their bearing, and by their unfailing charity towards their neighbours. Secondly, they must be ready to give an answer to every man that asks for a reason of the hope that is in them. For this, instruction is needed, and men and women must be trained in dealing with questions with which they are confronted, bearing upon the Christian faith and teaching. Thirdly, there must be a real sympathy and compassion as well as understanding and insight. They must know how to deal with men in the light of God's purpose and in the power of his love. Such men and women can become Christian pathfinders in the labyrinth of modern life, and for such a purpose they should be able to look for their training at the hands of the ordained ministry. To such a purpose we must call the laity and for it we must prepare them.

But God is the Creator of the world. His kingdom must be prepared, not only in the souls of men, but also in the work of creation in which man is permitted to share. The Church must therefore claim for God's purpose, and seek to baptize into the service of Christ, all the manifold skills and capacities and the scientific and technical discoveries which have been entrusted to mankind. This can be done only through the laity in their various callings and occupations, in their professions, in industry, and in politics: only by them will it be done at all.

This means that the Christian will be seeking to do God's will, and to be loyal to his vocation, not only in religious activities, but in the doing of the job in which he earns his livelihood during the week. That is an essential expression of his share of the priestly ministry of the whole body. Not everything in the Christian life is specifically and technically religious: but for Christians nothing can ever be merely secular.

I. ST AUGUSTINE'S COLLEGE, CANTERBURY

The Committee has examined with care the Report submitted to the Archbishops and Bishops of the Anglican Communion, and desires first of all to express its appreciation of the fact that so much has been achieved in so short a time. There is considerable evidence to show that the College is meeting a real need in the Anglican Communion, and in spite of initial handicaps and difficulties its life is firmly established. There is also evidence to show that those who have undertaken either a full course of study, or shorter courses, at the College have derived considerable profit.

Reference should be made to two main difficulties. First, the College has been handicapped by having no capital resources of its own, either to complete the work of establishment or to act as a cushion to meet rising costs. The Committee is satisfied that every economy is shown in ordinary expenditure, and so far the budget has just been balanced year by year. But there is no margin even for modest modernization, let alone necessary extension. The second difficulty is inseparable from any new venture, that of securing sufficient numbers to take advantage of what is provided. The College should have regularly in residence thirty priest students and ten ordinands. Numbers are improving, but these figures have so far not been reached. Therefore if the Conference approves the continuance of the College until the next Lambeth Conference, it is essential that bishops should ensure that suitable men are set free for a period to take advantage of the opportunity. Generous bursaries are available to suitable men. It may not be possible yet for other provinces to emulate the example of the Episcopal Church of the U.S.A. in sending six priests to the College each year and in providing for those who are sent. But, if the College is to fulfil its proper task, every part of the Anglican Communion needs to be represented.

The College would be very glad to receive for its library copies of diocesan or parochial histories and indeed any books relating to the history and development of the Anglican Communion.

WALTER H. GRAY
Bishop of Connecticut
Chairman

4. The Reconciling of Conflicts between and within Nations

MEMBERS OF THE COMMITTEE

ENGLAND
T. Bloomer, D.D. [Carlisle]
W. D. L. Greer, D.D. [Manchester]
R. P. Wilson, D.D. [Chichester]
W. L. S. Fleming, D.D. [Portsmouth]
A. S. Reeve, D.D. [Lichfield]
C. K. N. Bardsley, C.B.E., D.D. [Coventry]

UNITED STATES
H. W. Hobson, D.D. [Southern Ohio] (*Vice-Chairman*)
W. F. Lewis, S.T.D. [Nevada]
B. W. Harris, D.D. [Liberia]
T. H. Wright, D.D. [East Carolina]
C. F. Hall, D.D. [New Hampshire]
W. J. Gordon, D.D. [Alaska]
T. N. Barth, D.D. [Tennessee]
W. C. Campbell, D.D. [West Virginia]
W. R. C. Powell, D.D. [Oklahoma]
W. H. Marmion, D.D. [South-Western Virginia]
A. R. Stuart, D.D. [Georgia]
A. P. Stokes, Jr, D.D. [Massachusetts]
R. R. Brown, D.D. [Arkansas]
P. L. Simoes, D.D. [South-Western Brazil]
N. B. Nash, D.D. [U.S. Churches in Europe]

CANADA
P. R. Beattie, D.D. [Kootenay]
N. R. Clarke, D.D. [James Bay (Suffr.)]

INDIA, PAKISTAN, BURMA, AND CEYLON
H. L. J. De Mel, D.D. [Kurunagala] (*Secretary*)
P. Parmar, M.A. [Bhagalpur]

NEW ZEALAND
J. T. Holland, M.A. [Waikato]
W. N. Panapa, C.B.E., L.TH. [Aotearoa (Suffr.)]

SOUTH AFRICA
J. de Blank, D.D. [Cape Town] (*Chairman*)
R. A. Reeves, M.A., S.T.D. [Johannesburg]
T. J. Savage, M.A. [Zululand]

WEST INDIES
G. L. G. Mandeville, M.A. [Barbados]

JAPAN
I. H. Nossé [South Tokyo]

CHINA
R. O. Hall, M.C., B.A. [Hong Kong]

WEST AFRICA
J. E. L. Mort, M.A. [Northern Nigeria]
R. R. Roseveare, S.S.M. [Accra]
St J. S. Pike, D.D. [Gambia and the Rio Pongas]

CENTRAL AFRICA
F. O. Green-Wilkinson, C.B.E., M.C., M.A. [Northern Rhodesia]

EXTRA-PROVINCIAL
F. Lutaya [Uganda (Asst.)]
Y. M. Omari [Central Tanganyika (Asst.)]
T. R. Parfitt, M.A. [Madagascar]
A. E. Chadwell, A.K.C. [Korea (Asst.)]
D. I. Evans, C.B.E., B.A. [Argentina and Eastern South America with the Falkland Islands]

. PREAMBLE

At the heart of the Christian revelation lies the truth of faith that God was in Christ reconciling the world unto himself. For all man's disregard, denial, and neglect of this truth, mankind made new in Jesus Christ remains the promised goal of God's redeeming love; and it is the Church's privilege, as it is its greatest glory, to declare that word of reconciliation which God has committed to it.

It has a word of God to speak to every age, whether men will hear or whether they will forbear. This word is not an utterance of a detached observer, but is mediated through the knowledge and experience of men fully involved in human affairs. It is in and through the conflicts of life that God speaks to his people.

Moreover the word of reconciliation committed to Christ's Church is more than one of words, it is that of the Word-made-Flesh. The Church dares to address God's word to men only if in its own life his word of judgement and mercy finds expression, first, in faithful worship and devotion, and then reaching out to the world in a ministry of compassion and service.

1. RECONCILIATION THROUGH CHRIST AND HIS CHURCH

The Committee has been entrusted with the subject, "The Reconciling of Conflicts between and within Nations". Its discussions have been held in a tragic awareness of the increasing toll of misery and unhappiness in the world. There are still millions of people who have been driven from their homes and are living in great distress as unwanted refugees in many lands. The nations move uneasily from crisis to crisis, and the future is dark with uncertainty.

It is in circumstances such as these that the reconciling word has to be proclaimed, not in any vague and indefinite manner, but addressed specifically to the situation in which twentieth-century man finds himself. This calls first for some understanding of the causes which lie behind the present unrest and conflict.

A. CAUSES OF CONFLICT

Present-day tensions arise from many sources. The long-established nations are suffering from a terrible insecurity. They realize that nuclear war would completely wreck their civilization. Perhaps even more they dread what might happen to them if ever they became subject to a totalitarian system that would mean enslavement. This insecurity and fear have led to a view of life that is essentially selfish. They prefer to enjoy the good things of this life as much as possible while the going is good, living simply for the day. "Let us eat and drink, for to-morrow we die."

On the other hand, the newly independent nations, having little to lose, are probably much less afraid either of war or of Communism. Very large numbers of their people are insufficiently fed and clothed. Stark poverty is all too common. Most of them have been ruled by other nations, and all else pales beside their fervent desire to be really free and to express their nationhood. The emerging nations still feel that the colonial powers are unwillingly yielding their privileged positions inch by inch. They demand to be thought of as in no way inferior to the nations of the Western world.

At the very time when these rapid and momentous developments in the history of the nations are taking place, the generality of mankind, the West included, has no firm philosophy of history to give it confidence in its destiny, or to justify the sufferings it must bear. Many, even in so-called Christian lands, had based whatever hope they had on secular progress. This outlook has been shattered by two world wars, and nothing has come to fill its place.

There is a further element in the situation which has particular significance. The Committee emphatically accepts the validity of the scientific method in its own domain and recognizes the wide range of benefits which science has brought to humanity. Though science has placed immense and rapidly increasing power in men's hands, it does not provide, nor in the nature of the case can it provide, the key to its right use. Thus the physical power of nuclear fission and fusion, or the possibilities open to man to make changes in himself (e.g. in the spheres of psychological manipulation, or genetics), are as much a threat to man's future life in this world as they are a potential source of great advantage to humanity.

The whole world has not only been profoundly affected by the dazzling material achievements of science and technology, but has been so progressively conditioned by a scientific climate of opinion that people come to look upon any knowledge other than that obtained by scientific method as suspect. This attitude is reinforced by Marxist doctrine, but even in the West the dogma that scientific truth is the only kind of truth is prevalent, though often less so among scientists themselves than among other people.

This is one reason why the Christian revelation is so often discounted and so frequently considered irrelevant. There is a widespread failure to appreciate the nature of the existential truth which the Bible contains and which the Church teaches. The neglect of this wide range of truth carries with it a depreciation of the dignity and worth of man, and of the ultimate purpose of his life. There is a tendency to think of man's ideals and his destiny in terms of biological or psychological necessity or in terms of economic advantage. Man looks upon his fellows much as an observer, from the outside. Such an attitude of impersonal detachment lowers his sense of sympathy and obligation. He begins to treat people like things. His actions become careless, callous, and even cruel.

All this contributes to an insecurity that breeds suspicion, finding its expression in a distrust of a class, an economic or some other group, or, in greater issue, a nation, an empire, or a race. People on both sides of such a conflict may have as their motive a legitimate desire for significance and for what might be fullness of life. But as a result people are pitted against people as all strive for significance. Fear is hypnotic: at last someone makes a desperate move, and fear is discharged in strife.

To live amid these conflicts, man needs inner resources. Escape is impossible. Group insecurity and frustration are not only external facts; they are generated from within. The germs of social disillusionment are found in individual disillusionment, and so are the germs of social antipathy and fear. Many an aggressive move is born of insecurity. Many an accusation is the confession of unfaced guilt. Many a destructive hatred is the projection of a hidden mistrust of human nature, an unacknowledged mistrust of self. Man's need is self-knowledge—a doctrine of the whole man and, more important still, a sense of purpose rooted in the doctrine of God. The gap between man's need and God's purpose is the area in which we must look for reconciliation.

B. THE NATURE OF CHRISTIAN RECONCILIATION

When differing views and interests meet, the result may be a head-on collision in which both parties suffer; or one side may give way to the other and suffer deprivation in the process; or there may be a readiness on the part of both sides to make concessions, so that the difference is reduced to terms on which compromise can be reached. But differing forces and tensions can also be resolved positively in a creative partnership yielding fresh powers for good. This is the true way of reconciliation.

It can only be achieved, however, when each party is prepared for the sake of some greater good to abandon and offer up its own exclusive interest despite the contingent risks involved. Renunciation and self-sacrifice are essential conditions for reconciliation. Its realization is not a monopoly of the Church, but Christians believe that in the Person of Jesus Christ the powers of self-sacrificial love have been revealed and released in full and unique manner. Thus we proclaim that God was in Christ reconciling the world to himself and has entrusted to the Church the word of reconciliation.

This reconciliation means that man, rebelling against God's love or living in ignorance of it, cannot achieve full reconciliation with either God or his fellows. Not till he seeks the divine love as the dynamic of his life can he grow as a free person in his human relations. Only a humble and thorough-going acceptance by all men of the forgiveness and help of God can fully and finally resolve the conflicts in the heart of man, and bring him to the measure of the stature of the fullness of Christ.

It follows that the Church's primary contribution to the peace of the world through the ministry of reconciliation is to continue faithfully the task of preaching Christ crucified in his ministry of reconciliation, and of drawing men into the reconciled and reconciling, forgiven and forgiving, redeemed and redeeming, community of faith. We dare not forget that his ministry, which created this community, led him to an ignominious death. The Church is Christ's Church only when its members live together in the spirit of Calvary, as those ready to pay the price as well as to inherit the blessing of the peacemakers. Each of us is to bear his share of the suffering and injury caused by the sins of the world. By our sacrificial living and self-giving to relieve others' needs, we share Christ's Cross, doing this not with any self-righteousness but knowing that our own sins are being borne by Christ and his Body the Church.

This full reconciliation is the goal to which the Church looks. This is its hope and for this it must labour. Yet it must be acknowledged that in most conditions of conflict the opposing sides accept no Christian obligation or authority. Here the Christian must not allow his ultimate concern to blind him to his duty to be a peacemaker, even though the way be frustrating and exacting. Here compromise, temporary solutions, relative justice, and partial achievement have their place.

Furthermore, the Church sometimes has to take the responsibility for creating conflict, never, legitimately, on its own behalf but to remedy injustice and to halt oppression. Though it has no weapons other than spiritual and moral ones, it can help to create a climate of public opinion wherein constructive action becomes possible.

Facing its reconciling task, the Church must in penitence confess its own failures. For the Church is not only the Body of Christ; it is also, in its human aspect, a company of sinful and fallible men, caught and infected by sin, ignorance, and frailty. As such it stands under the judgement of God. The Church has not infrequently failed to contribute to the resolution of conflicts in the social and political fields. Sometimes it has complacently and uncritically blessed an unjust *status quo* in the belief that the sinfulness of the world so easily leads to anarchy that any order, however unjust, is preferable to chaos. Sometimes it has confused social and political issues by proclaiming its perfectionist ethic as directly applicable to specific situations, and so has avoided the costly process of dealing with questions of relative good and evil. In particular we must confess our share in the sin and scandal of the disunity of the visible historic Church. Our sorry inability to find the reconciling truth that shall restore visible unity to Christ's Church weakens our witness to the love of the one God and the one Lord. It therefore behoves us as Christians to speak with great humility since we are ourselves infected with the disease for which we seek a cure.

But the Church is not only a company of sinful people, in daily need of God's continuing forgiveness. It is also the Body of Christ, and the word of reconciliation has in our own time brought into being the Ecumenical Movement, which has been used by God to heal in no small measure the wounds in Christ's Body.

In this Movement, as in the frank and friendly facing of the differences within our own Communion, we have learned that conflict can be constructive as well as destructive. When religious differences are accepted as tensions within a family, they can either be resolved, or, at the least, continue as differences within a loving brotherhood of believers. We therefore feel able to claim that the Church has something from its own life and experience to teach the world about the reconciling of conflicts.

We welcome the various agencies which have been established and which help us to bring Christian insights to bear upon social, industrial, racial, and international problems. These deserve our interest and support, but will scarcely prove effective unless Christians are willing consciously to bring their faith to act in areas hitherto regarded as secular. In many conflicts the part which a Christian must play will be determined not by the application of some ready-made Church directive but by technical knowledge combined with Christian judgement, and a sincere desire to be led by the Spirit. The Christian layman, be he shop steward, employer, politician, or statesman, can do much to reconcile the conflicts of which we have been thinking. He must take the risk of being wrong; the risk, too, of standing alone.

The Church of Christ and every member of it is called to practise love and forgiveness in every human fellowship from the home to the family of nations: in parish, in diocese, and in national and international, denominational and interdenominational, Church life. Especially we must ask God to teach us how to pray for those who neither forgive nor love us, and who do not pray for us, and how to take advantage of every opportunity for manifesting our desire to establish friendly relations with them.

We undertake this ministry of reconciliation not in despair but in hope. God now, as always, is making peace among men. He reigns; his love is ultimately invincible; and we, his children, sure of that reconciling love, continue in faith, sustained by his forgiveness and peace. In some measure we can share to-day in the final triumph of his Kingdom. "The kingdoms of this world are become the kingdoms of our Lord, and of his Christ; and he shall reign for ever and ever" (Revelation 11.15, A.V.).

C. THE CHURCH'S MINISTRY OF RECONCILIATION

In this ministry of reconciliation there must be, within our parishes, Christian fellowship on a far deeper level than is often found. There must be welcoming and forgiving love for persons of all types and conditions, and of any racial, social, and economic background. The grounds of such fellowship will go deeper than superficial congeniality to the level of a shared life in Christ. Unless individual Christians within the parish experience this deep family life, there is little value in calling the Church at large to its reconciling task.

Too often we think of the Church merely as an institution. The Church's primary vocation is to be a community in Christ. The Church's work is not to be done only for people—but by and with people. The Church does not merely declare God's love or his forgiveness or his power. It calls people to share in that love, forgiveness, and power, and to communicate these to others. The parish family gathered around the altar must go out to express its Christian fellowship in homes and parish activities and community life. This is the ministry of every member. How shall the Church reconcile conflicts unless in every parish the clergy and laity are forgiving and understanding and helping their brethren in a real experience of Christian community?

This beloved community extends beyond the parish and includes the whole Church of God. Recent years have seen a development of diocesan, provincial, and international gatherings. These are fruitful for good, and opportunities for personal contacts between Church people of different races and nations should be encouraged and initiated. Those at Lambeth have rejoiced in the fellowship they have experienced with bishops from all parts of the world. Their hope is that all Church people may in greater measure appreciate the inspiration of the wider fellowship that exists both in Anglicanism and in Christendom at large. Such contact should be recognized as a means of reconciliation, and those taking advantage of such opportunities should, by preliminary prayer and study, as well as, later, by personal friendship, work to build bridges of confidence and understanding between differing economic, political, cultural, and national groups.

Yet the Church does not exist exclusively to serve its own members. It must always move out into the world to seek and to save. To this end it must identify itself with all men whom it can reach and willingly share their conditions of life. To-day the whole world, including the most industrialized countries, is a mission field with which we must establish contact and for the sake of which we must be ready to sacrifice comfort and luxury.

The apostleship of the laity is vital, if the Church is to carry out its work of reconciliation. It is not enough to ask men to come out of the world and into the Church. Christians must go back into the world, expressing their lay ministry in offices and shops, in labour unions and in management, in public service and in domestic life. As Church members they can welcome the lonely, the refugee and the disheartened. As citizens they can take their responsible place in the community, on a voluntary and also governmental level. Some can influence world affairs in public life, but all can make their presence felt in creating public opinion. The quality of each life makes either for conflict or for peace.

A dedication to Christian vocation is the chief way in which Christ's Church can to-day carry its influence into every sphere of human activity. Every layman is called to be the Church in each situation where he finds himself, making himself an instrument of Christ's reconciling love. This outgoing ministry demands recruitment and inspiration, encouragement and training. In Christian education new emphasis must be laid on this responsibility of every member, and in the parishes special sources of fellowship and instruction must be available to help those who bear their witness in the complexities of modern commercial and industrial affairs.

This activity must be undergirded by prayer—the vocation of every Christian. We must pray with new imagination and new devotion, not only for those we love and care for, but also for those whose counsels we oppose. For it is God from whom reconciliation comes.

To Christians, who amid conflict give themselves to Christ's reconciling ministry through his Church as members of his Body, there come new strength and courage to go forward unafraid even as through them God gives new hope to all his children. "Wherefore, my beloved brethren, be ye steadfast, unmoveable, always abounding in the work of the Lord, forasmuch as ye know that your labour is not in vain in the Lord" (1 Cor. 15.58, A.V.).

2. CONFLICTS BETWEEN NATIONS

This is God's world. His purpose for man has been declared in Jesus Christ. Irrespective of race or colour, all men are equally the object of God's love, and are called to love and serve him. All men are made in his image; for all Christ died; and to all there is made the offer of eternal life. Yet this life cannot be lived in isolation. Each one is born into a particular family, and through it into the larger community of the nation.

A. NATIONS AND NATIONALISM

The nation, like the family, is part of God's ordering of human life. Within this order man grows in character through obedience to God in the duties of common life. The interdependence of nations is evidence of this divine order in the realm of international relationships. Nations, like individuals, are members one of another. If nations are to live together in harmony, their people need to learn from one another and to seek out and value the good in those from whom they differ.

In a world in which nations are increasingly becoming interdependent, it is important to appreciate the place and worth of true nationalism. For so often it can be perverted. Where it becomes the expression of political, racial, or cultural supremacy, it denies the sovereignty of God and threatens the freedom and security of mankind. For the Christian, true nationalism must be rooted in Christ as well as related to his country.

Our concern here is with the conflicts between nations. It is clear that these arise both from human selfishness and from the tensions that are inherent in the normal change and development which take place in human societies. For this reason we must recognize the effect of corporate selfishness and lust for power, which is often expressed in an exclusive or militant nationalism, and in the complete subordination of life to some particular ideology which denies the purpose of God. We must also recognize among the sources of conflict, the pressure of starvation and over-population; the drive for access to raw materials; the fear of insecurity or disintegration; the desire to protect a culture or a way of life; the yearnings of peoples coming to maturity. In all this we acknowledge in penitence before God our share in the sins of nations, and our unwillingness, corporately and individually, to face the cost of Christian discipleship.

B. THERMO-NUCLEAR WARFARE

The consequences of conflict between nations have been heightened by the startling development of modern weapons which threaten destruction on a world scale. The situation created by these weapons makes a new challenge and demand upon us, both as Christians and as citizens. There is grave danger in delay. While nations drift, nuclear bombs are being multiplied with the damage, real though difficult to measure, of continuing tests. As more nations come to possess nuclear weapons the situation will become more inflammable.

We need to create a better informed public opinion without which effective control will be impossible. At present the threat of nuclear warfare mainly arouses fear, which, while it is natural, can be largely self-centred. Christians are to consider, rather:

(a) Their responsibility for inflicting untold suffering by sanctioning nuclear bombing.

(b) The wasteful expenditure of wealth and effort upon weapons of destruction, when such resources could be used constructively for satisfying human needs in the vast undeveloped areas of the world.

There are those who, on grounds of sincere pacifist conviction, hold all war to be indefensible in all circumstances. To such the present issue does not pose any new decision, though it will strengthen their convictions. The Committee is unanimous in re-affirming that "war as a method of settling international disputes is incompatible with the teaching and example of our Lord Jesus Christ."[1] The existence of

---

[1] Lambeth Conference, 1930 and 1948.

nuclear bombs, and other weapons capable of similar indiscriminate destruction, compels the Committee to draw attention again to these words, and to urge that the use of such weapons should be abolished by international agreement. They recognize, however, the difficulties that lie in the way of achieving this agreement, and are divided over the practical steps that ought to be taken immediately.

Some of the Committee are convinced that in the present uncertain situation, and until international agreement is reached, individual nations are justified in retaining these weapons as a lesser evil than surrendering them and increasing the possibility of an unscrupulous attack.

Others of the Committee are convinced that the use of such weapons is morally unjustifiable in any circumstances, and would advocate unilateral renunciation of their possession, use, and testing even before international agreement has been reached.

The Committee is aware that Christians are longing for one clear answer. To give such an answer would be to gloss over the complexity of the situation. But the fact that the Committee is divided does not absolve any of us from personal decision. Each one of us has to try to understand the issues involved and face the consequences of any action that he advocates. Insofar as we do this seriously we shall help to make others conscious of what is at stake and overcome the apathy into which it is so easy to fall. Therefore we urge that:

(*a*) At every level of Church life Christian people should subject their attitudes to intense prayer and study, recognizing that God is calling us to a costly choice and that, as individuals, we share responsibility for the public decisions which our countries make.

(*b*) Despite the technical difficulties in discriminating in nuclear research between development for peaceful and for military purposes, Christians should press through their governments for international control of the production and testing of nuclear weapons as a matter of the utmost urgency, recognizing that the nations concerned are morally bound to make unceasing effort to secure this, and to accept such limitations of their own freedom as effective control will demand.

(*c*) The Church should seek means whereby it can consult with scientists and political leaders about the many problems of ethics and conscience which may arise from the discovery and development of nuclear fission and fusion.

C. POSITIVE MEANS OF ACTION

There is a danger of thinking of conflict in terms of its ultimate consequence in war. The Church, however, is called at all times to the positive work of reconciliation. The reconciliation of conflicts between nations to which Christians are committed involves:

1. The duty and opportunity of every individual Christian to be a channel of reconciliation in all personal relationships. In international, industrial, and other negotiations, this encounter of person with person may frequently spell the difference between success and failure.

2. The acceptance of the necessity for an international organization for the prevention of armed conflicts and the development of mutual help between nations. The Committee acknowledges with gratitude the efforts and achievement of the United Nations, which has been created for these purposes. It has played an important part in the prevention of war and has kept open the means of communication between peoples at variance with one another. Despite the apathy of people and governments, the United Nations has worked effectively in the field of health, welfare, and education. The Committee calls upon Church people to assume a greater sense of personal responsibility in becoming informed about its plans, purposes, and needs; in encouraging community study and concern; in working through their governments to strengthen and develop the United Nations. It pleads for serious consideration of the revision of its charter; the provision of a more effective organ for international justice; and the creation of adequate means for enforcing its decisions, in order that the United Nations may achieve the purposes for which it was formed.

3. The determination in every sphere of Christian endeavour to create a climate in which reconciliation becomes possible. It must be remembered that the Christian Church is not to be identified with any particular political or social system. The Anglican Communion is a living demonstration of this and furnishes within its own membership opportunities of deepening and extending the fellowship of people of different nations.

4. The acknowledgement that God has set us in a world in which certain tensions and conflicts are essential elements in growth. This means that we must accept the cost and discipline of living in such a world. The discipline that God requires of us involves the ready sharing of material resources with those who need, and the overcoming of prejudice, self-interest, and suspicion.

Above all, the Christian, remembering that conflicts in the world reflect conflicts in the heart of man, must be faithful to his calling. Christ calls him to pray for his enemies; give wherever there is need, expecting nothing in return; forgive those who wrong; love when tempted to hate; live as a redeemed sinner whom Christ has reconciled to God.

3. CONFLICTS WITHIN NATIONS

NOTE: *The Committee has confined itself to areas within which the Anglican Communion is to be found in some strength.*

A. THE RACIAL PROBLEM

The Committee asks that attention should not be confined to any one section. It has been thought good to make a general statement in the context of one area in order that, when seen more vividly in that context, its importance for others may be the better appreciated.

Within any land in which members of different races meet, there are the seeds of racial tension and conflict, not least in those territories into which the white man has penetrated. Tensions there will always be in every part of the world; yet it is one of the primary tasks of the Church not so much to resolve such tensions as, by the power of Christ through whom man is reconciled to God, through whom man's *at-one-ment* has been wrought, to reconcile man to man, and race to race. In Christ the Church is to transform all tensions from being fruitful for evil to being fruitful for good.

At the root of every conflict lies human sin, provoking situations which may become inflammatory and problems which may seem to be insoluble. Yet, for Christians, the fact of man's essential unity in Christ is paramount. In every sphere of his activity man is called to unity and brotherhood in the Family of God, the Church. Therefore no permanent class or racial separation, no oppression of the weak by the strong, no denial of opportunity for advancement, can be justified.

The Church itself must bear witness to this truth in its own life. Inter-racial worship, inter-racial meeting, both formal and informal, freedom of all races to enter and use educational, social, and health facilities, equal economic opportunities—these and other activities must be seen within the pattern of the Church's life and witness without compromise, self-consciousness, or apology. There may be no easy answers to special and local difficulties; nevertheless the Church must affirm that any form of segregation or separation solely on the basis of race is contrary to the Divine Will.

(i) Areas of Unrest

(a) United States of America

On 17 May 1954 the Supreme Court of the United States handed down a decision ruling racial segregation in the public schools to be unconstitutional, and brought into focus one of the most acute social problems the nation has faced in generations. Together with other religious bodies, the General Convention of the Episcopal Church has also declared it would "consistently oppose and combat discrimination based on colour or race of every form, both within the Church and without, in this country and internationally",[2] while its National Council has passed a separate resolution regarding the Supreme Court's decision as "just, right and necessary".[3] No diocesan council or convention of the Church is segregated according to race. More and more Church organizations are disregarding colour lines.

Unquestionably these independent actions of Church and State have combined to make possible some of the encouraging progress now being seen in the attainment of broader civil rights for minority groups. The Negro is entering upon a new era of educational and political freedom in the United States. Better housing and greater economic opportunities are becoming available to the people of many races and tongues. Many social barriers are coming down.

However, the degree of this attainment has not been the same everywhere. There are still unresolved conflicts resulting from the influx of immigrants into seaport cities; the special problems connected with Puerto Ricans, Poles, Jews, and Irish still demand attention; the South-West is at grips with its Latin-American difficulties; the West Coast is concerned with its proper relation to Orientals; the position of the American Indian has not yet been clarified. Beyond all these conflicts of varying intensity, the Negro is now moving North in great numbers, and already this area is being increasingly faced with the necessity of solving this fresh integration problem.

Meanwhile the eyes of the nation and of the world are fixed upon the problem as it presents itself in the South, where Christians are finding themselves on opposite sides. The Negro with natural impatience is exercising a persistence which many whites find irritating. Mutual fear and suspicion and prejudice are, as so often, delaying the process of reconciliation. The controversy has engendered deep differences not only between the white man and the Negro but between members of the same family and race. The situation, with its accompanying political implications, has also prompted the passage of many segregation Bills by Southern State legislatures in an attempt to circumvent the Supreme Court's ruling. This has created a further division of loyalties.

These are some of the elements of a complicated and confusing situation in which the Church is speaking and living. Its clergy and, in increasing numbers, its laity are working, not only to ensure to members of all races a free participation in divine worship, but also to ensure that educational and health services as well as equal economic opportunities are available to all. This the Church is consistently trying to accomplish without submitting to any tempting policy of expediency. It is striving to go forward in the knowledge that to stand still is a denial of its belief in God's guidance and its own responsibility to its brothers in Christ.

There is no easy solution to the differences which exist in regard

---

[2] General Convention, Boston, 1952.
[3] Cf. National Council Pamphlet entitled *Just ,Right and Necessary.*

E+

to race relations in the United States in general. The complexities compel a sympathy for all who are involved. But this Committee believes that men of goodwill in all races can point the way to greater peace and harmony through the exercise of mutual understanding, calm reason, and constant prayer.

(b) *Israel and the Arab World*

The events which led up to the establishment of the State of Israel in 1948 have been the cause of increasingly bitter conflict between Arab and Jew during the past forty years. Few would fail to appreciate the desire of the Jews to find a new home and nation in a land so closely linked with their history and their faith, or would withhold sympathy from a race which has suffered such appalling persecutions through the centuries.

No responsible person would minimize the problems with which the Mandatory power was faced as it tried to implement promises to Arab and Jew which in the event proved irreconciliable. Neither can Christian people face with equanimity the fact that nearly a million Arabs lost their homes in a land which they had inhabited for centuries, and that they are convinced that a cruel injustice has been done to them.

To-day Arabs and Jews are still in a state of war though, thanks to the courage and devotion of the United Nations observers, who have the heavy task of preserving the armistice, frontier incidents are kept in check.

In the absence of a settlement, hundreds of thousands of refugees still depend upon the inadequate resources of agencies of the United Nations for their meagre existence. We are thankful that the Anglican Communion both in Israel and Arab lands, though not strong in numbers, has ever sought to exercise a ministry of reconciliation. In addition, the work of Inter-Church Aid and World Church Service operating through the Near East Christian Council (and supplementing other agencies), is an example not only of true Christian charity of the highest order but also of a type of co-operation within the divided Church which is infinitely precious.

The Committee urges all Christian people to support such work wholeheartedly, to offer sanctuary and the deepest charity to those who for whatever cause have lost their home and citizenship, and to work and pray for the day when (through the United Nations) a just settlement may be reached and some of the causes of continuing bitterness removed.

(c) *India, Pakistan, Burma, and Ceylon*

In India and Pakistan the acute conflicts between Muslims and Hindus, which were intensified at the time of the partition of the country, have come to an end and the two countries have shown commendable religious toleration. In India the Constitution provides for freedom to practise and propagate any religion; this freedom has been impartially preserved by the Central Government, and any local infringements have been remedied on appeal. In Pakistan, though a professedly Islamic State, Hindus, Buddhists, and Christians carry on their customs and worship unmolested at any level. What internal strife has appeared here and in Burma and Ceylon from time to time has generally been engendered by linguistic and cultural antagonisms; there is hope that such differences may soon be overcome. When the deep cultural traditions of a race are violated there may be a sense of grievance and sharp reactions. As experience of self-government grows, such potential sources of conflict are likely to be avoided.

The Church of India, Pakistan, Burma, and Ceylon has a fine history and inheritance and is fully alive to its immense task as a mediator amongst the people of the nations in which it exists.

(d) The Far East

The emergence of Independent States in the Far East is producing a situation in which the Church is not only facing new problems but also new and great opportunities and responsibilities, especially in areas where a multi-racial society exists—e.g., constructive co-operation within new nations learning the art of self-government; the prevention or reconciliation of racial conflicts. In Malaya the presence of Malays, Indians, Chinese, and Westerners is a potential source of conflict if only because of the very marked differences of traditions, language, and patterns of life.

The 25 million Chinese dispersed in S.E. Asia represent a rather different aspect. Torn between loyalties to the ideologies of their parent land and to others which pervade S.E. Asia, they also suffer, in some areas, from varying degrees of hostile discrimination.

Throughout this area a growing Church may well find itself one of the greatest sources of reconciliation and inter-racial unity.

(e) Australia

Whereas Australia is without racial conflicts, it is included here since strong criticism of its unwillingness to accept non-white immigrants is made in some quarters.

While it is natural that a young nation may feel justified in maintaining a high standard of living and safeguarding itself against the possibility of racial conflict, the Committee believes that the present unwillingness to receive non-white immigrants should as soon as possible be modified in order to allow for the controlled entry of members of any race or nation. In the meantime the Committee welcomes the policy whereby, under the Colombo Plan, an increasing number of Asians is accepted into Australian educational institutions, sometimes for considerably extended periods.

(f) *Great Britain*

While there is no evidence of widespread racial discrimination in Great Britain, nevertheless some hotels and boarding-houses and a few places of amusement still refuse to receive coloured people, and there have been, from time to time, local community expressions of antipathy towards foreigners, for the most part caused by fear of unemployment or for other economic reasons.

Furthermore, there has been all too frequently a general failure to welcome immigrants from other parts of the world. Often foreign students have returned to their native land conscious that they have not been made to feel at home in Britain.

The Committee urges Church congregations to do everything in their power to welcome overseas visitors at church and to integrate them with natural friendliness into their Church fellowship. Furthermore, the Committee would stress the value of priests overseas commending members of their congregation to incumbents in Britain so that they can be met on arrival and given hospitality.

The Committee expresses the hope that all those who are responsible for sending men and women overseas to live and work amongst other races will take pains to ensure that they are wisely prepared for the new conditions into which they will go, not least in the matter of their future relationship with those of other races.

(ii) *The Awakening of Africa*

The extent and nature of racial tension in this vast continent are not the same in every part. It is advisable to treat four of these parts separately.

(a) *West Africa* has never had to face the problem of the white settler who has made his permanent home in a new land. During the past 100 years or so much of West Africa has been under British Colonial rule. Ghana is now an independent State within the Commonwealth; Nigeria, already with federal self-government, is expected to achieve independence within a year or so; Sierra Leone is likely to follow a few years later.

Whatever may be the political difficulties of newly-won independence, there is to be seen a very obvious sense of release from former oppression and tutelage, however paternal it may have been. The new future independent West African States are to be secular States. While they guarantee freedom of worship and assembly they are not likely to provide for Christians those quite unofficial and indefinable privileges which were to some extent present under British rule. The Church must therefore learn how to live and extend its evangelistic frontiers in quite new circumstances and must not overlook the fact that Islam will inevitably be afforded increased opportunities of influence and advance.

The white man is welcomed in West Africa if he comes as a co-operator to help the African through trade, through technical assistance of every kind, and through other channels, on terms now being fixed by the African.

(b) *East Africa* is still a long way behind West Africa in the development of natural resources and the provision of educational facilities. The most significant example of conflict since Lambeth 1948 in this area occurred in the multi-racial society of Kenya where the bewilderment of rapid social change was very acute. Here there have been movements of regression in which certain common features were evident: they have tended to be tribal; they have sought to re-establish a sense of communal security by retreating, as it were, behind re-erected tribal barriers and by extruding those features of the new life of a mixed society which the retreating group is unable or unwilling to absorb. The movement of Mau Mau terrorism in Kenya is illustrative of this.

The experience of the Church's rehabilitation workers has shown quite clearly what is the Church's duty not only in seeking to assist in the healing of such situations after disaster has befallen a tribe, but also in seeking to anticipate the conflict. The Church must demonstrate beyond all doubt that it is the Family of God into the fullness of whose membership all may come without distinction or difference. There, in Christ, they will find strength and grace both to face all the baffling bewilderment of rapid social change unafraid, and also to contribute actively towards the solution in society of the problems which society has itself created.

(c) *Central Africa* is yet another sphere in which the white settler exists in growing numbers. Some of what is said later applies to this area. There is now a Federation uneasily reaching out towards a policy of partnership, in which the relatively small numbers of white settlers will share with the Africans (who far outnumber them) the government of a fast developing group of countries where an increase of industrialization is inevitable.

The Committee believes that, if true partnership is to be achieved, there must quickly be an end to many of the old ideas associated with patronage and even paternalism, and that the African should be allowed and encouraged to take a fair and just share in the government of the Federation and its constituent parts—not only a just share but one seen to be just. Here, as elsewhere, the African can only become a responsible person by having responsibility. It is clear that considerable sacrifices will have to be made by both partners, and we would urge that nothing should be done by the British Government which would have the effect of enhancing the already powerful advantages of the white settlers over the Africans.

Here the Church, and the Church pre-eminently, must exercise a spirit of reconciliation between white and black for their mutual enrichment.

(d) *The Union of South Africa* is involved in acute racial conflicts, though the facts are not always accurately known. The danger of over-simplifying the issues is very great. In general the white South African, still ridden by fear that the black South African will displace him and rob him of his home and livelihood, seeks to maintain his supremacy while according to the non-white what he (the white South African) regards as a generous measure of self-development. The policy of *apartheid* (separate development) was acceptable to some, provided that the non-white was granted sufficient land in which to live and develop; but such separation is now impracticable for economic and industrial reasons, even were white South Africans willing to surrender much of their own land for occupation by non-whites. Others regard a limited separation as the only practicable course, providing relatively good conditions of living and education, but increasing the social separation between white and black and insuring that the latter will in no way compete with the former nor expect any place whatever in his society. Furthermore, this is to be the policy towards other non-white racial communities (coloured, Malay, and Indian). Here (as in East and Central Africa) the white settler claims title to his home and property and will strive to defend them. Yet his whole economy depends upon the presence of a contented non-white population.

Although disharmony among white South Africans themselves is a tragic feature in this deeply complex pattern, nevertheless the Church of the Province (through its bishops and other clergy and increasingly through its laity) fights bravely to keep open the lines of communication between the races, and protests vigorously against injustice. It also consistently refuses to divide the Church racially, encourages inter-racial worship, and summons inter-racial synods.

To say anything in this situation is to run grave risk of misunderstanding or distortion, but this much must be said. The white South African is as much an African as a black or coloured South African. There must therefore, at the earliest possible moment, be a reconciling of every colour and race. With the Church of the Province of South Africa the Committee condemns the injustices perpetrated against non-white men and women in South Africa under the policy of *apartheid*. It holds that every citizen of South Africa of whatever race should have equal rights before the law; and that the non-white should be given a fair and just share in the government of the nation of his birth and citizenship. It believes that, if the present pattern of multi-racial community is to continue, any form of *apartheid* is less just and righteous than a gradual and mutually enriching growth into responsible interdependence of all the races which now share this fertile and beautiful land.

It would be faithless to conclude that the situation is without hope for either the white or the non-white South African, or for both. A renewed attempt by the sundered parts of the Church of God in South Africa is surely required to break down the barriers which divide them. Made in penitence, faith, and humility, such an encounter might well be the most powerful action which Christians could take in the immediate future. For no power less than that of Christ working in and through his Church can bring unity of heart and mind to this torn and perplexed nation. Few nations have a greater claim upon our prayers.

(iii) *Freedom of Opportunity*

The Committee wishes to add the following statement which, though set in the context of racial unrest within the continent of Africa, is in fact, *mutatis mutandis*, applicable to other nations and countries where the existence of powerful racial groups may have produced situations in which injustice, discrimination, or even oppression continue to a greater or lesser degree.

(*a*) Year by year the desire of the African (Christian and non-Christian alike) is deepened, and his determination strengthened, to manage his own affairs and to call Africa his own—one African people throughout the whole continent. His white fellow-African must become wise and humble enough to come to terms with him while there is still time to do so peaceably and justly.

(*b*) The African must be allowed his just share in the control, the development, and the rewards of the natural resources of his country.

(*c*) In industrial development the Committee believes that the African must be encouraged and enabled to advance to the highest level of attainment: and that he should be free to combine on terms of equality with his fellow-workers of all races through trade unions and similar associations.

(*d*) The Committee believes that neither race nor colour is in itself a barrier to any aspect of that life in family and community for which God created all men—men for whom Christ died and to whom the Holy Spirit is promised. God's revelation fulfilled in Christ lends no support to the belief that any race can claim permanent supremacy over another.

B. CENTRES OF INDUSTRY

The growth of industrialism has created acute tensions and difficulties which have never yet been fully resolved. It is only necessary, for instance, to see the mines in southern Africa and the large urban populations which spring up in every centre of industry, to realize that the flow of simple country people into industrial communities produces a revolutionary change in the pattern of personal and community life. Again, in the U.S.A. there is to-day an unprecedented movement of vast numbers of people to and between different industrial centres. Similar movements of population are taking place in many other parts of the world. In such cases, people become detached from their age-long surroundings, from their traditional family and tribal life and customs, and from whatever religious traditions have nurtured them.

Little that is good and much that is evil is immediately available to take the place of deep-rooted habits and patterns of life.

The rapid spread of industries into many more areas of the world to-day is a sharp reminder to the Church of the urgent need for being better prepared to bring the Gospel, with all its implications, to industrial and urban communities. The normal missionary and parochial pattern of the Church's life cannot alone grapple with the totality of this task. In a sphere which inevitably contains the seeds of conflict, in which previous ideas about the dignity of labour and man's place in society are less apparent, or which have not been re-interpreted in terms of a very different order of society, the Church needs to understand afresh its place and purpose within what is commonly known as industrial society. Though it may only rarely be either wise or necessary for it to intervene directly in an industrial dispute, the Church must learn the meaning and significance of the standards and methods which characterize this society. It must also equip itself to exert such influence both upon industrial society itself and upon the members who compose it as shall aid and inform the growth of good relations within a community which, like any other, has its own very special contribution to make to the service of mankind.

Of recent years some experiments have been made and much may be learnt from them. The Industrial Mission in Sheffield is one of these, and there are many others being made in Great Britain on a small scale, largely unco-ordinated, with varying success. In Canada, to give another instance which includes a measure of multi-racialism, the extremely rapid expansion of industry, especially in the North, has shown a notable spirit of co-operation between Government, Industry, and Church. These experiments have not been confined to the Anglican Communion and in France, for instance, a somewhat different approach has been made but towards a very similar end.

The Committee is convinced that it is now time for the Church to make some new and imaginative attempt to study and define more closely the direction in which it should move towards a deeper penetration into industrial society in all its aspects, not only in those countries in which large industries have existed for many years but also in underdeveloped countries in which its rapid growth is producing fresh and sometimes terrifying problems.

The Committee here summarizes some of the points which seem to call for special attention in this context:

1. New, long-term, and understanding encounter between the Church and the workers, especially in countries where an estrangement has existed between them over many years or even generations;

2. Personal friendship with workers and managements as such in workshop or factory, as also with leaders of industry and trade unions and, in highly developed nations or areas, with those who

are concerned with the framing of policy at the central points from which big industrial organizations operate;

3. Knowledge of the social, industrial, and economic history of the particular nation or area in which the Church is involved;
4. The most careful opening up and maintenance of new lines of communication between the various classes and ranks within industry and, by so doing, helping to create a new structure of engagement designed to provide communication, impact, and reconciling influence within industrial society;
5. An ability to inspire the Christian layman within industry to involve himself deeply in the common life of the working community in which he finds himself and to engage in it, as a Christian, in a natural and attractive manner;
6. Readiness to re-assess and, if necessary, radically to alter the training of priests who are to work in industrial areas, and to encourage priests of suitable quality to offer themselves for this form of parochial or extra-parochial ministry.

C. POLITICAL CONFLICTS

Although particular attention has been given to racial problems, the Committee is equally aware of the political conflict in the world. As has been said earlier in this Report, the conflict of ideas is often a means of growth; but there is a profound difference between those conflicts which can be resolved by peaceful means, and those where changes are made through civil strife or outside interference.

Even this poses the problem too simply. It is important to recognize the question-begging nature of a phrase like "peaceful means". A Government may be brought to power without the use of military or physical force, but this is no guarantee that it commands the free support of the majority of its citizens. In the first place, much depends on the conditions that determine the right to vote. Where there are minimal qualifications for the franchise, these should apply to all, and there should be no discrimination on grounds of race, religion, class, or caste.

Secondly, there are forces which, though not physical, are nevertheless improper and immoral to use in pursuit of power. There is, alas, no doubt that in many countries there are political groups and factions working to get the better of their opponents by such dubious exercise of force as intimidation, bribery, blackmail, and social and other pressures.

It is generally taken for granted that democracy is the most suitable mode of political action in the world to-day. This is not to criticize dynastic, patriarchal, or similar forms of government, but it cannot be disputed that as people acquire knowledge they desire, quite naturally, to have a say in their country's affairs.

E*

If this be so, it is necessary to give consideration to the subject of democracy in action. The Committee rejects all forms of totalitarian rule as denying basic human rights, but it does not give its unqualified support for the principles of democracy unless at the same time there be a firm resolve to put those principles into practice.

There are questions which Christians need to ask, and there are situations in which Christians need to act. One such fundamental question is: Do the existing democratic governments truly represent the clear convictions of the majority of their citizens? This leads to a further question: Are there countries where governments, though acknowledging democratic forms, have in fact come to power, and perhaps remain in power, by undemocratic means? And when, if ever, is such procedure morally justified?

Nor can a further question be avoided: If a government stays in power against the wishes of the majority of its citizens, what are the resisting citizens to do?

The Committee holds that these are not abstract questions. In our twentieth-century world they apply to specific situations in both hemispheres, and they trouble the Christian conscience. Believing that "God has made of one blood all nations of men for to dwell on the face of the earth", the Christian accepts the solidarity of the human family. It is laid down as a principle of the United Nations that no member nation shall interfere in the internal affairs of another; but how can a nation that has accepted the Declaration on Human Rights stand idly by while that Declaration is being openly defied by one or more of its neighbours?

The Committee believes that in the political situation the Church has its own duty and responsibility. Through its teaching and through the loyalty given to it by peoples of strongly differing political convictions, it can ever act as a reconciling agent. Never is this of more moment than when political disagreement threatens civil strife.

At times of acute political conflict, the Church must keep before the people the principles of disinterested justice. It must call upon the conflicting groups to renounce all bitterness, and it must work to create a temper of mind in which inflamed emotions can calm down and disagreement can be resolved by a dispassionate consideration of the facts. It must also strive to keep the well-being of the community as a whole before the warring groups—the good of the whole community must come first, and party advantage must be kept secondary.

Normally the Church will not intervene directly, but it will seek to strengthen its own members in their understanding of Christian principles. As a result, they should be able to bring new Christian influence to bear on commercial, civic, and public life. But occasions may arise when the Church should act as a corporate body in support of freedom and justice. Such an issue was clear, for instance, to the Church in Germany during the Hitler régime. Nevertheless, all available evidence indicates that the Church should not foster clerical political parties. They not only make for faction but strain the Church allegiance of many Christians who cannot honestly square their own political convictions with the official policy of the clerical party.

There are glorious pages in world history when warring parties sought the Church's reconciling ministry. The Committee prays that by God's grace the Anglican Communion may be such a reconciling power in our time.

4. CONCLUSION

The Committee has surveyed in small compass some of the conflicts that trouble the world to-day. Its findings may here and there be questioned, but a disagreement in detail in no way vitiates the need for reconciliation. With this need the Committee has been primarily concerned, and in this need the Committee speaks with unanimous conviction.

Its urgent prayer is that, throughout the world, men of goodwill may continue to work unceasingly in the cause of peace as the fruit of reconciliation—peace between nations, and peace within nations. This peace remains the will of God, and the hope and inspiration of all men everywhere.

JOOST CAPE TOWN
Chairman

5. The Family in Contemporary Society

MEMBERS OF THE COMMITTEE

ENGLAND

P. M. Herbert, K.C.V.O., D.D. [Norwich]

L. S. Hunter, D.D., D.C.L., LL.D. [Sheffield]

B. F. Simpson, M.C., D.D. [Southwark]

E. M. Gresford Jones, D.D. [St Albans]

J. L. Wilson, C.M.G., D.D. [Birmingham]

A. H. Morris, D.D. [St Edmundsbury and Ipswich]

G. A. Ellison, D.D. [Chester]

IRELAND

E. C. Hodges, D.D. [Limerick, Ardfert, and Aghadoe]

A. H. Butler, M.A., M.B.E. [Tuam, Killala, and Achonry]

SCOTLAND

D. MacInnes, M.B.E., M.C. [Moray, Ross, and Caithness]

UNITED STATES

C. C. J. Carpenter, D.D. [Alabama]

R. Mallett, D.D. [Northern Indiana]

H. I. Louttit, D.D. [South Florida]

J. E. Hines, D.D. [Texas]
(Joint Secretary)

S. F. Bayne, S.T.D. [Olympia]
(Chairman)

J. W. Hunter, D.D. [Wyoming]

G. M. Jones, D.D. [Louisiana]

D. S. Stark, D.D. [Rochester]

A. E. Swift, S.T.D. [Puerto Rico]

F. J. Warnecke, D.D. [Bethlehem]

D. B. McNeil, D.D. [Western Michigan]

C. A. Cole, D.D. [Upper South Carolina]

C. G. Marmion, D.D. [Kentucky]

J. S. Minnis, D.D. [Colorado]

J. W. F. Carman, D.D. [Oregon (Coadj.)]

E. C. Turner, D.D. [Kansas (Coadj.)]

CANADA

E. S. Reed, D.D., D.C.L. [Ottawa]

INDIA, PAKISTAN, BURMA, AND CEYLON

J. Amritanand, B.A. [Assam]

F. R. Willis, D.D. [Delhi]
(Joint Secretary)

AUSTRALIA

J. S. Moyes, D.D. [Armidale]
(Vice-Chairman)

NEW ZEALAND

R. H. Owen, D.D. [Wellington]

SOUTH AFRICA

R. S. Taylor, M.A. [Pretoria]

WEST INDIES

D. R. Knowles, O.B.E., L.TH., B.A. [Antigua]

WEST AFRICA

D. R. Oyebode, B.A. (Dur.) [Ibadan]

P. J. Jones, M.A. [Sierra Leone (Asst.)]

EXTRA-PROVINCIAL

D. Deng Atong [Sudan (Asst.)]

W. L. M. Way [Masasi]

A. L. E. Williams, M.A. [Bermuda]

PREFACE

Everywhere in the world there is restless concern for the well-being of the family as a basic institution in society. This is most vividly clear against two backgrounds in particular. One is the swiftly-increasing degree of what is variously called the "urbanizing" or "industrializing" of our society (whether in terms of the elaborate industrial life of England or North America, for example, or those of tribal society in Africa facing the expanding needs of industry for manpower). The other is that of the urgent and mounting problems of population growth in many parts of the world—a growth the result of improved medical care and higher health standards, and measured in terms of dramatically reduced mortality rates, particularly among young children.

Each of these throws into sharp relief problems of concern to Christian and non-Christian alike. For it hardly needs saying that the family is not a peculiarly Christian institution. Yet it is certainly true that through Holy Scripture, and supremely through Christ's teaching, God has led his Church to uniquely deep insights into the nature of the family and its necessities and possibilities. Thus Christians not only share (or ought to share) the universal concern of all men of good will, but have also a particular and commanding obligation of their own. This report examines, first of all, the family as Christian faith understands it; then explores more briefly both the strains and the possibilities of family life in our society, against the backgrounds mentioned above.

In its thought, the Committee has been very greatly indebted to the report published under the title of *The Family in Contemporary Society*,[1] written by a group convened at the behest of the Archbishop of Canterbury, with supplementary reports from the American, Canadian, and Indian Churches, and warmly commends it to the study of all interested people.

1. THEOLOGY OF SEXUALITY AND THE FAMILY

THE PURPOSES OF MARRIAGE

First of all, the family is rooted in the elemental processes of life itself. Human reproduction—human parenthood—is vastly more complicated than the reproduction of plants or the simpler animals. Mankind has rightly come to see depths and possibilities in the process, and in the relationships which it establishes, which are, at best, only faintly suggested (if indeed they exist at all) in the lower orders of life. Still the human family, even in its richest and noblest complexity,

---

[1] S.P.C.K., 1958.

is at one with all of nature in its function as the means by which new life is begun.

The commandment in Genesis to "be fruitful and multiply" reflects this biological function. More significantly, it raises it to the level of God's creative purpose. Underlying the insistent drive of all life to reproduce itself is the creative activity of God himself, who ordered nature in this way and established the process and the urgent impulse, and reveals to mankind something of his purpose in so doing. Indeed, the revelation expressed in Genesis implies that in this fruitfulness, to some degree, man shares in God's creative work, that he is admitted to a quasi-partnership with God in the establishment of new life. Therefore the process of human reproduction, from the earliest levels of Biblical revelation, has been seen as invested with a special and responsible dignity.

The Biblical revelation, however, does not limit the function of sexuality and the family to the reproductive purpose. Equally deep-rooted in Genesis is the reflection of a second factor—the need of man and woman for each other, to complement and fulfil each other and to establish a durable partnership against the loneliness and rigour of life. It was not good for man to be alone, and God made a helpmeet for him. This relationship of man and woman—of husband and wife —is rooted in God's creative purpose equally with the procreative function of sexuality. "For this reason shall a man leave his father and mother and be joined to his wife".[2]

Thus, in the heart of the Biblical teaching about creation, two great insights into the nature and purpose of sexuality and the family are lodged. They are not subordinated one to the other; they are not directly related to one another; their relationship, in the developing experience of Israel, is to be found in yet a third area—that of the place of the family in giving responsible security to the children born of the love of husband and wife.

Indeed the extraordinary helplessness of the human infant and his long need for protection and care alike awoke a special sense of responsibility in even the most primitive society. Sometimes, in its simplest forms, this responsibility was seen as little more than a property right, or an obligation to preserve the integrity and heritage of family groups, or to ensure their continuing power and prestige. More fully, as in the elaborate safeguards of the Roman mother in classic times, responsibility for the stability of the family reached a markedly high level. The Old Testament reflects this range of responsibility, and moves towards the developed doctrine of the monogamous and responsible relationship of the Jewish family of New Testament times, protected by the strictest rules of marital fidelity and economic security.

Christ's teaching about marriage deals directly with only the second of the three purposes mentioned, that of the personal relationships

---

[2] Gen. 2. 18–25; Matt. 19. 4f.

between husband and wife. Here, in response to a question about the Jewish law of divorce—a question designed to discover what school of rabbinical interpretation he favoured—he recalls his hearers to the true nature of the marriage relationship as God created it. The tie between husband and wife is, by God's ordinance, a life-long one, not to be broken by any act of man. In his answer he quotes two texts from Genesis: that God created sexuality in mankind ("male and female created he them"), and that the right relationship between the sexes was the union, life-long and life-deep, of the two in "one flesh".[3]

Characteristically, the teaching establishes a principle and, equally characteristically, it is in the form of a return to the essential truth about life as God has created it and therefore of life as it must be in the Kingdom of God on earth. The fact that Christ says nothing of the procreative function of the family or of its rôle in the nurture of children is of no significance here; he is not dealing with those matters but with the specific issue of divorce. It is not suggested, therefore, that he neglects the parent-child relationship but that he is rather setting forth what all would feel to be one of the primary necessities of parenthood—that it grow out of a faithful relationship between two free souls who can give to their children both the security and the richness of a stable, full, mature, unquestioning partnership. The parental love that speaks in the parable of the Prodigal Son is possible because of the standard of marital love he sets forth in his teaching about marriage and divorce.

To summarize, three purposes—three functions—are interwoven in human sexuality. Each of them is profoundly rooted in human experience and in God's revelation. The procreation of children, the fulfilment and completion of husband and wife in each other, and the establishment of a stable environment within which the deepest truths about human relationships can be expressed and communicated and children can grow up seeing and learning what mature life is really like—these are the great purposes which, in God's loving will, marriage and the family are created to serve.

RELATIONSHIP BETWEEN THE PURPOSES

It has been common, in Christian theology, to mention the procreative function first, as if to say that it is the ruling purpose. So it is, in the sense that no marriage would be according to God's will which (where procreation is possible) did not bear fruit in children. But it is clearly not true that all other duties and relationships in marriage must be subordinate to the procreative one. Neither the Bible nor human experience supports such a view. Where it has been held, the reason generally lay in a fear of the misuse of the sexual relationship or in a false sense that there is, in any sexual relationship, an intrinsic evil.

---

[3] Gen. 1. 27; 2. 24.

Neither fear nor a false sense of what is "evil" is a helpful guide for humanity, in this or any other matter.

Responsible parenthood is both a more complex relationship and a far richer one than merely the reproduction of the species. Granted that the institution of the family is inescapably rooted in the biology of procreation and that this must always form part of the moral structure within which the decisions of husband and wife must lie, still the heart of family life—the heart of the marriage which is the cornerstone of the family—is the responsible freedom of the partners who make the marriage to begin with.

Indeed the whole enterprise of marriage and the establishment of a family is perhaps the most vivid expression we know of responsible human freedom under God. A man and a woman, free and competent to do so, agree before God and society to take each other as husband and wife, without reservation, for life. Any such adventure of free people carries with it both the privilege and the obligation of making the choices with which life confronts us.

Marriage does not merely happen to us. It is something for which Church and State can only provide the setting and the protections of law and doctrine. It is something which husband and wife create and maintain, with the help of God, by means of the multitude of choices of which the day-to-day texture of a marriage is woven. Indeed it is those very choices which are signified by the promises "to love and to cherish", for love is something people *do* far more than merely something they feel; it is an act of the will as well as—often before— it is an emotional experience. And the most important of all those choices are those which involve the fundamental purposes of marriage and family life.

This is no new discovery. What *is* new, in our society, is the well-nigh fatal ease with which those purposes can now be separated from one another. It was suggested earlier that in God's revelation there is no automatic unity among them. This is paralleled in human experience everywhere, which has taught us how easy it is to dissociate sexual pleasure from the sober duty of procreation, and to sever them both from the third group of obligations of family loyalty. To keep all three sets of relationships and duties together, in one frame of moral reference, is an art man has had a long fight to learn, and must still steadily fight to preserve. This unity or harmony of purpose in marriage can never be taken for granted: it is always threatened by sin and ignorance—and never more so than in our time.

Techniques and devices for controlled conception now make it generally and easily possible to plan for parenthood at will. Thus the old, direct relationship between sexual intercourse and the procreation of children has been broken. The fear which has so often dominated sexual intercourse has largely disappeared, and with it many of the accustomed disciplines of sexual conduct. And, in this new situation, there appear new problems for conscientious choice, and new possibilities for the marital relationship.

So, too, have a variety of changes affected the structure and function of the family as a unit in society. To mention only the most dramatic, women are increasingly finding a new place in economic and social life; the State has assumed vastly greater responsibility for the care and nurture of children; far greater freedom of divorce has radically altered the psychological climate of marriage, particularly in the loss, in the hearts of many young people, of any expectancy or assurance of permanence; changing social and industrial patterns have done away with much of the economic dependence which once tended to establish family solidarity as an economic necessity. Such changes, while some of them, at least, doubtless offer new possibilities for good, have also had the effect of dissolving the traditional moral patterns of family life, of separating the great triad of purposes which family life exists to serve, and, again, of confronting husbands and wives—and, indeed, children as well—with perplexing and unprecedented new choices.

It is not the purpose of this Report to attempt to evaluate all these new factors. Such evaluation would be premature, in many cases; and, in any event, the Committee's purpose is rather to suggest the lines along which the Christian conscience moves in making the often bewildering choices which these new factors pose.

The commanding problem, as was said above, is the problem which every husband and wife faces, of maintaining a right relationship among the three great purposes of their marriage. The two most critical areas for this are, first, the question of family planning and, secondly, that of the permanence of the marriage bond.

FAMILY PLANNING

The responsible procreation of children is a primary obligation. The questions, How many children? At what intervals? are matters on which no general counsel can be given. The choice must be made by parents together, in prayerful consideration of their resources, the society in which they live, and the problems they face.

It may be said, however, that responsible parenthood implies a watchful guard against selfishness and covetousness, and an equally thoughtful awareness of the world into which our children are to be born. Couples who postpone having children until certain financial goals are reached, or certain possessions gained, need to be vigilant lest they are putting their own comfort ahead of their duty. Similarly those who carelessly and improvidently bring children into the world trusting in an unknown future or a generous society to care for them, need to make a rigorous examination of their lack of concern for their children and for the society of which they are a part.

In general, the earlier in a marriage children are born, the better—

both for them and their parents. And there is every reason to suggest to young men and women that it is far wiser to postpone marriage for a time than to enter it in constant fear of accidental pregnancy. Sexual relationships scarred by fear are tragically incapable of bearing either the strains or the joys of full and happy married life.

But the procreation of children is not the only purpose of marriage. Husbands and wives owe to each other and to the depth and stability of their families the duty to express, in sexual intercourse, the love which they bear and mean to bear to each other. Sexual intercourse is not by any means the only language of earthly love, but it is, in its full and right use, the most intimate and the most revealing; it has the depth of communication signified by the Biblical word so often used for it, "knowledge"; it is a giving and receiving in the unity of two free spirits which is in itself good (within the marriage bond) and mediates good to those who share it. Therefore it is utterly wrong to urge that, unless children are specifically desired, sexual intercourse is of the nature of sin. It is also wrong to say that such intercourse ought not to be engaged in except with the willing intention to procreate children.

It must be emphasized once again that family planning ought to be the result of thoughtful and prayerful Christian decision. Where it is, Christian husbands and wives need feel no hesitation in offering their decision humbly to God and following it with a clear conscience. The *means* of family planning are in large measure matters of clinical and aesthetic choice, subject to the requirement that they be admissible to the Christian conscience. Scientific studies can rightly help, and do, in assessing the effects and the usefulness of any particular means; and Christians have every right to use the gifts of science for proper ends.

Continence, self-control, and chastity have often been advocated on the basis of a view of life that identified the principle of evil with the "material" or "the flesh". Though we can no longer accept the dualism expressed in Puritanism and in the theology of St Augustine, yet the Church holds as strongly as ever that continence, chastity, and self-control are a positive and creative element in Christian living. They are indeed an ingredient in an heroic and sacrificial response of man to the costly redeeming love of God. If Christian living were to be so influenced by current hedonism as to allow free rein to biological and sexual urges, it would lose the dimension of holiness and its power to challenge "the world".

In the man–woman relationship, not only before marriage but in it, chastity and continence are virtues of positive worth, sustained by the grace of God, for they release creative power into other channels. If the sexual relationship is to be truly an expression of partnership, the male has to recognize that his sexual urge may be the stronger and therefore he has more consciously to exercise self-control. Nothing that is said hereafter about the use of contraceptives in family planning takes away from the beauty and strength of abstinence mutually accepted.

Some of the means which are not acceptable to Christians are listed, together with the reasons for that judgement, as guides to parents in their choices:

The wilful withholding of one partner from intercourse with the other, sometimes mis-named "continence", cannot be endorsed, for such persistent one-sided denial of the right of bodily love of husband and wife is a denial of one of the supreme conditions and purposes of marriage as God has established it. (This, of course, does not refer to a mutual decision of husband and wife to agree to abstain from intercourse for a time as a particular and special offering to God.)

The Christian conscience rightly rejects any means which interrupts or prevents the fulfilment of *coitus* and thus precludes, in husband or wife, the full completion of the sexual act.

In the strongest terms, Christians reject the practice of induced abortion, or infanticide, which involves the killing of a life already conceived (as well as a violation of the personality of the mother), save at the dictate of strict and undeniable medical necessity. The plight of families, or, indeed, of governments, trapped in hopeless poverty and over-population, may well help us understand why they think abortion more merciful than the slow starvation which looms ahead. Still, the sacredness of life is, in Christian eyes, an absolute which should not be violated.

The Christian rightly accepts the help of responsible physicians in making conception possible, where it may be prevented by some physical or emotional abnormality. Artificial insemination by any one other than the husband raises problems of such gravity that the Committee cannot see any possibility of its acceptance by Christian people. The Committee calls attention to the report on *Artificial Human Insemination*[4] made in 1948 by a Commission appointed by the Archbishop of Canterbury.

The question of sterilization, whether therapeutic, genetic, or contraceptive in its intent, presents a complex ethical problem. It is an urgent matter, in many parts of the world, where it is put forward either as a general solution to overpopulation, or as an easy way out for couples who wish no more children. Because it is a decision often casually and thoughtlessly made, the Committee examined it with special care.

The Committee agreed that sterilization when an imperative medical necessity (as in hysterectomy or the treatment of cancer) is justified. All likewise agreed that any government policy of compulsory sterilization as a means of population control is unacceptable to the Christian conscience, at least in our present state of knowledge and understanding; some indeed felt that such a policy could never be justified.

[4] S.P.C.K., 1948.

Voluntary sterilization, either as a government policy or only as an individual choice, raises many grave questions. It is urged, in some quarters, that sterilization of husband or wife, after the procreation of a proper number of children, seems to be little more than a particularly safe and easy method of family planning, and as such is proposed, for example by the Madras government in India, for populations where poverty and illiteracy make any widespread use of contraceptive devices or techniques unlikely. The factor of relative certainty weighs heavily with peoples and communities wrestling with the grievous problem of overpopulation, and as well introduces a degree of freedom from fear which is held to promote a deeper and happier relationship between spouses.

The Committee thinks it right, however, to state that sterilization, now generally an irreversible process, limits the ability of the man or woman to meet changed circumstances (as in depriving a future spouse of the possibility of parenthood), and as such is a major and irrevocable abdication of an important area of responsible freedom. It has psychological and physiological consequences that are as yet unknown and unmeasured, and represents as well a violation of the human body, a body which is God's gift and trust, and only in a limited sense ours to do with as we wish. All agreed with these considerations, although some members felt that in the present state of our knowledge, we ought not to attempt to judge finally for the future.

The choice of sterilization is a grave one, to be made only in deepest and most conscientious thought, with full agreement between the spouses. Often this is not the case; and it is noted that the operation is increasingly being sought, or even recommended, without any adequate appreciation of its gravity as a moral decision. In the Committee's judgement, before any such decision is reached, the most prayerful and serious consideration should be given, before God, and with the best counsel from pastor and physician which can be gained. In this connection the Committee urges the study of *Human Sterilization*, a report of a group of Anglican theologians.[5]

The discussion of these specific questions has illustrated the complexity of the choices husbands and wives are daily called upon to make. They have a duty to bear children; they owe an equal duty to each other, of tender and completing love; and these two duties interpenetrate and lighten each other. Neither one should master the other, for then marriage is distorted and untrue. To keep them both in true balance is never easy, and the use of effective contraceptives, with its persistent invitation to sensuality and selfishness, is an added hazard.

Yet to say this is to say no more than that no human relationship or dignity is easy to achieve. Marriage is a vocation as well as an estate of nature; it is an essay in responsible freedom; and we have no

---

[5] *Human Sterilization: Some Principles of Christian Ethics*, published for the Church of England Moral Welfare Council by the Church Information Board, 1951.

more right to expect it to be without its problems than we might expect good citizenship or personal integrity to be painless. Freedom is the condition of every human virtue and of every grace.

Freedom is also the way towards the attainment of all that is excellent and true. And, perplexing though the choices in contemporary marriage are, it must also be said that the new freedom of sexuality in marriage in our time is also, and equally, a gate to a new depth and joy in personal relationships between husband and wife. At a time when so much in our culture tends to depersonalize life—to erode and dissolve the old, clear, outlines of human personality—Christians may well give thanks for the chance given us to establish, in marriage, a new level of intimate, loving interdependence between husband and wife and parents and children, freed from some of the old disciplines of fear.

It must be said once more that this will not happen automatically. It will happen only when we deliberately choose it, and pay the cost of it in self-discipline, in courtesy towards one another within the marital tie, and in willingness to receive and give the fullest communication of love, physically as well as in every other way.

FAMILY AND HOME

The second of the two great, critical areas of choice is that of the depth and permanence of the family ties themselves. "Permanence" and "depth" are rightly associated, for no family life can find true depth except where there is the firm assurance of steadfast faithfulness. This is not to idealize "indissolubility" alone, in the legal sense, which, if it is not accompanied by the other necessities of true family life, can poison and destroy. It is rather to say that the relationships of husband and wife and children to and among each other are *given* relationships. A man may be a bad brother or an unworthy son, but brother and son he is, regardless of whether he lives up to it or not.

This is to say something of what is meant when we speak of the family as God's creation as a basic unit of society. The relationships within a family are not the only relationships we have, nor necessarily the most important ones. They are the *first* ones, in point of time, and they are so ordained of God in the natural order to provide a given status and place for children as they begin their earthly course.

The time will come, and rightly, when the family unit will develop into other family units (and parents have a duty to prepare for this inevitable change). So too will the time come when the family unit must give place to wider associations. The tie of blood is the first tie in life but not the final one. The final one is the fellowship established in Holy Baptism, the fellowship of grace, of redeemed humanity, in which we are all called to take our part. The Prayer Book, looking back at the deep teaching of the Epistle to the Ephesians, speaks of marriage as the closest thing we can know to the unity which exists "betwixt Christ and his Church". Only the bond of the redeemed, in

Christ, is closer than that between husband and wife; yet, by that same token, marriage is not a final end in itself but must serve the body of Christ. A like thought may be applied to the family, this intimate unity of life and blood—close as it is, the bond of redeemed humanity in Christ is yet closer. The family is the training ground behind which stands the wider world, for which the life of the family prepares, and to which it must give place. "Who are my mother and my brothers?" asked Christ, and gave the answer: "Whoever does the will of God is my brother, and sister, and mother".[6]

The family is the God-given environment within which souls are born, to learn first the lessons of human individuality and dignity, of responsible freedom and redemptive love: the lessons which in due course must be lived out in the wider and deeper associations of humanity in Christ.

Men and women who marry undertake not only a love to each other and a fulfilment of their duty of reproduction, but also a specific obligation towards the establishment of a secure family within which these great lessons can be learned. The family is not the only unit of society but it is the *root* unit; all else grows out from it; and no society will be stronger than the family life which prepares its citizens for their part in it.

Therefore society owes a most solemn obligation to families. The State has a responsibility to serve them, quite as truly as families may be expected to serve the State. And husbands and wives owe an equally solemn duty to their families. Children are a trust with a prior claim on parents, even before the claims of their own personal liberty. The husband or wife who puts personal happiness before the need of his family for stability is once again denying the true claims of his or her responsibilities and the just balance of the purposes for which marriage and the home were created. There is no God-given "right to happiness" which can over-ride the profound claims of children to a stable and dependable home. No Christian man or woman has the right even to consider such abandonment of duty save where, after fullest counsel from his parish priest as well as every help and reconciliation skilled Christian marriage counsellors can give (where they are available), it is clear to all that the continuance of the family and home will work greater harm than will a separation.

CHRISTIAN FAMILY IDEALS

It is right to speak so seriously of the claims of family life, for it has never been so exposed to the acids of carelessness and selfishness as now, nor has the world ever had greater need of the gifts family life can make. Some of these gifts are:

In a true family, children learn that there is one God. They learn

---

[6] Mark 3. 33, 35.

it first from their parents, and from the disciplined and thoughtful obedience parents and children alike pay to the same God. Parents who force on a child an obedience they are not willing to accept equally for themselves are committing one of the deepest offences of family life, for they are giving to their child a false view of the one God who rules over all life and in whose will is our peace.

In a true family, children learn what love and judgement mean, for a family ideally is a society in which all bear common pain and share common grief, and all give and receive equally of love.

In a true family, children learn, little by little, how to be free; they practise how to make the choices life requires of them, within the protection of loving concern and watchful care.

In a true family, children learn the essential standards of judgement—how to tell the important things, how to distinguish the true and the excellent and the right, how to speak rightly and listen with courteous love.

In a true family, children learn how to accept themselves and, in time, how to accept others on the same basis; for membership in a family comes not by earning it nor buying it, nor is it given only to those who deserve it. Like life itself and the grace of God, it comes without deserving; and the self-acceptance of healthy childhood is a precious preparation for a humane and tolerant manhood.

In a true family, children learn how to be themselves, in true individuality, and how to accept others in their equally true individuality, with patience and kindness.

Of such qualities is a true family made. To bear witness to these things is part of the vocation of a Christian family in our society. In that society, sympathetic to its good influences, critical of, or resistant to, its unwholesome influences, the truly Christian home should be salt and leaven. To be this it has to be sure of itself and of its basis in the will of God and the Gospel.

Such a home is the one place where Christians can live by the Gospel, as they cannot fully do in a society where other sanctions come in. The marks of "living by the Gospel" are the care of each for other, the value set on persons for their own sake without regard to merit or demerit, to success or failure. Where there is this warm understanding and love there is both freedom and responsibility. Each member feels free to be himself. This sense of freedom is one of the marks of a Christian in the world—all too rarely found in Church or in society.

Such a home gives to boy or girl support and direction, the discipline and happiness of living together without fear or favour, and the courage to launch out. The discipline will be related to the children's stage of development and will avoid unnecessary conflicts of will. Where a child has to be punished it will be a "safety-first" precaution. Punishment will be once for all, neither with petulance or excessive moralizing, nor with the intention to shame or to assert superior power. Its best and most remedial form may well be deprivation. Well-ordered, free, family life of this sort is nearer to the Kingdom of God than anything men and women are likely to experience in this life. It is the best that society and Church can give to young people. There are no substitutes for such homes. They are made and sustained when their life is integrated in Christ, reproducing his passion for social justice, his discerning care and astringent love, and are enfolded in the larger family of his Church.

Such a home will be welcoming to young and old, to strangers and lonely persons. Unlike many families in the world it will not be turned in on itself, keeping itself to itself and so losing touch also with God. In so far as it is open and exposed to the Spirit of God, it will share in the ministry of the Church to society, caring for friend and neighbour, near or distant, not seeking privileges only for itself, a forgiving society where free and fresh starts are always possible, a beacon-light to a factious, unforgiving, and suspicious world. The Church has to be vigilant on its behalf, receptive of the influences in society, friendly to good home-making, critical of the pressures which may become hurtful, remembering that, in the past, Christians and philanthropists have been far too ready to deplore, and far too content to do no more than ambulance work. Our duty is to be, as far as we can, at the creative end of social processes, as the . Church unfortunately failed to be in the early days of the industrial revolution in the West. This is a challenge and opportunity for the Church in countries which are beginning to be industrialized; and they must be accepted and seized by laymen in industry. Because Christians are sensitive to the evils and injustices in society, they must not allow themselves to forget the fact that this is God's world, where his will has to be discerned and done.

RELATED MATTERS

1. It remains, in this section, to speak briefly of some related matters. First, what of the marriage that fails? The Committee calls attention to the report of the Committee on Marriage of the 1948 Lambeth Conference and fully and wholeheartedly makes its own the conclusions of their study. In the intervening years, much thought has been given to the problems raised by divorce and much has been learned. All that has been learned re-emphasizes the imperative duty of the Church to bear faithful witness to life-long monogamy as the standard of its teaching; we cannot challenge our world with any lesser standard than the one our Lord gave us.

2. The Committee notes the experience of the Church in the United States in attacking the difficult and ambiguous problem of the marriage where "there is no marriage bond recognized by the Church".[7] In particular, the procedure of that Church in exploring the degree of

---

[7] *The Lambeth Conference, 1948*, Resolution 94.

freedom and competence to marry in a given situation seems to permit the gathering of helpful evidence leading toward better preparation for marriage and deeper pastoral care; and we commend to all our provinces a study of this procedure and its results.

3. Christian teaching about monogamy introduces revolutionary changes in a polygamous society, and involves both individuals and the Church in costly and distressing differences. Polygamy, in most societies where it exists, is a basic economic and social pattern, and not merely a sexual one. The early societies of the Old Testament were polygamous; and the part that the larger or extended family played in establishing a balanced and self-sustaining community was an important one, as it is still in some parts of the world. To teach and require monogamy in such a society means a radical alteration in the pattern of life, with possible breakdown of the structure of economic life and of traditional social values; it introduces most complex problems in the lives of the men and women affected, and in the understanding and establishment of new patterns to replace the old.

There are no easy answers to these problems, to which devoted study continues to be needed and given. Simply to require monogamy, with no provision for the social dislocations and the persons involved, would be intolerable. Yet it would be equally intolerable for the Church to falter in its teaching of the true nature of marriage. For, just as the polygamous societies of the Old Testament gave place to monogamy and finally to the supremely high principle of life-long marriage of one man with one woman, so must go the universal witness of Christian faith. Monogamous marriage, especially as it developed among the people of the Middle East and in the New Testament, is not the idea or invention of western civilization, or of so-called Christian countries. It is a fundamental truth about the nature of man and woman as God has created them, reinforced by the explicit teaching of Christ, valid for all mankind, in every society.

Thus, the Church must steadfastly uphold the standard of life-long monogamy. Yet, in doing so, the Church must be prepared to face, frankly and sympathetically, the problems this teaching creates, and must accept responsibility to work wholeheartedly towards their solution. Discipline in this matter may sometimes differ in various provinces of the Church, according to what is thought to be wise. But the proclamation of the truth and responsible willingness to face the cost of it are alike inescapable obligations laid upon the Church.

Equally must there be responsibility on the part of individual Christians in this matter. The Christian principle of life-long monogamous marriage is one of the greatest of all God's blessings. It brought, and still brings, to the world a new and precious valuation of human life, particularly in the new dignity and status of women. It reinforces the ideal of responsible freedom, and enhances in every way mature and deep human relationships, freed from old dependencies, and released for new possibilities of personal development. To educate ourselves for this, to commit ourselves to it, to revise old patterns so as to make the new ones possible, to help to prepare ourselves and our society—these are urgent tasks for individual Christians as well as for the Church.

4. It will be generally agreed that the most valuable contribution the Church can make toward the stability of the marriage bond is to help young people to marry in the right way. This is very largely the responsibility of the parochial clergy. We would urge all our provinces to provide for pre-marital interviews between pastors and people concerned, where instruction can be given, along the lines of this report, in the nature of marriage and family life and their problems. Where specialized physical or other counsel is needed, such interviews can well discover the need, and provide means to meet it. They will be spiritual opportunities for young people who are about to make solemn promises to each other and to God, who will and do welcome such help. In explaining the meaning of the marriage service and its implications, pastors are provided with unique opportunities of relating the whole Christian faith to the lives of such people.

In addition, special thought should be given to more remote preparation for marriage, both in the Church (as in confirmation preparation and youth groups) and in community and school activities. To this end, the provision of special training courses for the clergy and for Christian men and women are needed. The Committee is glad to observe that in many dioceses, in recent years, such courses for clergy and laity have been held, and warmly urges their extension.

5. The clergy should also note their obligation to maintain a continuing relationship with the couples they marry, not only by showing a special concern for them during the early months of their marriage (a time when marriage counselling and instruction may be especially useful and fruitful) but also by commending them to the clergy of other parishes where they may go to set up their homes.

Splendid work is being done in many countries, and especially in the United Kingdom, by Marriage Guidance Councils in providing courses in preparation for marriage and in helping men and women whose marriages are breaking down or are imperilled. These Councils consist of married men and women who give their services voluntarily. They undergo a course of training and are required to pass an examination before being accepted as counsellors. There is an urgent need here for happily-married, convinced Christians to offer themselves for this work. The witness of a Christian home in a community is of the greatest value; and there must be many Christians who, out of gratitude to God for what their Church and home have given them, would be prepared to carry their witness to a further stage by becoming Marriage Guidance Counsellors, or the like. The Committee suggests that the clergy should be urged to bring the claims of such service to the notice of their loyal Church members.

6. This report deals hardly at all with single men and women, but no one of mature years can ever be other than intensely sympathetic with the young unmarried people of to-day and with their problems. They came to birth in war years, within world revolution, when standards were being overthrown, when parents were overstrained, and many marriages broken.

The strain upon their early adult life with the force upon them of sexual urges and the new freedom youth has attained, together with the possibility of sexual intercourse with but little fear of physical consequences, is a frightening thing; and their behaviour where it has fallen below Christian standards demands comradely help rather than stark condemnation. The Committee urges that they should keep before themselves not the pleasures of this moment but the vision of true life and family in the days ahead.

Pre-marital intercourse can never be right; it is selfish and sinful in its irreverence for the sanctity of both a man's and a woman's life; and it tends to make impossible the really happy fellowship that belongs to a marriage when the partners bring to each other a complete offering of selfhood unspoiled by any liaison. The full giving and receiving of a whole person which sexual intercourse expresses is only possible within the assurance and protection of the faithful, life-long promise of each to the other, "forsaking all others".

7. It is clearly the will of God that the great majority of mankind should marry and have families. But to some of both sexes there comes a call to the celibate life. For the individual the question to be faced is not, "Which of these two vocations is the 'higher'?" but, "Which of the two is God's will *for me*?" Throughout Church history the Religious Orders have made a very large contribution to the building up of God's Kingdom, not only by what they *do* but by what they *are*. There is an obligation for all who counsel youth to see to it that deliberately-chosen celibacy—whether for a time or for life—is presented as a real vocational possibility, along with the vocation of marriage.

The community also owes much to the single man or woman— perhaps particularly to the single woman—who sees the unmarried state as offering opportunities of full-time dedicated service to the Church, to families, to society, in many capacities. An unmarried person can do tasks that married people cannot do; and in many spheres a single woman can minister to children, the sick, and the aged in ways which for a married woman would be impossible. The frustration and bitterness so often associated with the single state is both unjustified and often un-Christian, for it results from the neglect of the truth that God's vocation of humanity is universal and unfailing, and that every state in life can be a good and full and Christian opportunity for service.

8. The Committee notes the destructive effect on family life of intemperance, particularly in gambling and drinking. Quite apart from the questions of individual morality involved, the unfair and selfish misuse of limited family means by such intemperance is harmful in the extreme.

Without entering into the vexed question of the ethics of gambling, the Committee says quite frankly that the habit of gambling has become so excessive and widespread in many places that the Church must speak clearly against it. It repeats the warning given by the 1948 Lambeth Conference, and again urges that the Church should not only resolutely refuse to raise money by gambling methods but should also steadily remind people of the persuasive invitation to selfishness which gambling offers. State support or encouragement of gambling is equally to be deprecated.

In many areas there is dangerously increasing intemperance in the use of alcohol. Personal influence and example are needed to oppose this; all Christian families should examine their own practice in this respect, and the witness they bear for Christian temperance and self-control. The rehabilitative work of Alcoholics Anonymous is particularly commended in this matter; and such ministry, by many groups as well as by individual doctors, is to be encouraged and supported by the Church. But alcoholism as a pathological problem is only part of our concern. Intemperance, over-indulgence, gluttony is the greater enemy; and this is a matter for Christian witness and discipline.

The Committee recognizes that these evils are very largely due to the insecurities of a turbulent and rapidly-changing world. There is very great cause for thanksgiving for the firmness of character of young people to-day, despite the emotional problems of our time. Church people everywhere should not waste their energy in condemnation of the erring but should assist in every possible way in promoting, through the wholesome example of responsible and disciplined family life as well as through their individual discipleship, a restored awareness of the security and richness of life in God's world.

2. THE FAMILY IN AN INDUSTRIALIZED SOCIETY

Society almost everywhere is becoming industrialized and urbanized. For the favoured few, rural life allows for a deep appreciation of nature, enjoyable pursuits, and a happy tempo of living; but down the centuries the lot of the peasant and his family has very often been penurious and relentlessly hard. The drift to the town with the onset of industry has been inevitable. It has confronted families with other and more complex problems, of which not a few are unsolved, and it has led to conditions of living and to a secular culture which are proving unfriendly to Christian values and to many of the good things of the cultural heritage of Europe and Asia. Some of these problems and tensions we now proceed to discuss.

HOUSING AND OVERCROWDING

The world over, in new countries and in old, there is a terrible shortage of decent and suitable housing, accentuated by the existence of refugees—families crowded in one house, often a family in one room. "You can have television in one room but not a family." Because sometimes, by the grace of God and a good mother, a family survives successfully living in one room, that is no excuse for churchmen acquiescing in these conditions of home life for people less fortunate than themselves.

The depressed state of problem families, in which the parents have not had strength and intelligence to stand up to these conditions, is a condemnation of society as much as of them. The heroic work of Family Service Units and other secular and religious agencies, which have tried patiently to rehabilitate and restore self-respect to such families, is a Christian work beyond praise.

There is a sacramental relationship between good housing and good homes which does not allow churchmen to be indifferent to the basic need for more and better housing. We have to urge this continuously, and as citizens to act responsibly in regard to it. The provision of good housing is an obligation on the community, local and national, and cannot be left only to private enterprise. And just because the bad habits generated by history under bad conditions are not removed overnight when a family moves into a new house in unfamiliar surroundings, the Church in such a district has work to do in helping these people to achieve a better way of life.

CHILDREN AND YOUNG PEOPLE

There must always be a gap and even a tension between the generations. That is specially the case to-day, when the young are often much better educated than their parents, and, in countries like Africa, where they may also have a religion with another cultural pattern from that of their grandparents. It is also difficult for the older generation to-day to appreciate what it feels like to be born and bred in a world so insecure as this—on the one hand a higher standard of life, and on the other the possibility of genocide or extinction. Almost inevitably, the resulting effect on youth is restlessness and psychological instabilities, not to say "angry young men".

The security of a Christian home will not, however, be that of escapism and make-believe, but the assurance that stems from the Cross. As the boy or girl approaches adolescence, he or she will be encouraged to be adventurous, to face life unafraid, to be ready for responsibility and sacrifice as the price of freedom. This will come about because the members of the home are at once thoughtful each for the other and pray for one another, and at the same time have toward other families an active sense of responsibility and a modest sense of privilege. They will be mindful of such words as Mark 10. 29, 30, and Matt. 25. 31 ff.[8] When the members of the younger generation begin to go out to make their own life in the world and to start new homes, parents will accept the inevitable loosening of the old ties realistically and without grudging, and the family will set about making a new pattern of family relationship. In a society where many homes are over-crowded and the day's work monotonous, the older generation has to be not so much disapproving of the outbreaks and delinquencies of youth as wise to direct frustrated energy into more constructive and satisfying activity, and forgiving. There are no wrongs done by the members of the family of Christ to one another which are unforgivable. A sense of rectitude or of injury should never be allowed to take priority over forgiveness. Where a costing forgiveness leads to repentance, and through repentance to reconciliation, a new start in living together is made possible.

CULTURAL PRESSURES

A new secular culture has been growing and permeating social life in countries where hitherto a Christian culture has been the heritage. This is partly because a large proportion of industrial workers has never been effectively within the Church and is for this reason the more exposed to secular influences. It has grown where the masses have become increasingly subject to the pressures and salesmanship of commercialized amusements, advertising propaganda, popular newsprint, and more recently of television which comes right into the home.

There are two concerns at issue.

1. The spread of literature has exposed the population to newsprint which has only an emotional appeal, and to other reading matter which does not create any appetite for the finer works of man. The habit of watching what is put on the screen and of listening without reflection, coupled with a pre-occupation with the machinery of life and its novelties, may atrophy the imagination and the appreciation of poetry and the love of truth, which have been the mainspring of art and science alike. If these are enfeebled or sterilized the spiritual life of man will indeed decay. For poetry and imagination are of the soil in which true religion grows and flowers. The Bible, moreover, which supplies the imagery and symbols of our faith and liturgy, speaks directly

---

[8] Mark 10. 29, 30: "There is no one who has left house or brothers or sisters or mother or father or children or lands, for my sake and for the gospel, who will not receive a hundredfold now in this time, houses and brothers and sisters and mothers and children and lands, with persecutions, and in the age to come eternal life."
Matt. 25. 31 ff. is the Parable of the Sheep and the Goats.

through and to the kindled imagination. The great truths of God's revelation cannot be translated into a language of a debased currency without loss of fullness and power.

2. The use of "depth psychology" in advertising in place of honest argument and an appeal to sound judgement is a menace to democracy and Christian living. So, more obviously, is the sheer silliness and the low standard of social morality which are the content of much that meets the eye and assails the ear to-day.

We would appeal to those who control newsprint, television, and advertising to recognize and respect the power for good or ill that they exercise, and not to allow themselves to be ruled only by sales and profits.

At the same time the members of the Church, in co-operation with all who care for truth and the good life, must not acquiesce in the penetration into our homes and lives of these corrupting influences. Home, School, and Church have to build up a resistant attitude to them, helping young and old to exercise control of their thoughts, to discriminate, to prefer truth to the lie, and to exemplify a fine quality of life. In addition, clergy have to understand the frustrations and limitations of the press at its various levels and to be ready to co-operate with it and with other organs of publicity.

INDUSTRIAL PRESSURES

To a man or woman in a small restricted job the forces governing industry and the pressures that ensue may seem to have the relentless power of the laws and forces of nature. That is a fallacy and a defeatist attitude. Industrial pressures are the work of men; often they have not been consciously organized, but have grown up gradually. They can gradually be changed if those at the controls so determine. The Church has to make clear to its members in industry that their daily work, with all its relationships and responsibilities, is the sphere of Christian service. They have to bring to their decisions not only technical and administrative competence but Christian insight and understanding, and not to be afraid to accept responsibility. The ministry of the laity has to be exercised outside the Church organization as well as within it. Some men and women ought to be told firmly that their Christian service may be the accepting of responsibility in a trade union or some form of community service or political life rather than in taking part in "Church work". It will usually be more valuable service to take an active part in a trade union, on the shop-floor, or in administration than to count the collection in the vestry! For the Church's influence on industrial organizations can for the most part be exercised only by laymen in industry, because they carry responsibility and have the technical knowledge. There are, however, some industrial pressures and problems affecting family life on which the Committee ventures to comment.

1. The expensive plants of industry and the labour force to keep them running more or less continuously demand expert management and technical ability, skill in machine-minding, good human relationships within industrial units, and an adequate supply of labour, fairly rewarded. It is not unnatural that those responsible for production should think that production is the primary, if not the only, consideration. Industry (owners, management, and labour alike) needs to be reminded that production is not the only yardstick by which to measure the value of the contribution of industry to the life of the community. In the discussions and bargainings between the various groups within an industry the welfare of the State and of different sections of the community should not be disregarded.

2. If the cost of machinery requires for its economic use the three-shift system, the system should as far as possible be manipulated so that it does not hinder the worker from enjoying wholeness of life and doing his part as a member of a family and as a citizen.

3. If efficient production and large-scale industrial organization require that management, technicians as well as manual workers, be frequently moved from place to place, and even that a works should be transplanted, the economic benefit of this mobility should be carefully balanced against the loss of civic responsibility, the rootlessness, and the dislocation and strain on family life which may ensue—and which may in the long run reduce the efficiency of the worker.

4. Migrant and contract labour obviously can have a disastrous effect on family life. It is an industrial demand, therefore, which the Church must watch very closely and do what it can to ameliorate. The careless, and at times callous, employment by industry of the African, for example, for long periods at a distance from his home and family which involves complete separation, is an evil which will in time bring its own nemesis.

   Where government services require families to move about a country, or from country to country, the Church has not only to be for them the focus of their community life, it has also to draw them as fully as possible into association with the community of the place or country of which they are temporary members.

5. Industry, on any decent or Christian principle of social obligation, cannot be content to argue: "Our only job is to produce and to pay the market price for such labour as we can attract." It has a further obligation towards its employees, towards their family life, and towards the local and national community of which it is a

part. The greater the power exercised by those who control industry over the life of the total community, the more scrupulous and tender in conscience must they be in the exercise of that pervasive power. If (any more than the social and educational services) it cannot function without the employment of married women, industry ought to be ready "to bend its regulations" to facilitate their employment, to put up with the inconvenience of part-timers, to have intelligent, trained, and sympathetic personnel managers. The employment of married women at lower wage-rates is not a proper alternative to paying a man good wages and providing working conditions which encourage full output.

6. In the employment of young people in industry and commerce both management and trade unions are showing an increasing care. Provision for part-time education, training schemes, recreational facilities, better working conditions, the care of personnel managers and welfare officers, more pastoral responsibility on the part of foremen and shop-stewards, the welcome to trained industrial chaplains, are pleasing signs of the times in many countries. Nevertheless there is still a great deal of wastage of youth in industry, too many over-paid dead-end jobs, too much insensibility at a crucial time in a young life. While the support of youth organizations by industrial and commercial organizations is all to the good, these cannot heal the hurt done to boys and girls leaving school when they meet with rough treatment and corrupting influences on the shop-floor or in offices. The transition from school to working-life should not be so harmful to character as it often is. The Committee hopes, therefore, that those responsible for the employment of youth, and trade unions, will not be content merely to develop "vocational" training, but will also have a concern for the whole life of young employees, and will help them to become responsible citizens and to grow up good and dutiful members of the family. The Church, on its part, through clergy and school-teachers, ought to give guidance to boys and girls, and to their parents, in regard to what they are to do when they leave school.

MOTHERS IN JOBS

There are good reasons why married women in increasing numbers respond to the demand for their labour. For example:

1. To supplement the amount their husbands earn or give them for household and family maintenance.

2. To provide more amenities for the family, including holidays, education, and saving.
(These two motives are re-inforced where there is a time lag between a rise in the cost of living and an increase in wages.)

3. To enlarge their own interests and relieve the monotony and lack of full occupation in their lives, or to resume professional work.

It is generally agreed that if a mother leaves a family with children under school age in other people's care, it is bad for the children—unless the substitute is a person who can mother a child and win its trust and affection.

When the children have reached school age, and especially if the mother's hours of work are limited to the hours when the children are at school, the family life as well as the mother's may gain. As the children grow older, her work outside the home may result in shared interests, thereby reducing the educational gap between parents and children, especially in the families of manual workers. It may lead to more partnership in the running of the home, joint-planning, budgeting, and spending—a happy expansion in the area in which married love operates.

Not only do the benefits of a mother's going out to work depend on right motives, they also depend on her physical strength and her ability to organize her time and her work well. If she lacks strength and ability, the strain may affect her health, and the home may suffer.

It is most desirable, therefore, that there should, on behalf of the community, be a continuous watch and a scientific study of the changing situation as it operates in all countries.

THE IMPORTANCE OF THE SMALL COMMUNITY

While the general migration from rural to urban areas has tended radically to change the ratio of city dwellers to country dwellers, it should be noted that there are still great numbers of citizens in most lands who live in rural areas or in small towns. For instance, in the U.S.A. there are still over 54 million persons living in rural communities (under 2,500 population).[9]

Such rural communities have, of course, been seriously affected by the results of industrialization. Depletion of population has in many cases denuded such communities of valuable leadership. Local schools have been replaced by regional schools, resident clergymen have been replaced by clergymen ministering to several congregations often at considerable distances from each other, and all social and medical services have tended to suffer.

It is important to be aware of the vital rôle of the rural community as the place in which family life may be more easily nurtured, in which opportunities for leadership can be exploited, and in which Church life and cultural pursuits can be more closely identified with the life of the people than is sometimes possible in large urban centres. Surveys have indicated that the majority of those who form the backbone of a city

---

[9] *The Family in Contemporary Society*, p. 170.

F*

congregation had their Christian life nurtured in a small country Church. It has often been observed that many leaders in business and national life were born in small communities and in them found opportunity for the development of their gifts in a way that might not have been provided in the impersonal atmosphere of urban centres. For the constant cultural renewal of the city and the continual vitalization of the city Church, serious attention must be given to the small community.

Family life in such communities now often suffers deeply because of the loss of so many central factors in community life. Life in the home itself is distracted because of growing dependence on services in distant areas; the small village or town increasingly is an incomplete community; there are fewer opportunities for recreation and education. The Church should take serious note of the challenge of such socially-impoverished areas, not only in the provision of trained and adequately supported clergymen, but also in presenting and supporting the opportunity of service in those communities of doctors, teachers, social workers, etc., as a vocation of special urgency in our time.

THE FAMILIES OF THE CLERGY

The clerical family, no less than others, faces stresses and strains, some of the same nature, some of a different kind. It has the same temptation to accept and live by a false scale of values. Since people look to the clerical home to set an attractive pattern of Christian living, there is laid upon the clerical family a responsibility which it cannot escape. Though the Committee would not advocate a double standard, one for clergy and their families, and another for the laity,

1. It is desirable that all young clergymen before they become engaged to marry should consider their marriage in relation to their calling, and ask themselves whether or not the Christian mission in the world would be served better if they remained single for a time. When they do marry they should think out honestly and carefully with their partner not only all that concerns the life of the family, but also the working relationship between the home and the ministry, and the contribution of a friendly, hospitable parsonage home to the life of the Church. From time to time they should review the matter again in the light of growing understanding and changing circumstances. If in the past some husbands and wives had done this, some unhappiness and mis-understandings would not have arisen. It can never be easy for a good priest to keep a fair balance between his responsibilities as husband and father in the home and the demands of his ministry. Success in doing this becomes an effective part of his witness in the community, and it depends much on the wisdom and good management of his wife.

2. Much of the good influence of clerical families has been due to

the spirit and devotion of the wives of the clergy, who have made their homes attractive examples of the Christian way of life.

In the first years of married life some of these would be helped if provision were made for them to have the counsel and guidance that other parishioners would expect to get from the parish priest. Some of their problems are new to our time, when many more wives of the clergy have had a professional training and experience. It is not unreasonable that they wish to return to their profession, part-time or whole-time, when their children are passing out of childhood, and that they resent the assumption that the parson's wife is the unpaid curate.

At the same time, a clergyman's wife with varied interests and professional qualifications should be helped to find a satisfying vocation in her position. We recommend that the experiment being made by some theological colleges of arranging courses for the fiancées of ordinands, and the practice in some dioceses of allowing wives as well as licensed workers to attend the post-ordination classes with their husbands, should be developed and spread more widely. Both in the Church and in society there is more than ever a valuable service which a well-educated woman can render without undertaking a full-time salaried appointment (for example, as counsellors under a Marriage Guidance Council).

Many of the houses of the clergy are still unsuited to modern conditions and should either be replaced or modernized and made more labour-saving. While much has been done, much remains to be done. This is a financial responsibility which the laity should shoulder. Adequate, well-planned, but not out-of-size houses would help the wives of the clergy to maintain their homes in simplicity and with good taste. This would not only reduce fatigue and strains but also be a visible Christian witness in all types of communities. Also, clergy stipends and allowances, particularly in times of rapid inflation, should be under constant scrutiny by bishops and laity.

We should like to think that every clerical home has in its bishop an accepted pastor and friend. We note with strong approval that bishops and dioceses are providing more occasions for clergy and their wives to share in worship, study, and recreation through retreats and conferences, and are trying to secure for them adequate holidays with a rest from house-work for the wife. We know that this has benefited the spiritual and intellectual life of the home and has brought much-needed relief and refreshment. We also suggest that they be given opportunities of meeting and discussing with men and women of other professions who are also serving the community.

3. POPULATION

A Christian discussion of population must take account of faith as well as of facts. We believe that each person is of eternal worth before

God, and that his family life is ordained by God. Within the family, men and women have responsibilities which they must be encouraged to sustain, and areas of personal decision in which their liberty must be affirmed. While it is the function of governments to establish a social order in which those duties can best be discharged and the good life be pursued, there are areas of family life in which personal freedom and family integrity must be respected, and into which the State must not intrude. Similarly, it is the duty of the Church, recognizing its responsibility for the physical and mental as well as the spiritual well-being of persons, no matter to what race they belong, to co-operate with governments both in promoting personal and family welfare, and in protecting their freedom and integrity.

It is on the basis of faith that the facts must be assessed. Preliminary study has assembled some of these in *The Family in Contemporary Society*. It is there stated that "The rate of population growth in the world has never been so rapid as at the present time, and it is estimated that in one generation the world population might increase by 45 per cent; in certain areas the rate of acceleration in population growth is probably without precedent in human history. The relationship between population trends and family life is so intimate and complex that the problems of the one cannot be separated from the other. Statistical material exists to indicate population trends; the effect of these changes on individual families may be conjectured, but, over a wide area, cannot be measured with any accuracy. Nevertheless, the pressure of population on raw materials, and on food supplies in particular, must have an effect on the standard of living in economically under-developed countries where the population is increasing rapidly." [10]

It is important to note that the main reason for this rapid increase in population is that: "Death rates have fallen all over the world, and are still falling, because of better health and medical practice, control over famine and infanticide . . ." [11]

There are here two distinct problems: the first, a *world* population multiplying at such a rate that the future adequacy of resources is being questioned; the second, certain *regional* populations already so dense that life is lived at the lowest levels of poverty, and multiplying at such a rate that local resources at the highest predictable rate of increase cannot be expected to keep up with them.

At present the increase of *total* world resources is keeping a little ahead of world population. There is insufficient evidence on which to conclude that it can continue to do so, if the rate of population growth is maintained. It is known, however, that since the potential for increasing resources lies at present overwhelmingly with the wealthier regions where population is relatively stabilized, only a willingness and

[10] P. 35.
[11] P. 221.

ability to share that potential with the under-developed and over-populated regions can distribute resources adequately to meet the needs of the world of the future, and of particular regions now.

As these problems of population have been created, in a measure, by a Christian concern to combat disease and to save life, so they can be met only by a redoubled concern to help those in need.

We quote an important paragraph from the report already mentioned:

". . . Christians who are also citizens of the materially advanced countries have a clear field in which to interpret the divine precept, to give to those in need. They ought, in our view, to use every influence to secure such sacrifices in their nation's relatively high standard of living as may make some contribution at least towards meeting the needs of the under-developed countries; they ought themselves to remain sensitive to a distinction between the necessities of an already ample life, and the luxuries which are continually attaching to it, and to commend this distinction to their nation. They ought to resist the erection of prohibitive tariff and other barriers by which their own national economy is protected at the expense of the much more precarious economies of countries which must market their few commodities in order to live. They ought to exercise a liberalizing influence on public opinion, disposing it towards accepting a concern for other peoples in need, and against inverted national or sectional self-interest; inculcating sympathy with the sensitiveness of the communities which they seek to help, their self-respect and desire for autonomy, and their suspicion of gifts trailing political 'strings'." [12]

The giving and receiving between nations, as between individuals, requires the exercise of a spiritual grace on both sides; and the Church is called to be an instrument of the mediation of such grace.

While stating the Christian obligation in these terms, the Committee must also record its appreciation of work to this end already being done by governments, the United Nations, and other international agencies; the Committee would urge the Church to support them in every way, not least by encouraging Christians to work, fully trained, in their service.

MIGRATION

In the past, migration has proved an effectual relief to an over-populated region, and it is necessary to consider how it may contribute a solution now. The possibilities are now severely limited. The wealthier lands are already taken; the poorer lands awaiting development would require expensive capital investment in order to produce any significant return in the critically short time. Immigration is almost everywhere subject to political controls; acceptable immigrants, chiefly those with technical or other skills or the ability to develop them, are precisely

---

[12] P. 10.

the people most needed for the rapid extension of the economy at home; the unskilled, the peasant family which is at the heart of the home problem, is seldom wanted elsewhere. Individuals, indeed, are sought for the labour supply, as in the contract or migrant labour forces in many areas; but in most cases their work is possible only at the expense of their family life.

Generalization, however, is inadequate in this matter. Churches, therefore, in sparsely-populated countries which have yet untapped resources, ought to engage in serious local study and discussion with their own specialists and governments, in order to determine whether a more liberal immigration policy would be possible and beneficial, and to use their influence accordingly.

In some countries, e.g. Ireland, the rate of emigration itself constitutes a problem, and points to the need for strengthening the social forces which would encourage a settled family life.

The tragic plight of refugees and of stateless people should be brought to the notice and laid upon the conscience of all Christian people. Unfortunately the tragedy of these lonely and destitute people is a continuing feature of the post-war world, and in many areas it is the cause of political unrest. The size of the problem and the intensity of the suffering are not sufficiently appreciated. To settle families in new countries requires more sustained action than has yet been forthcoming by the United Nations and the several States which compose it. What is required is that receiving countries should be willing to accept a family as a unit even when one or another member is unfit or aged. Otherwise families are broken up and a remnant of the aged folk is left in refugee camps with perhaps one or more sick relatives to the end of their lives. Sometimes if one member is ill the rest of the family, either individually or corporately, will be denied the chance of a new start in life by being refused admission by immigration authorities. Churchmen have a responsibility to keep their governments alert to this need, and also to join in supporting Inter-Church Aid and Refugee Service. Such work involves pastoral and spiritual care, patient administration, and first aid in material things.

SOCIAL DEVELOPMENT AND PLANNING

When policies designed to increase resources and to distribute them more fruitfully are advocated, it must be remembered that "man shall not live by bread alone". The rapid economic development of a country, especially by means of industrialization, must inevitably disrupt a long-established social order and, if no other provision be made, must create a perilous void in the lives of its people. Life in community is precious, and necessary for man. The Church everywhere should concern itself with the social life of its region. In areas of new development it should strive to secure from the beginning the best social foundations upon which family life can be built whatever its local cultural form. The Church should give the best of its experience, its support, and, above all, its people, fully trained, to educational and social development, co-operating wherever possible with government and with other agencies by which it is directed. In particular there is a call for women, especially unmarried women, to assist in social welfare and education among women and girls, upon whom the quality of family life so much depends.

The Committee stresses the importance of social development, not simply as a necessary adjunct to industrial development, but because of its own vital contribution to the solution of the population problem. High birth rates and high death rates (especially of infants and children) are themselves the product of social conditions which are amenable to change. A true education both inculcates a concern and respect for the person and makes it possible to exercise them; it promotes a sense of responsibility for family integrity and well-being; it ought also to promote a quickened awareness of and reverence for marital love and procreative powers. Given all these, attitudes to the size of the family begin to change; fatalism and mere indulgence give place to concern and conscientious decision. The "population problem" is brought back to its source: the personal life of husbands and wives in their own homes.

In view of what has been stated, the Committee has reached the conclusion that some form of family planning, particularly in those areas of rapidly growing population, is an urgent necessity. By "family planning" is meant an extension of the responsible use of science into the realms of procreation, within the permissible range of Christian ethics, in the immediate interest of the family and the more remote but no less real interest of society at large. As a means to the exercise of responsibility in procreation it is to be distinguished from other means by which the birth rate and size of the family are reduced.

THE OLDER PERSON

Our concern is for the whole family, old as well as young. Just as the Church and society in general have been interested, rightly, in ensuring that children and young people have adequate opportunity for true development, so it is necessary at this time for special thought to be given to the older person whom industrial society confronts with many hazards and frustrations.

The proportion of older persons in the total population has risen sharply in many countries as a result of improvement in medical and social care. This situation calls for serious research to ensure that such older persons should have a meaningful place in society and should not be regarded simply as a problem.

Changes in various regions leave the aged less protected socially and economically. Many have to leave the area in which they have lived most of their lives to reside in cheaper quarters, are deprived of the emotional support which comes from fellowship with kith and kin, and face the unhappy realization that they are not needed or, indeed, wanted.

In Asia and Africa, as well as in the West, the old are often left relatively alone when industry and social change carry the young people of their families away.

In the face of these situations the Church must constantly teach the integrity of the family and the mutual responsibility for each other of young and old. It is also the duty of the Church to work for the right social conditions in which that care can be given. It is commendable that in many countries serious study is being given to the question of the aged so that they may have a meaningful part to play in society. Pioneering efforts in housing for older people and provision for day centres for fellowship and recreation and for cultural pursuits are being developed, often under the inspiration of the Church. Much more needs to be done.

Older persons should be encouraged to use their leisure constructively. Many after retirement may seek re-employment in some light occupation wherein their talents can still be used, and industry and society are challenged to make such employment possible. Indeed, industry should examine carefully the possibility of planned schemes for the part-time employment of retired men and women, both to conserve their skills as a social asset and also to help remove the sense of uselessness which often burdens older people.

Some will wish to give their services to the Church and community. Imagination and patience will be required to make proper use of their services. The clergy could do a great deal to develop this in their parishes. It is also suggested to parish clergy that they seek the more active participation of their older parishioners in the work of worship and intercession, and encourage them to use their new leisure as a privileged ministry of prayer and to regard themselves as workers together with those of all ages in the family of God.

APPENDIX
CERTAIN RESOLUTIONS OF THE LAMBETH CONFERENCE OF 1948 ON THE CHURCH'S DISCIPLINE IN MARRIAGE

94. The Conference affirms that the marriage of one whose former partner is still living may not be celebrated according to the rites of the Church, unless it has been established that there exists no marriage bond recognized by the Church.

95. Mindful of the needs of those who are in deep distress and claim the Church's sympathy, the Conference urges that provincial and regional Churches should consider how best their pastoral responsibility

towards those who do not conform to our Lord's standard can be discharged.

96. Confirmed members of the Church who marry contrary to the law of the Church, as accepted in the provincial or regional Church to which they belong, should be regarded as subject to the discipline of the Church in respect of admission to Holy Communion. Their admission to Holy Communion lies within the discretion of the Bishop, due regard being had to their own spiritual good and the avoidance of scandal to others. It is important that the practice within each province or regional Church in this matter should be uniform. We restate Resolution 11 (b) of the Lambeth Conference, 1930, as follows:

"That in every case where a person with a former partner still living is re-married and desires to be admitted to Holy Communion the case should be referred to the bishop, subject to provincial or regional regulations."

STEPHEN F. BAYNE, Jr.
Bishop of Olympia
Chairman